Siblings

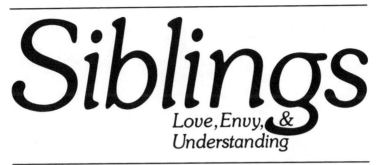

Siblings

Love, Envy, & Understanding

Judy Dunn and Carol Kendrick

GRANT
McINTYRE

First published in Great Britain in 1982 by

Grant McIntyre Ltd
90-91 Great Russell Street
London WC1B 3PY

British Library Cataloguing in Publication Data

Dunn, Judy
    Siblings.
    1. Brothers and sisters   2. Child development
    3. Interpersonal relations
    I. Title   II. Kendrick, Carol
    155.4'43   BF723.S43

    ISBN 0-86216-04-5
    ISBN 0-86216-07-8

For Sophie, William, Paul, Nicho, Jacob, and Laura

Acknowledgments

The study we describe in this book was supported by the Medical Research Council. We are deeply grateful to the families who took part for the patience, interest, and good humor with which they helped — they taught us so much. We should also like to thank the Health Visitors and General Practitioners of the Cambridge (England) area for their assistance.

We have changed the names of the children in the book to ensure their anonymity. Except where incidents involving particular children are described, we have referred to the firstborn as "he." This convention, while imposing some problems, does distinguish between our references to the mother and to the child.

Many people helped us in the course of the project: Pat Altham, Anne Campbell, Irene Hudson, and Rosanne MacNamee with statistical advice; Jeremy Cherfas and Phyllis Lee with computing; Beverley Bevis, Lynn Ferguson, Christine Outhwaite, Becky Williams, and Jackie Woolcott with coding of transcripts; Ann Hills, Christine Keefe, Pat Naylor, and Christine Reed with preparation of the manuscript; Les Barden with formulation of the figures. We collaborated with Claire Sturge of Northwick Park Hospital (Middlesex, England), who is carrying out a parallel study, on the initial planning of interviews; we are grateful to her both for permission to use her Temperamental Characteristics Assessment interview and for many helpful discussions. We are indebted, too, to Robin Stillwell-Barnes, who generously allowed us to draw from the interviews she conducted with the children when they were 6 years old, and to quote some of her preliminary findings. Several friends read and commented on parts of the manuscript: Patrick Bateson, Nick Humphrey, and Heather and David Wood. We should like to thank them for their assistance, and we are especially grateful to Eric Wanner of Harvard University Press for his perceptive suggestions on the entire book, and to Vivian Wheeler for her meticulous attention to the manuscript.

Our greatest debt is to Robert Hinde and John Dunn, whose interest, enthusiasm, constructive criticism, and intellectual imagination sustained and encouraged us throughout the study.

Contents

Siblings

Introduction

With the birth of a sibling the world of a firstborn child is transformed. Never again will his mother be his alone. "Why have you ruined my life?" a precocious 4-year-old asked his mother when his brother was born. Beyond the impact of the event itself — overwhelming for many first children — the sibling is there for life.

We know from our experience as parents, as siblings, or simply as observers of the families around us that the sibling relationship can be a profoundly important one. It is a relationship of poignancy and power that is watched and worried over by parents, explored and illuminated by novelists. Yet psychologists have paid scant attention to it. The single relationship of overwhelming importance in the preschool years has been assumed to be the one between mother and child. Consequently, relations between very young siblings have been considered principally in terms of rivalry for maternal affection.

There is, of course, much advice in parent manuals about how to handle jealousy between young siblings: there are pronouncements on its origins, on the significance of the age gap between siblings, on the advisability of permitting the older child to witness breast-feeding, and on much else. Parents are held to be largely responsible for the amount of disturbed behavior the first child shows, and for the quality of the sibling relationship:

one

Whether the fires of jealousy will flicker safely or flare up danger-
ously depends on our attitudes and acts (Ginott 1969).

The family climate and the parents' overt and covert message about
sibling roles decisively condition the interrelations between the siblings (Einstein and Moss 1967).

Often the advice offered is contradictory, and these con-
tradictions raise questions about the nature of the evidence
underlying "expert" opinion. Certainly it is not evidence from
systematic research; of that there is pitifully little. It was in
part our concern over this gap in what is known about the
early relations between siblings that led us to carry out the
study described in this book. Clearly, reliable information
about the way a young child will react to such a major event
in his life, and how young siblings will relate to one another,
are both issues of central importance to parents.

But we did not look at the beginning of the sibling relationship solely because it is potentially a cause for concern to
parents and physicians. It also provides an extraordinarily interesting opportunity to consider how a child's understanding
of other people develops. The change in the child's social
world at the time of a sibling's birth is profound: his relations
with his father and mother alter dramatically, and he is faced
with someone who is not only a rival for the love and attention of the parents, but who, unlike the adults in his world, is
not sensitively tuned to understand and respond to *him*. How
does he relate to someone who is indeed human, but in no
sense culturally sophisticated — someone who expresses
distress, contentment, excitement, yet who communicates in
such a very different way from adults? How does a young
child respond to such a change — a change that must involve a
major reorientation in his understanding of what other people
are like and why they behave as they do?

Research on parent-child communication has suggested that
it is through parental sensitivity to the child's interests, inten-

tions, and actions that the child begins to understand the meaning of his actions for other people and begins to use the "conventional" forms of communication. How then does a young child communicate with a still younger being who does not have a sophisticated understanding of his cognitive level, or of his motives and intentions? To what extent do young children differentiate between the other members of their family, in the ways in which they communicate with them? How much do 2-year-olds understand of the baby sibling's emotional state, intentions, or attempts to communicate? These questions raise very broad issues about the degree to which young children can understand and communicate with other people.

Studying the child with someone other than a mother (who is almost always highly motivated to interpret his intentions and to build a world of shared meanings with him) presents us with a new view of the child's abilities to understand and relate to others and gives us an opportunity to examine his beliefs about other people's states of mind and feelings. When we observe children with their young siblings, our attention is drawn not to the process of cultural initiation of the child by an adult, but rather to the child's capacity to understand and relate to another human being as a human being without following essentially *cultural* cues. Here we see unmistakably how the range of considerations that psychologists have judged to be important in development has been constrained by the particular ways in which they have set about studying children. Observing young siblings highlights aspects of human growth that may simply go unnoticed if development is studied solely in the context of parent and child. And it suggests a marked discrepancy between the capacities which psychologists will be led to attribute to children according to whether they are studied inside or outside the family context. As early as their second year, some of the secondborn siblings whom we studied demonstrated a pragmatic understanding not only of how to comfort and console, but also of how to provoke and annoy the elder. The firstborn children, for their part, even those only 2 years old, "explained" the baby to us. Their sensitivity to the emotional expressions of the baby, and their interpretations of this behavior—freely given in their discussions with their mothers and with us—presented with splendid clarity their beliefs and their understanding of the other child. They did *not* respond to their sibling's feelings simply by projecting their own feelings onto the baby, as studies of very young children's responses to the emotions of storybook characters have suggested.

Our interest in the interaction between the young siblings grew, therefore, to include more general questions about the nature of their relationships and about their understanding of other people. We were interested also in exploring the ways in which the various family relationships affected one another. If you reflect on families you know well, you immediately recognize that the relationships a young child forms with members of his family other than his mother are extremely important even in the first two to three years, and that these relationships may influence one another in complex ways. To consider mother and child as a dyad isolated from these other relationships within the family can be extremely misleading, as research on fathers in particular has already shown (Lamb 1976; Clarke-Stewart 1978). A second reason for studying the young siblings, then, was to try to see how the mother-child and the sibling relationships might influence each other. We were particulary interested in how these relationships evolved. Did the relationship between the siblings change as the children grew up; how was it affected by the age of the children?

A third issue concerned the period when the baby sibling was born. The birth of a sibling is frequently cited by clinicians as a source of long-lasting difficulty and stress to firstborn children—a major event that has the potential, surely, to alter the child's relations with his mother but, beyond that, also to affect his personality in a profound and durable way.[1] As yet, however, the effects of this change in family structure on the bonds between firstborn children and their parents have been little studied in a systematic way. So we decided to begin our study *before* the birth of the sibling, and to follow the firstborn children from a point late in the mother's pregnancy with the second child through the infancy of the secondborn.

It is well known that children vary in their response to sharp changes in their environment, or to stressful events. Some children appear to be much more vulnerable to such changes than others. Even though these individual differences have been repeatedly noted by clinicians, we have very little understanding of why some children seem more vulnerable than others. How far are differences in the temperament of the children significant — or differences in their relations with their parents? What is the prognostic significance of various forms of reaction? In examining the response of children to the

---

1. It is not of course the case that the importance of birth order has been an unexplored topic. For children over 5 years of age there is an extensive literature showing that the position of an individual in his family, and the sex and age spacing of his siblings, does influence his interests, preferences, style of thinking, self-esteem, conformity, and his eminence and achievement as an adult (see for example Jones 1931; Brim 1958; Harris 1964; Sutton-Smith and Rosenberg 1970; Schooler 1972; Cicirelli 1973, 1975, 1976a and b, 1977, 1978; Zajonc and Markus 1975; Majoribanks, Walberg, and Bargen 1975). Koch's work (1955a and b) shows that as early as age 6 there are systematic differences between children that can be related to their "sibling status."

Can these differences be attributed to the influence of the sibling directly? Or are they primarily the results of differences in parental treatment of first and later children? As Sutton-Smith and Rosenberg pointed out (1970), there is in fact a curious imbalance in the research on birth order, an imbalance that makes it difficult to answer questions about the early development of these differences. Studies of children over age 5 have examined *sibling* influences but not the interaction between parent and child according to sibling status, while research on infancy has examined *mother-child* interaction with first and later children but not the behavior of siblings together.

Since Sutton-Smith and Rosenberg's thoughtful discussion of the subject there have been a few studies of sibling interaction in infancy (Lamb 1978a and b; Abramovitch, Corter, and Lando 1979; Abramovitch, Corter, and Pepler 1980); however, only one of these has followed the children longitudinally, observing them in their own families.

events surrounding the birth of the sibling, we are addressing questions that may be of much more general clinical importance than is apparent at first glance.

Our findings show that the birth of a baby, and the accompanying change in the firstborn's life, have a dramatic effect on the behavior of the firstborn child. Almost all the children we followed showed signs of disturbance and unhappiness in addition to their interest in and affection for the baby. Their relations with their parents changed sharply. But there was a wide range of responses among the children: some became demanding and difficult; others became withdrawn, miserable, or clinging — and these reactions had quite different long-term implications. As we followed the children for 14 months after the birth of the second child, continuity with the first child's initial reaction was remarkably strong. The firstborn's response to the events surrounding the birth was linked to his behavior to the sibling 14 months later, to his response to his mother and sibling playing together, and, most strikingly, to the baby's behavior toward him.

Our planning of this study, then, reflected four chief concerns: the relationship between mother and first child before and after the sibling's birth; the reaction of the first children to the constellation of events surrounding the birth; the nature of the relationship that developed between the siblings; and the patterning of the several relationships within the family. To try to answer such a variety of questions, we decided to use a variety of techniques; these we describe in the next chapter.

two

The Children and the Study

This is a study of 40 firstborn children living with their mothers and fathers in Cambridge, England, or in villages close by. What kind of world did the children live in? What kinds of lives did they lead before the new baby arrived? Cambridge is a small provincial town, on the edge of the flat East Anglian fen country — a rich farming area. The town, known for its large university, also has a number of light industries, which in recent years have been declining in prosperity. For the great majority of the families, who were (in terms of the father's occupation — Registrar General 1973) working class, the world of the university was one with which they had absolutely no contact. Many of the mothers of the children, who had themselves grown up in Cambridge, had never been to the west side of town where the university is situated. Cambridge and the surrounding area has had a relatively stable working-class population with little immigration or mobility. The housing consists of new estates of houses and apartments — some council (public), some private — built in the last 20 years or so on the edge of the town; older and rather more run-down council estates, areas of Victorian and Edwardian terrace and semidetached housing more centrally; and larger detached houses with spacious gardens on the south and west sides of the town. The housing situation, in comparison with many inner-city areas, is relatively good. The newer council estates, in particular, are well planned and comfortable; the houses have bathrooms and indoor toilets, and usually as much space as those on the private estates. The poorest housing is, by and large, in the rental accommodation of the Victorian and Edwardian housing in the town, or in the more decrepit older council houses.

These two features, the stability of the working-class population and the relatively good housing, had a direct and important effect on the lives of the children we studied. The stability was reflected in the network of relatives (cousins, aunts, uncles, and more distant relatives) that many of the children had in the area, a network that extended over several generations. And most of the families lived in houses on the newer estates, either council houses or apartments (43 percent), or their own semidetached or terrace houses (38 percent). The remaining families lived in rented rooms or semidetached houses — usually the turn-of-the-century housing of the main town. The housing conditions on the estates and the stability of the population meant that while the social class of the sample was, in terms of the father's occupation, far from homogeneous, the pattern of the different children's lives was in many respects remarkably similar. A predictable routine of continuous close contact with the mother, regular visits from the grandparents, visits to local shops, and frequent contact with other children was common to most of the children whether they were living on council-house estates or in private housing, and whether the housing estates were at the edge of Cambridge or in a nearby village. The children's lives were very much focused on the estates where they lived: bus trips to the center of Cambridge to look at the stores were rare, and very few mothers had the use of a car.

Play space was quite plentiful for most children: the houses or apartments usually had a large living room, in which the family ate their meals, talked, and watched television, and in which the mothers did the ironing or sorted and mended clothes. Here the children played — and toys were abundant. Books were less common, but magazines and catalogs were numerous and very popular with the children. There was often a small garden or yard, though it was not always available (or rather, sanctioned) as play space for the children, since the families used the gardens for a wide range of purposes: for growing vegetables; for rearing rabbits, guinea pigs, or pigeons; for car maintenance; or as a general dumping ground. Sand pits (sandboxes) and climbing frames (jungle gyms) in the gardens were rare, but there was sometimes a swing; and for most children there was a playground not far away, to which trips were frequently made.

When we first met the children, each was the only child in the family, but the mothers were within a few weeks of the birth of their second child. Twenty-one boys and 19 girls, they ranged in age from 18 months to 43 months at the actual birth of the second baby, but over half the sample were between 19 and 23 months at the birth. So at our first visits, a month or so before the sibling's arrival, most were between 1½ and 2 years of age.

Daily life was, for almost all the children, a life spent close to the mother—following her around the house as she cleaned and tidied, "helping" her to hang out the wash, playing in the kitchen as she cooked, going to local shops with her, having a drink and a biscuit with her in front of the television. Most of the children were not used to even brief separations from their mothers. Six had never been separated, even for an afternoon, and 14 more experienced separations only about once a month. Only 3 were used to daily separations. Longer departures from the mother, for a night or for 24 hours were also rare: 28 children had never experienced such a separation, and only 3 had been away from their mothers for more than a week. During these periods all the children except one had been looked after by a relative.

While the children were accustomed to a life with their mother constantly present, their social world was far from being restricted to mother and father alone. The estates on which most of them lived were full of young families, and many children saw other children frequently. Twenty-three of the 40 saw other children more than twice a week, and 12 of these had a relationship with another child that their mothers felt was very important to them. Because they were so young, only 5 attended a play group or nursery school at this stage of the study.

Contact with grandparents was close for most of the families. Half the children saw their maternal grandmother at least once or twice a week; only 7 saw her rarely. The father's mother was also seen frequently in many families: at least once or twice a week in 14 families, and in 18 others one to three times a month. Visits to or from other relatives and (less commonly) friends of the family were frequent. Only 2 mothers reported having social contacts with either friends or relatives less than once a week. Of course, life on the housing estates did have for many women real disadvantages. Some found it hard to make new friends; others found the size and bleakness of the estates, and the distance from the center of town, depressing. To take the children to a paddling (wading) pool on a hot summer day, for instance, was a major and complicated expedition.

The amount of time the children spent with their fathers did vary considerably between families. All the fathers reportedly played with the child, and most took him out occasionally and helped at bedtime and mealtimes. Some regularly helped with diaper changing, dressing and undressing, and bathing, whereas others never took part in these aspects of child care. But it was notable that the actual time most fathers spent playing with or looking after the child was reported by the mothers to be relatively short. For 73 percent it involved a brief play period in the evening and perhaps half a day on the weekends. Most of the children seldom had their fathers to themselves at home: if the fathers were present, so were the mothers. The amount and type of help the fathers gave in the house also varied greatly. All apparently helped with repairs; some regularly washed the dishes, but very few cooked, shopped, or did the laundry. Almost all the families had dogs (often very large Alsatians) or cats, budgerigars or goldfish, to which the children were often extremely attached.

The daily pattern for the children differed not only in the role of the fathers, but in the family routines of eating and sleeping. In several families there were in fact no regular mealtimes, in the sense of the entire family's sitting down at a table to eat together; bowls of cereal, bread, or packets of crisps were consumed in front of the television more or less as it suited the children. In other families the child was expected to sit through a family meal. There was a similar range of differences in sleeping routines. Some children were not put to bed until the parents went to bed, but simply fell asleep in a chair or sofa. Others were put to bed much earlier and had a definite bedtime with a predictable routine of bath and story.

In considering the findings of our study — the nature of the children's relationships with their sibling and parents, the changes in their behavior with the birth of the sibling — we must bear in mind that we examined a particular and relatively small group of children, living in a particular place at a particular time. As we shall see, the pattern of the children's feeding and sleeping difficulties, their attention-seeking behavior and mood changes, in fact matched well the findings of large-scale studies of children of this age. But in other respects their lives clearly reflected the specific social world in which they were growing up. The closeness of contact with relatives and friends, the infrequency of separation from the mother, and the generally comfortable housing conditions of the majority of the children suggest that these children's lives were very different from, say, the lives of children brought up in many inner-city areas. Nonetheless, the birth of the sibling inevitably brought a major change in their lives — an irrevocable change from a life where, as one mother put it, "she's queen of the world." In the next chapter we describe the changes in the children's behavior and their experiences. First, though, we outline briefly the *methods* used to study the children, their personalities, and the changes in their behavior and relationships.

The Methods of the Study

How can we best investigate and describe a young child's wants and interests, his daily experiences and characteristic behavior, and his relations with his family? It is obvious that any one method of observing children or interviewing parents can give us only a partial picture, and that both observation and interviews are potentially biased sources of information. Not only is the presence of an observer intrusive, but there are clearly some features of the behavior of siblings toward each other that an observer would be unlikely to see during the limited time she or he is present (the response of an elder child to a younger one in danger, for example). It is also quite evident that a mother's description during an interview of her child's behavior will give *her* particular view of her child: in itself this is of course highly significant and interesting. Still, it might well differ from the description given by another person. We decided, therefore, both to observe the children directly, using a variety of ways of describing their behavior, and to interview the mothers at length about their children. We wanted to look systematically at these different sources of information in order to examine the extent of agreement between them (obviously important if we are concerned about the reliability of either technique), but also in order to assess which kinds of questions are most usefully addressed by interview techniques and which by direct observation.

It seemed to us crucially important to study the children in their own homes, rather than in a laboratory situation. It is true that a comparison of the behavior of different children under controlled circumstances provides a degree of standardization that we lose by observing these children in homes that vary substantially. Still, it is precisely these differences in children's normal experiences, and in their everyday behavior with their families, that we were anxious to study. If we are to understand what excites a child, what upsets or disturbs him, what kinds of theories and perceptions he has about the people in his life, then we are best placed to do so if we study him in a setting that has real emotional meaning to him — with his family and his friends — than if we study him in a laboratory playroom, however carefully this is presented as a "living room."

Our aim, then, was to observe the children at home with as

little disruption of their everyday life as possible. It is inevitable that the presence of an observer will affect the way members of a family behave towards one another — in real life there is no such thing as "nonparticipant" observing. To minimize the intrusive effect of the presence of a stranger, we made sure that the same observer visited each family at each visit, and that only one observer was present. Because we felt the premium should be on reducing the disruptive effect of the observer as much as possible, we did not attempt to remain silent and unresponsive but talked freely to the children and to the other family members if they spoke to us. This manner of observing turned out to have very real advantages. What the children said to us about their siblings was a revealing and fascinating source of information on their views and beliefs about the baby, a source that would have been lost to us if we had insisted on observing without talking. To argue that such "participant" observation can be both systematic and rigorous is hardly original: Charlotte Bühler's 1939 studies, in which her observers became "part of the family," showed long ago how useful this approach could be.

We contacted our families with the help of Health Visitors and General Practitioners. The Health Visitors made the initial approach when the mothers came for their prenatal checkups. Those mothers who were prepared to consider taking part then got in touch with us, and we visited them in their homes to describe the study in detail. All the mothers visited agreed to participate, and only one dropped out in the course of the study.

We decided to visit the families at four stages: during the last month or so of the mother's pregnancy with the second child; during the first month after the birth; when the baby was 8 months old; and when the baby was 14 months old. During each of these periods we made at least two visits, often three, and carried out the hour-long observations and interviews that we describe in more detail below. These included an assessment of the temperament, or personality, of the child. The framework of our study, then, was as follows:

Pregnancy visits
Mother pregnant with
  second child.
	Two observations: child with mother
	  ± father
	Interview
	Rating of temperamental
	  characteristics.

First-month visits
Two and three weeks after
  birth of second child.
	Two observations: child with mother
	  and baby sibling (including feeding),
	  ± father
	Interview

8-month visits
Second child 8 months old.
	Two observations: siblings with
	  mother, ± father.
	Interviews
	Rating of temperamental
	  characteristics.

14-month visits
Second child 14 months
  old.
	Two observations: siblings with
	  mother, ± father.
	Interviews

We chose 8 months and 14 months as age points for the follow-up visits because we were interested in the way the growing powers, independence, and mobility of the baby might affect the first child's relationships with both mother and sibling. At 8 months some of the babies would still be immobile whereas others would be able to get about; by 14 months all would be mobile and all would have well-developed powers of communication and understanding.

Observing the Children

Two major issues are involved in analyzing a young child's social behavior. One is the problem of making inferences about the meaning to the children of the particular interactions we are studying, and a second is the problem of moving from the level of describing *interaction* to that of describing *relationships*. Our assumptions about the cognitive ability, social understanding, and intentions of the child and about the nature of the relationship he has with the others in his world inevitably affect the kind of categories we use. Such issues are central themes of this book; they are extensively discussed in the chapters concerned with the relationship between the siblings, and the communication and understanding between them (Chapters 5 to 7). Here we merely give a brief outline of the kinds of observations we made.

"When he does that we call it 'smile,' and when he does that we call it 'laugh,'" is the way a 3-year-old explained to the observer the expressions of her 8-month-old brother. Her remark captures the element of choice and arbitrariness in descriptive categories of behavior. The way a psychologist chooses to describe the behavior of small children varies greatly according to the theoretical views of the psychologist, and according to the type of question she or he is addressing.

In the early naturalistic diary accounts of children at home that were kept by psychologists 50 or more years ago, the description often reflected the interest of the psychologist in the *educational* value of the child's activities. Stern (1924, p. 98) described his son's banging of his cup on the table: "With every blow that the child deals the table with his tin mug, he hammers into his little brain 'Noises can be made with things.'" In other early accounts psychologists viewed the child's actions within a more psychoanalytic framework. One example is Thorburn's (1938, p. 13) attempt to provide an account of the child's play in order "to help towards a realisation of just what it is to be a child." Other well-known examples are the observations of Dorothy Burlingham and Anna Freud (1944) of children brought up in a residential nursery, and, in a clinical setting, the observations of Donald Winnicott (1977).

In the past 15 years or so there has been renewed interest in the direct observation of children in naturalistic settings. Much of this research followed an "ethological" approach to observing the children: a characteristic feature (in the earlier studies) was that the observer attempted to avoid both descriptive units that implied emotional states (aggression, anxiety, and the like), and broader categories such as "attachment," at least at the time of the original recording of behavior (Blurton-Jones 1972; McGrew 1972). But the view that this restriction to "objective" terms somehow "freed" the information from the orientation of the psychologist who was observing is open to serious criticism. Description of human actions cannot be in terms of categories that are visually given; there is no way of describing human action without implying interpretation of it. Other psychologists observing children of this age do use categories that make explicit the interpretation which the observer places on the behavior. For instance, Mary Main (see George and Main 1979), in her work on children in day care, categorizes the children's social behavior as approach, avoidance, approach/avoidance, and aggression, and she follows Margaret Manning's methods of observing nursery-school children by subdividing behavior into harassment, teasing, and specific hostility (see Manning, Heron, and Marshall 1978).

For our study we decided to use a variety of descriptive units, including both measures that described single actions (one child giving the other a toy) and broader categories such as joint play (sequences of interaction when the child and his mother or sibling played with toys together, or engaged in games such as peekaboo). We also recorded particular categories of behavior that are of special interest to psychologists, such as imitations of actions or sounds, or actions where one person helped another. The details of these categories are given in Appendix B. (Appendix A comprises the tables that show the results of our analyses.) In selecting the categories for describing the interaction between child and parent and the methods for recording our observations, we drew heavily on the work of Clark-Stewart (1973). Our method enabled us to record the *duration* (in 10-second units) and the *frequency* of particular items of behavior. We also recorded some *sequences*. For instance, if a child made a verbal demand for something, we recorded whether or not this demand was complied with. The method also made it possible for us to keep a narrative record during our observations of particular aspects of the children's behavior that interested us; for instance we were able to note details of the children's play.

In observing the behavior of the siblings together at the 8-month and 14-month visits, we recorded each interaction, noting in detail their play, imitative and cooperative behavior, their visual attention to each other, encounters involving objects, and aggressive actions such as pushing or hitting. It was the *first* child on whom we focused, and we were therefore unable to record in fine detail the behavior of mother and baby together when the first child was not directly involved in their interaction. We were, however, able to record reliably the frequency and duration of such exchanges between mother and baby, and for the analyses reported in this book we categorized these exchanges simply as playful, restraining, caretaking, or vocal.

We tape-recorded the children's conversations during all the observations, using a small, portable, stereo tape recorder, and transcribed the conversations ourselves soon after the observations. This greatly lengthened the time taken to code and analyze the observation records, but provided us with a wonderfully rich source of data.

Reliability

It is of course important to know how reliable the two of us were in recording the children's behavior — that is, how consistent we were individually in recording a particular action or sequence of actions in the same way on different occasions, and whether or not we both were recording in the same fashion the behavior we observed. The extent of agreement between us, as observers, is given in Appendix B. A separate question concerns the length of time for which we observed, and the number of observations we made. How reliable a picture of a particular child's behavior and experience can one gain from observing such a tiny fraction of his behavior? A partial answer can be obtained by comparing the behavior measures of individual children from a given observation with the measures of the same children from observations carried out one week later. (This calculation of the "stability" of the measures is given also in Appendix B.) The results confirm that two separate observations of one hour each did give a relatively reliable picture of the differences between families in the measures we were using.

In one of the few studies that have examined the reliability of home observations of young children, Hughes and his colleagues (1979) compared the observations made on four separate visits to 4-year-olds in their homes. The second, third, and fourth visits gave very similar results, but observation on the very first visits gave atypical findings. (We did not observe on our first visits to the homes.)

Timing the Visits

When did we visit the children? During the visits made before the second child was born, we wanted to watch the children both in periods when their mothers were busy and in periods when they were more relaxed. We asked to come at an hour that suited the mother, but when she was carrying out routine household tasks. This could be afternoon or morning, according to her preference, but always included some time when she was busy washing, ironing, cleaning, or cooking, as well as some time when she was sitting with a cup of tea, watching TV, or talking to friends. After the baby was born, we arranged to include in our observations at least one feeding of the new baby. For all the families in the study this meant that in the first month after the baby was born (referred to as the first-month observations) we observed periods when the mother was occupied in caring for the baby, but also periods when the baby was asleep. At the 8-month and 14-month observations we arranged to visit at times when both children were at home.

How representative a picture of the child's behavior did this give us? We know from other studies that if families are observed at mealtimes or at bedtime, there is more confrontation between child and parent, and more parental control is exerted than at other times of day (Hughes et al. 1979). So while our results suggest that we were obtaining a reliable picture of daytime interaction, we should not assume that we would have obtained the same picture if we had observed at mealtimes and bedtime, or if we had observed on weekends: diary studies suggest that while family interaction is strikingly similar on different days during the week, it may be very different on the weekend (Douglas et al. 1968). By choosing to observe in the daytime and on weekdays, we missed the opportunity to observe systematically the children with their fathers. Our information on that relationship was therefore derived primarily from our interviews with the mothers.

The Interviews

At each of the four stages when we visited the children, we asked the mothers about the children's feeding, sleeping, and toilet habits, about attention-seeking behavior, independence and dependence, fears, worries, miserable moods, and so on. The interviews included questions on the children's medical history, their experience with other children, their relationship with their father, their response to separation from their mother, and "preparation" for the arrival of the sibling. The questions about the children's behavior focused on detailed descriptions of their actions in specific situations. The mothers were not asked to make general comments on their child's behavior; instead, they were asked to describe, for instance, how he had behaved at each mealtime over the previous 24 hours and what his sleep patterns had been over the past week. We should stress that not only were the interview questions open-ended, but most mothers talked freely and expansively about their children, perhaps in part because we were in their homes on several occasions and for long periods.

At the visits in the first month after the sibling's birth, the interview included also specific questions about the first child's reaction to the baby; about his behavior when the mother was feeding, caring for, or cuddling the baby; and about his response to his father's or grandparents' interaction with the baby. At the visits made when the sibling was 8 months and 14 months old, the interview included many questions about the relations between the siblings, about the behavior of the second child, about the father's relations with both children, and about the mother's view of similarities and differences between her two children. The details of these questions, and the way the mothers' replies were coded, will be discussed later in relevant chapters of the book.

Describing Differences in Children: The Issue of Temperament

Individual differences between children are marked from the moment they are born. Some babies are easygoing, placid, and calm; others are more tense and jumpy. Some seem predominantly happy and relaxed; others are much more moody and unhappy. Parents, doctors, psychologists — anyone who has to care for young children — cannot fail to be aware of these differences. To what extent do they influence the way other people behave toward the children? Do they persist through childhood? To what degree are they the results of the children's experience?

To investigate these questions in a careful and systematic way, we need precise and reliable techniques for describing and measuring these "personality" or "temperamental" differences. It is extremely difficult to devise such methods. The central problem the psychologist must face is that in the course of the first three or four years the new skills and understanding that a child acquires transform his behavior. This means that a particular item of behavior may *appear* similar at two ages, but its meaning and the circumstances and motives that elicit it and influence it may in fact be quite dissimilar. A baby crying at 3 months is often responding to very different factors from those that lead a child of 2 years to cry.

The problem thus is one of assigning meaning to particular items of behavior and then of assessing the significance of individual differences in the frequency with which this behavior appears. Psychologists have used a number of different strategies in trying to trace the patterns of continuity and discontinuity in individual differences over the early years. One approach has been to use a global characterization of *how* a child behaves, to describe his style rather than the detail of his actions, a form of description where the "traits" of temperamental differences are thought to be appropriate for characterizing children from infancy through early childhood.

The key study that first developed this approach to the analysis of individual differences in temperament from infancy onward was that of Thomas et al. (1963). On the basis of extensive interviews with parents these investigators developed a relatively broad classification of different aspects of temperament in children, which distinguished the following traits: "*activity level, rhythmicity* (regularity) of biological functions, *approach or withdrawal* to the new, *adaptability* to new or altered situations, *sensory threshold* of responsiveness to stimuli, *intensity of reaction, quality of mood, distractibility,* and *attention span and persistence*" (Thomas and Chess 1980). They did not assume that a child's temperament was unchangeable, but argued that the environment in which a child grew up could either heighten or diminish his "reactive style." Several more recent studies have used this type of classification of temperament differences among children. Although there are many conceptual and methodological problems inherent in the approach, these studies have been extremely important in drawing attention to the significance of individual differences, and they have indisputably shown that there are associations between the nature of a child's "temperament" and the likelihood that he will develop a behavior disorder (Rutter et al. 1964; Graham, Rutter, and George 1973; Dunn 1979).

We were aware that there were differences in the children's behavior that were not captured either by our direct observation categories or by the questions in our interview. So we decided to include an assessment of temperamental differences along the lines of the Thomas, Chess, and Birch (1968) study. We felt that this was particularly necessary because of evidence that differences between children along these dimensions do significantly modify their responses to stressful circumstances. Since we were particularly interested in *which* children reacted to the arrival of a sibling by becoming upset or disturbed, it seemed important to include an assessment of these temperamental differences, regardless of our theoretical reservations about some of the assumptions on which the assessment was based. At the time we carried out the first interview, therefore, we included an Assessment of Temperamental Characteristics interview developed by Claire Sturge from the Thomas, Chess, and Birch interview.

In this interview we asked the mothers for detailed descriptions of how their children had behaved in a number of situations over the previous day or so. Most of these were common daily or weekly events in the child's life — being dressed and washed in the morning, being told to stop what he was doing, being taken out for a walk to the stores, having his hair washed, having a toy taken away by another child, and so on. Other questions focused on the child's reaction to changes in his routine — how did he react when he last was put to sleep in a strange place, or was fed away from home? — and on his behavior when he did not feel well. Many of these questions, then, were concerned with the behavior of the child when faced with routine yet mildly stressful events, or when his behavior was being controlled. In Appendix B the detailed scoring of these traits and the reliability are given.

We used the assessment (for reasons discussed in the appendix) to dichotomize the sample, for each of the temperamental traits, into those children who were relatively extreme on the trait versus the rest. Some examples will give the flavor of this grouping. A child who was rated as extreme on the *intensity* trait would be a child who had reacted with great excitement and wild emotion (either pleasure or fury) to the ordinary events of life about which we were inquiring. And a child rated as extreme in withdrawal would be a child who had hidden when the doorbell rang, who had clung to his mother throughout a visit to the local clinic while other children happily ran off to explore, and who in a stranger's presence had been extremely shy. A child rated as extreme on the dimension of *negative mood* would be one who had been grumpy and bad-tempered when he woke that morning and who had fussed a great deal when taken for a walk, when his nails were cut, and when his hair was brushed. The group of children who were classed as extreme on *unmalleability* were children who were difficult to persuade to give up an activity when called for a meal, who were considerably bothered by a change in their routine or in their state of health, and who when "told off" reacted very defiantly.

The Relations between Observations and Interviews

At each stage of the study — the pregnancy visit, the first-month visit, the 8-month visit, and the 14-month visit — we examined the information gained from our direct observation of the children in relation to that gained from the interviews. We shall discuss the results at appropriate points in the book; they show an encouraging amount of agreement among the different sources of data.

We turn now to the children, and to their response to the arrival of the new sibling. How did they react to this change in their family world?

three

Arrival of the Sibling

> I keep wondering how she'll cope when the baby comes
> . . . Her world's going to change so much, and she seems
> so *little* to have it all upside down . . . She doesn't much
> like changes anyway, so what's she going to make of
> *this?*

A mother, concerned for her 22-month-old daughter as the
birth of the sibling approached, voiced worries felt by many
parents. Behind her question lie a host of issues. How likely is
it that a child will be disturbed by the changes? Which aspect
will be most stressful for the child — the separation from the
mother, the mother's preoccupation with the new baby, the
symbolic displacement? How will the age of the firstborn
affect her response? Which children are most vulnerable?
What will the birth of the second child *mean* to the first?
Freud had clear views on this last issue:

It is of quite particular interest to observe the behaviour of small
children up to the age of 2 or 3 or a little older towards their young
brothers and sisters . . . I am quite seriously of the opinion that a
child can form a just estimate of the set-back he has to expect at the
hands of the little stranger. (1948, pp. 251–252)

To many clinicians the birth of a sibling is seen as a potentially stressful experience for young children, especially for
firstborn children. The effects of the "dethronement" or "dis-

placement" that a sibling birth involves are frequently cited in case histories (Petty 1953; Aarons 1954; Black and Sturge 1979), although psychiatrists disagree on how far this stress should be considered a "normal" event. Some argue that the change in the child's life is an experience that the majority of children have to cope with, and that "it is so usual as to be called normal when a child is upset at a new one" (Winnicott 1964). Both Spock (1969) and Winnicott in fact suggested that the event is potentially valuable to the child: Winnicott commented that the experience of "finding hate" is one that is developmentally important, even though he noted (as well he might) that the difficulty for the child is finding a "legitimate expression of that hate."

In contrast, other psychologists have compared the birth of a sibling to a parental death, arguing that the significance of these experiences for later personality development may well be similar (Moore 1969).

Although sibling rivalry and especially response to the birth of the new sibling are frequently cited in the case histories of children referred to psychiatrists, our information on the reaction of firstborn children is extremely patchy. A number of interview studies have included reports on the reaction of children to the birth of a sibling. These indicate in broad outline what form we may expect the responses of children to take: an increase in behavior problems, but also an increase in independence. For instance, four studies indicate that a high proportion of children are likely to react with some increase in behavior problems. Henchie (1963) in a study of 66 children found that 89 percent of the children under age 3 at the birth of the sibling showed "overt negative responses." In Cleveland a group of pediatricians studying the effects of hospital visiting on a group of 31 firstborn children whose mothers were in hospital for the birth of a second child, reported an increase in behavior problems in 92 percent of the children (Trause et al. 1978). And Legg, Sherick, and Wadland (1974), interviewing the parents of 21 children over the period when a second child was born, found that regressive behavior was reported for most of the children. In the New York longitudinal study of Thomas and Chess (1977) a sibling was born in 18 of the families during the period of study, and over half of the children were reported to show disturbance. Other studies directed specifically at documenting the incidence of "jealousy" report that it is very common (Sewall, 1930; Valentine 1946).

But *which* children are likely to be most upset? What is the prognostic significance of the different kinds of reactions? And *why* are the children upset? The interview studies do not go very far toward helping us answer these questions. It is often assumed that maternal attention to the new baby must be foremost in the etiology of disturbance after a sibling birth. Yet the arrival of a sibling involves a whole constellation of changes for the first child, and no systematic information is available to enable us to distinguish the causal impacts of these changes from one another.

The studies do suggest that the behavior disturbance is greater in children under 5 years of age at the time of the sibling birth, though there is no clear indication that age differences in children younger than this are systematically related to the ways in which the children respond. Despite this lack of consistent evidence on very young children, it is still widely believed that age differences are systematically related to the degree of disturbance shown by the child who is under 5. Podolsky (1954) wrote that jealousy is more likely to be severe when the age difference between the children is between 1½ and 3 years, an age range that Sewall (1930) too found to be particularly vulnerable. Freud himself maintained: "Normally of course this attitude of a child towards a younger brother or sister is a simple function of the difference between their ages. Where the gap in time is sufficiently long, an elder girl will already begin to feel the stirring of her maternal instincts towards the helpless newborn baby" (1958, p. 252).

On the issue of how much the separation from the mother may contribute to disturbance shown by children after a sibling's birth, these studies cannot provide clear answers, for no adequate controls were provided. Nonetheless, it is notable that neither Trause and her colleagues nor Henchie found that differences in the *extent* of separation affected the indexes of disturbance they employed. Sex differences in the response of the first children were not found in most of the interview studies either, though in Sewall's study the firstborn children were particularly likely to be jealous if the new baby was a boy.

There are a number of striking gaps in the picture given by these studies. First, there is no indication of how far the quality of the relationship of the first child to the parent before the birth is associated with the first child's reaction to the arrival of baby. Yet this is seen by clinicians as centrally important. David Levy (1937) in his discussion of sibling rivalry (based on studies of children playing with dolls) links disturbance and hostile behavior directly to the closeness of the relationship between the child and mother. He commented that the closer the relationship of a child to mother, the greater was the disturbance and the demonstration of hostility caused by the "intruder." And Podolsky (1954) commented that the severity of the rivalry reaction depended on the degree to which the child was dependent on the mother. Stendler (1954) too argued that intense of sibling rivalry is most likely if the older child is displaced while still highly dependent on his mother.

A second gap, related to the first, is that there is little systematic information on how the child's relationship with the mother and father changes over the period when the second child is born. Yet if we are to understand why children respond in the way that they do to the arrival of a sibling, it is certainly important to study any change in their relationship with their parents.

A third notable gap concerns individual differences among children. There is little indication from the studies of how such differences might be related to response to the arrival of a sibling. Even so, it is often argued clinically that temperamental differences are of major significance in accounting for individual variations in children's responses to stressful events (Rutter et al. 1964; Graham, Rutter, and George 1973; Dunn 1979).

Finally, and most importantly, the interview studies do not give us information directly from the children themselves, but rest upon information that comes from the mothers' descriptions of their children. Any study of children that is based on parental interview is open to the criticism that reports of changes in children's behavior may simply reflect changes in parents' perceptions of the children. Direct and systematic observations of mothers and children before and after the birth of a sibling are extremely rare. Taylor and Kogan (1973), observing eight mother-child dyads in a playroom before and after the sibling birth, reported that both mother and child showed less warmth to each other after the birth. Because observations of families in more natural settings are lacking, we determined to use both observations and interviews.

The results showed that there were marked changes in the behavior of the majority of children, and in particular in their interaction with their mothers. The first question we need to consider, then, is, How common were the *different* changes in children's behavior that the mothers described to us?

The mothers gave us, in the interviews before and after the sibling birth, detailed descriptions of the child's feeding, sleeping, and toilet behavior, their fears, worries, dependence, and so on. The answers to the interview questions were coded on three-point or four-point scales, so changes in the children's behavior could be analyzed in terms of changes in these scores. For instance, there were detailed questions on the child's settling to sleep and on his waking during the night in the week before the interview; from these a four-point "sleep problem" rating was derived: 0 = no problem; 1 = occasional problem (for example, child woke once in previous week, took more than a hour to settle on one occasion); 2 = marked problem (child woke two to six times in the week); 3 = very marked (child woke every night in the week). Thus if a child had not wakened at all at the time of the pregnancy interview, and then had wakened three times in the week of the first-month interview this would have been coded as a two-point increase—a "moderate increase." (See Table A3.1 in Appendix A, which gives the incidence of changes in the children's behavior.)

In answering the detailed questions about the children's behavior, the mothers made vivid comments on how they felt the children had changed, comments that highlighted the unhappiness of the children and the difficulties their parents experienced in coping with them. The most common change was an increase in naughtiness and demanding behavior, particularly toward the mother, a change shown by 93 percent of the children:

> MOTHER OF SYLVIA S: She always was naughty, but now she won't do *anything* I ask. I send her up to bed and try not to smack [spank]. I don't really believe in it; anyway, it doesn't do any good. She's rude, cheeky, into things, defiant, disobedient.

> MOTHER OF JOANNE R: She's got very selfish—wants everything she can see. Gets very cross if she's told to wait.

More than half the children in the sample increased in clinging and tearfulness after the sibling birth:

> MOTHER OF JIM E: He cries at everything. I can't tell him off for anything.

> MOTHER OF DIANNE H: There's more tears over frustration. She's more sensitive to things. As though life's a bit hard all 'round—as if she's [got] more to cope with and she's not quite sure how to cope with it.

Several of the children were reported to show distinct signs of withdrawal:

> MOTHER OF ARNOLD H: It's not so bad now as it was at
> first, when he was naughty, crying, and difficult. He
> didn't do anything I asked. So bad-tempered. Anything
> you said no to, he cried. Now it seems as if he's in a wee
> world of his own. So quiet. I think he's feeling pushed
> out. If anyone comes, he used to get so excited. Now
> he's so quiet.

Sleeping problems increased for 28 percent of the children,
and toilet training difficulties for 2 of the 26 children who
were trained before the birth. (Feeding problems were so common among the children in the study that there was hardly
room for an increase! But 3 children who had been easy over
feeding did become more difficult.)

Signs of regression were noted by 28 mothers. For 15
children these were mild—occasional baby talk, demands to
be carried around, or requests to be fed. For an additional 13
children there was a definite regressive step over toilet training, or an insistence on being fed by a child who had
previously fed himself, and so on.

Jealousy of the Baby with Fathers and Grandparents

In many families the mothers felt that the most obvious signs
of jealousy were shown when the father or the grandparents
showed pleasure or interest in the baby. Over half the
children were said to show some jealousy—either by looking
unhappy, or by direct action or comment—when the father
held or played with the baby.

> MOTHER OF SUSAN S: She minds him [father] holding
> him much more than when I do. I think she takes me
> and him [baby] for granted. But she looks at her dad in
> a special way when he's with the baby.

One child put it very firmly to her mother, "Daddy is *not*
Ronnie's daddy." Fifty percent of the children were said to be

jealous of the grandparents' holding or playing with the baby too.

Nevertheless, the picture was not entirely a bleak one. Over half the mothers reported increased independence in their children. The most common changes reported were that the child showed a new insistence on feeding or dressing himself, a self-reliance about going to the toilet alone, and an increase in the time during which the child would tolerate playing alone. Several children also gave up the bottle in the first two weeks following the sibling's birth.

> MOTHER OF DEREK J: He's started feeding himself—first time for months he *insists* on feeding himself. Also he will go and play in the garden if she's in the pram [carriage].

> MOTHER OF DIANNE H: There's a new independence. She's started talking to people in the shops, which she never used to.

Similar changes—signs of the child's having become suddenly "more grown up"—have been reported in a number of other interview studies (Einstein and Moss 1967; Legg, Sherick, and Wadland 1974; Trause et al. 1978; and see also Freud 1965).

Behavior toward the Baby

While aggression and naughtiness directed at the *mother* increased in so many families, most of the children were interested and affectionate toward the *baby* (Table A3.2).

> MOTHER OF JIM E: He asks where she is first thing in the morning. He's happy when he can see her.

> MOTHER OF HARVEY M: He talks to him a lot. Shows him things.

Thirty-two of the children *talked* about the baby, 12 of these referring to him frequently. Twenty-two tried to entertain the baby with books, toys, or play, and 30 wanted to cuddle or caress him.

Many were also concerned when the baby cried: 24 were said to be upset at signs of distress.

> MOTHER OF SYLVIA S: She doesn't like it when he cries. She was in tears when he first cried.

> MOTHER OF BRENDAN F: When she cries he's very concerned. Gets her dummy [pacifier], then comes and tells me.

> MOTHER OF DUNCAN K: Every time he hears him cry, he comes running up.

Aggression to the baby — hitting, poking, or pinching — was not common, although 21 children were described by their parents as deliberately irritating the baby by overwhelming him with physical attention, by shaking the cot, or by taking away his bottle or pacifier (Table A3.3). This low incidence of aggression to the baby contrasts markedly with Sewall's study from the 1930s, where 26 out of 70 children were said to have made "bodily attacks" on the new baby.

Almost all (95 percent) of the children were extremely eager to help with caring for the baby and joined in with great enthusiasm if their mothers encouraged them (and indeed, even if their mothers did *not*). Imitation of the baby's noises, grimaces, and actions was described by 30 of the mothers; and 15 of the children were said to imitate the baby very frequently.

The Patterning of the Reaction

How closely were these different reactions related? Were the children who were most upset over sleeping and toilet training, for instance, also the children who were most clinging and tearful? And were they the children who were least interested in the new baby?

We examined the association between the different aspects of reaction using a method of log-linear analysis.[1] The results showed that the children who increased markedly in tearfulness also increased in clinging behavior, but that the other aspects of disturbance were *not* closely linked. The children who increased in sleeping problems, for instance, were not necessarily the children who had become particularly demanding, difficult, clinging, or withdrawn, and there were no associations between increases in demanding or naughty behavior and increases in tearfulness or withdrawal. In contrast, the different kinds of *friendly* behavior shown toward the baby were linked. Children who made frequent references to the baby tended also to want to help the mother with caring for the baby and tried to entertain him or cuddle and play with him.

The pattern of reactions showed that the children who were frequently warm and affectionate to the baby were often children who in other respects were clearly disturbed and upset by the events surrounding the arrival of the sibling. There was no simple association between the rise in behavior problems, and the interest displayed in the new baby. The only exception to this general finding is that children who showed no interest in the sibling were likely to have increased in withdrawal and clinging behavior in other contexts. The signs of being "more grown up," the increases in independence reported for more than half the children in the study, were often reported for children who also showed signs of disturbance and upset. The same child (Jill J) who was described by her mother after the sibling birth as now sucking her thumb all day, being desperately clinging, and insisting on having bottles of milk that she had previously given up, *also* now

---

1. The details of the log-linear contingency analysis and the linear logistic model regression analysis are given in full in Dunn, Kendrick, and MacNamee (1981).

insisted on going to the toilet on her own, and on taking her own shoes on and off. And Derek J, described by his mother as insisting on feeding himself and playing in the garden if his sister was in the pram, was also clearly very upset:

> MOTHER OF DEREK J: He keeps having tantrums and misery. Anything sets him off. He's just terrible.

It appears from these findings that a simple notion of "degree of disturbance" is inappropriate to describe the children's reaction to the arrival of the baby. And the follow-up data support this conclusion. The long-term implications of the various aspects of the reaction—their links with the problems that persisted over the following year and with the quality of the relationship that developed between the siblings—were quite different (Chapters 8 and 10).

These descriptions of changes in the children's behavior may of course reflect changes in the mothers' perceptions of the children. It was clear from the interviews that many of the mothers were extremely tired and under considerable stress during the three weeks following the sibling's birth. Twenty-two of the 40 mothers reported that they were getting less than five hours of sleep per 24 hours at three weeks after the baby's birth.

There were in fact links between the mother's state in the postpartum weeks and a number of features of the child's reaction: if the mother had felt very tired and/or depressed during the first three weeks after the baby was born, her first child was more likely to have increased in tearfulness, and she herself was likely to have had very interrupted nights, with few hours' sleep, and to be experiencing particular difficulties with the new baby (Table A3.4).

Several felt that the strain was not attributable solely to tiredness:

> MOTHER OF PATRICIA R: I don't think it's simply tired-ness, though the nights aren't very good. I was *afraid*

when my husband went back to work. I felt like an abandoned child. I did want help.

And two mothers were quite explicit about the ambivalence they felt toward the first child under these circumstances:

MOTHER OF LAURA W: I'm very low. I feel like murdering her. I dread the sound of her feet along the corridor. I've wept for two weeks.

MOTHER OF SYLVIE S: I'm not quite as exhausted as last week — still, very tired. Very edgy and irritable. I've got so I can't stand her. She has me in tears every day. It's bad really.

This extreme degree of irritation with the first child was not common, although the numbers of women who described themselves as very tired and depressed three weeks after the baby was born was distressingly high (Fig. 3.1). Obviously we should bear this tiredness and strain in mind when considering the mothers' description of their children's behavior.

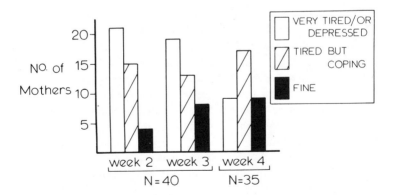

Figure 3.1 Mothers' descriptions of how they are feeling two, three, and four weeks after the birth of their second child.

It was clear too from the interviews that some of the descriptions of the children's behavior, especially toward the sibling, presented particular problems of interpretation; they could be viewed as reflecting very different kinds of feelings or intentions on the first child's part:

> MOTHER OF ALISTAIR M: He wants to play with her but he's so rough. Lies on top of her. Then she cries. He wants to roll all over her. I have to keep her away from him 'cause I can't let her be bashed about yet.

The categorization of a child's behavior as deliberately irritating the baby or as physically affectionate toward the baby both present obvious difficulties. Similar behavior shown to the baby by a 2-year-old might well be described by one mother as "showing affectionate interest" and by another as "unnecessarily interfering with or irritating the baby." Mothers often described behavior that they called protective, for instance, which might well be labeled rather differently by others:

> MOTHER OF JOANNE R: She's very protective. She stands by the cot for hours, sucking her thumb.

This issue of the relation between the mothers' perception of the children's behavior, their description of changes, and the observed changes in the children's behavior is one that we shall take up in the next section, when we consider our observations of the children before and after the sibling birth. Before turning to the observations, however, we should note that not only were some children described by their mothers as showing both frequent physical affection *and* as often irritating the baby, but that our own observations suggested that some children did show individually a range of behavior to the baby that included both affectionate, gentle caressing, and behavior that was much more clearly categorized as "irritating"—pulling the dummy (pacifier) out of the baby's mouth and throwing it away, for instance. (This ambivalence was reflected also in the comments made by the children about the new baby, comments we shall discuss in the next chapter.)

Changes in Observed Behavior

When we compared the behavior of the children with their mothers before the sibling birth with their behavior after the birth, a number of striking changes were apparent. First, confrontation between child and mother increased significantly after the birth (Table A3.5) and was reflected in a number of measures, both verbal and nonverbal. Second, the time that child and mother spent together in joint play, or in focusing together on a common item of interest, decreased markedly. The frequency with which the mother helped the child; showed, pointed out, or gave things to the child; or made suggestions to highlight features of whatever was the current focus of attention for the child — and the time during which the child was held or cuddled — all decreased by more than 24 percent of their level in the pregnancy observations.

Third, there was a change in the initiative of mother and child in starting interaction. Mothers started fewer bouts of joint play, and the part the children played in starting bouts of either mutual attention or joint play increased (Table A3.6).

Analysis of the conversations between mother and child revealed the same pattern of change. The conversations were coded into episodes, and these episodes categorized as being concerned with control, play, books, or other topics (see Wootton 1974). After the sibling birth there was a significant increase in the number of episodes of conversation concerned with control, although the frequency of the other categories did not change significantly (Table A3.7). And while there was a *decrease* in the number of conversational episodes initiated by the mother, there was an *increase* in the number started by the child. The children, in other words, were taking a larger role in initiating communicative exchanges. The mothers, on the other hand, were less likely to begin a conversation by making a friendly comment on the child's activities, by offering a suggestion for a new activity, or by starting a verbal game or fantasy. A marked exception to this pattern was the frequency of verbal exchanges that began with the mother's *prohibiting* the child. These increased in frequency: indeed, the ratio of friendly positive verbal initiations to negative prohibitory initiations by the mother decreased sharply after the sibling birth.

In our observations before the sibling was born, we had found certain marked patterns of association between the ways in which mother and child behaved toward each other (Table A3.8). In some families the children spent a large proportion of time wandering around aimlessly or sitting without playing; in these families there was relatively little joint play between child and mother and a relatively high level of confrontation and dispute between mother and child. On the other hand, the families where there was frequent play and little disagreement or prohibition by the mother tended to be families where the children played in a focused way and initiated a good deal of conversation with the mother. After the baby was born this picture changed dramatically. Some of the children whose mothers had been among the most playful and permissive now spent a high percentage of time in aimless wandering or sitting without playing (Table A3.9).

This change in the linkage between the behavior of mother and child could have arisen in a number of different ways. It could reflect primarily changes in the individual differences between mothers, with some mothers, relative to the other mothers, suddenly becoming much more restrictive and prohibitive after the sibling birth. Or it could reflect changes in the individual differences in the children — or indeed in both mothers and children. It is possible, too, that the changes described reflected *developmental* changes in the interaction between mothers and children, rather than changes in response to the events surrounding the sibling birth. Finally the change could be a statistical effect, mirroring a change in the variance of the measures of mothers' and children's behavior.

These different possibilities were examined and the results showed, first, that the differences between the mothers in the study remained very stable from before to after the sibling birth. The families where the mothers had been relatively playful were still the families with the most playful mothers after the second child was born, although, as we have seen, for the sample as a whole there was a decrease in maternal attention and play and an increase in confrontation. In contrast, the differences between children observed before the sibling birth were not consistent with the differences observed after the sibling birth. Some children who before the sibling birth had played in a focused way and spent very little time sitting, using comfort objects, or wandering around aimlessly, suddenly after the sibling birth became the children who spent *most* time in such activities. There was no consistency from before to after the sibling birth in the relative rank orders on the frequency with which the children fussed and cried, made demands on their mothers, wandered around, or sat without playing (Table A3.10). Of course these changes in the behavior of individual children may well have been responses to the changes in interaction with the mother that had been found for the sample as a whole. The point to be stressed is that the pattern of change after the events surrounding the birth was very different in different children.

Since we do not have data on a control group of children of the same age, temperament, and family background who did not experience the birth of a sibling, the possibility that the changes we observed reflect developmental changes cannot be examined directly. However, the, sample did include 20 families where the interval between the observations before and after the sibling birth was less than two months. When the observations for these families were examined separately, the results were found to be, without exception, similar in direction and as marked in extent as in the full sample. While this does not rule out the possibility that developmental changes were involved, it seems highly unlikely that such sharp changes in interaction and behavior could be solely — or even strongly — related to an age change of less than two months. What we have to explain, then, is the occurrence of changes, including very sudden "advances" in children's behavior, an issue to which we shall return.

The Effects of Maternal Care for the New Baby

Were the changes in the behavior of child and mother a direct consequence of the mother's involvement with the new baby? Superficially it seems entirely plausible that a decrease in attention and play, and an increase in confrontation, may straightforwardly reflect the problems facing a mother who is having to bathe and feed a new baby while coping with a demanding toddler. We examined the issue by comparing the interaction between the mother and first child when the mother was feeding the baby; when she was holding, caring for, or playing with the baby; and when she was not involved with the baby in any direct way.

The comparisons revealed some surprises. First, the mother and first child spent *more* time in joint play and attention when the baby was being fed than when the mother was not occupied with the baby. They spent more time looking at each other in a friendly way, and the mother made more "child-centered" suggestions referring to whatever was the focus of the child's attention. However, there was also more trouble between child and mother during the feedings — more confrontation, prohibition, and mutually hostile looks than in the periods when the mother was not occupied with the baby. When the mother was holding, playing with, or changing the baby, the pattern was the same: there was more friendly attention and play between child and mother, but also more confrontation than when the mother was not involved with the baby (Table A3.11).

So the periods during which the mothers were occupied with their second babies were *not* occasions when they ignored their first children. How then can we account for the overall general decrease in joint attention and play that we observed to occur with the arrival of the sibling? To find out, we compared the behavior of mother and child during the pregnancy observations and during those parts of the first-month observations when the mother was not directly involved with the baby. What we found was that while there was no increase in confrontation and prohibition after the sibling birth except when the mother was dealing with the baby, there *was* a marked decrease in the overall time spent in joint attention and play. When the mother was not occupied with the baby, the change in her attention to and her playful interest in the first child was particularly marked.

The increase in confrontation that was so striking when the mother was caring for the new baby might have reflected either an increase in naughtiness and/or aggression on the part of the first child, or a change in the patience or restrictiveness on the mother's part — or, indeed, a change in both. In an attempt to separate these possibilities, we examined the frequency with which the children were "deliberately naughty" while we were observing. The criteria for putting an act in this category were highly conservative. Only if a child performed an act that had been explicitly forbidden while we were present, or if the child physically attacked the mother, was the act coded as deliberately naughty.

The results were impressive. There was a threefold increase in the frequency of such incidents after the birth of the sibling, and the incidents were three times more likely to occur when the mother was busy with the baby than when she was not (Table A3.12).

This analysis suggested that the children did tend to become more naughty and difficult after the sibling birth. Of course, it does not exclude the possibility that the mothers also became more restrictive. Since the categorization of an act as deliberately naughty depended on the mother's having

previously forbidden a certain kind of action, clearly an increase in her restrictiveness would be likely contribute to an
apparent increase in the deliberate naughtiness. There is no
way we can completely resolve the issue, but we must emphasize that the great majority of acts classified as deliberately
naughty according to these criteria were, to a detached and
not particularly exhausted or irritated observer, in com-
monsense terms both *naughty* and *deliberate.* Two examples:
One child, whose mother and baby sister were gazing at each
other in a long absorbed exchange, picked up his cup, which
had a lid with holes in the top, and looking across to the
baby and his ecstatic cooing mother, started to sprinkle his
milk all over the sofa. A second child ran into the garden and
laughingly let down the line with a full load of clean washing
onto the muddy grass. The number of times that a mother
repeated a prohibition during an incident of naughtiness increased after the sibling birth. Again, this could reflect either
increased recalcitrance on the child's part, or increased restrictiveness and impatience on the mother's part, or both.

This difficulty in separating changes in the mother's perceptions and behavior from changes in that of the child brings us
back to the question we raised in discussing the mothers'
reports of increased behavior problems after the sibling birth.
To what extent do the observations agree with the picture
given us by the mothers?

We looked specifically at the mothers' reports of increased
tearfulness, clinging, withdrawal, demanding behavior, and
negative reactions to the mother, by comparing the frequency
of relevant observational measures in the groups of children
who were said to have changed in these ways, with that in the
groups of children reported not to have changed. The findings
showed that mothers' descriptions agreed well with our observations of the children (Table A3.13). Children described as
having become more tearful had indeed increased in the extent
to which they fussed during the observations significantly
more than those not so described; those reported to have increased in clinging spent more time being held in the first-

month observations; those said to have increased in demanding behavior did make more demands in the first-month observations. In families where the children were said to have increased in negative behavior to the mothers, there were indeed significantly greater increases in several measures of confrontation than in the other families. (We should bear in mind, of course, that this pattern could result from a change in the child, the mother, or both.)

The mothers' descriptions of the childrens' behavior to the baby also accorded well with our observations. Children described by their mothers as showing frequent physical affection to the baby *held* the baby more during the observations and caressed the baby more than the children whose mothers said this occurred rarely. Those reported to be very helpful with the baby were significantly more likely to comply with the mothers' suggestions during the feedings. And those reported to be interested in the baby were observed to hold the baby more than the rest.

The mothers had also been asked during the interviews about the first child's behavior during the feedings, and while the mother was caring for the baby (when she changed, comforted, or cuddled the baby). Again, we found some good agreement between the mothers' descriptions of how the children behaved in these situations and what we had recorded during the observations.

The extent of this agreement is encouraging. It is true that since the interviews were carried out after the observations, there may have been a contributing halo effect: the interviewer may have been biased in her rating of the mother's replies. But the interview questions were focused on detailed descriptions of the child's behavior and were far less open to halo effect than more global ratings would have been. The comparison between observation and interview suggests that under the circumstances in which the mothers talked to us about their children they gave accurate descriptions, and that the changes they described in their children's behavior were not simply the biased descriptions of exhausted and stressed mothers. Interviews and observations both showed that there were very marked differences between children in the ways in which they reacted to the arrival of the sibling, and it is these individual differences that we consider next.

Individual Differences in the Children's Reactions

How closely were the variations in behavior problems, in altered interaction with the mother, in the first child's interest in the baby, and in the signs of becoming more grown up related to the child's age at the time of the sibling birth, to temperamental differences, to sex differences, or to differences in the quality of the relationship with the parents before the birth? Was the child's experience of separation from the mother important? We have seen that several mothers were extremely tired and depressed after the birth of the baby; did these mothers have children who were particularly disturbed or difficult? Did the choice to breast-feed or bottle-feed the baby relate in any systematic way to the first child's reaction? Did differences in the ways in which parents prepared their first child for the birth, or differences in the manner in which the baby was introduced to the first child, affect their reaction?

To answer these questions we examined the impact of the different variables by means of a multiple regression analysis. We wanted to see to what degree the various changes in the children's behavior could be attributed to our variables, either separately or in combination. The multiple regression analysis made it possible for us to look at each aspect of a child's reaction — increase in withdrawal, breakdown in toilet training, increase in sleeping problems, and so on — and to assess the extent to which each of the different "independent" factors was linked to the change in the child's behavior.

The results (see note 1) showed that temperamental differences between the children, differences in the quality of their relationship with their mothers before the sibling birth, the mother's state in the postpartum weeks, and the age and sex of the child were all of particular importance to the form of the first child's reaction to the birth, but that there were different patterns of association for the different aspects of reaction. It is to these patterns that we turn next.

Temperament

Children who were characteristically extremely "negative in mood" on the temperament assessment carried out before the sibling birth were more likely to increase in withdrawal and in sleeping problems after the birth, and children who were both "negative in mood" and "extreme in emotional intensity" were likely to respond by increased clinging. The children who were rated as "withdrawing" children were less likely to show positive interest and affection to the baby.

Sex

Boys were likely to become more withdrawn after the baby's birth than girls.

Mother's State

In families where the mother said she felt extremely tired and/or depressed in the postpartum weeks, the first children were more likely to have increased in withdrawal. While we obviously cannot draw any conclusions about the causal direction of this link, it is important to note that there were interactive effects among the various factors. If the mother was tired and depressed *and* the first child was a boy, the likelihood of an increase in withdrawal by the first child was significantly increased.

One possible interpretation of these patterns of association is that they are the result of a consistently biased perception of the first child by the mother. For instance, the link between a first child who is described as being "negative in mood" and

"intense in emotional expression" — a child with a "difficult"
temperament — and an increase in reported sleeping problems,
clinging, and withdrawal could be seen as a consistently
critical description of the child by a biased mother. But we
have a number of lines of evidence against this interpretation,
as explained in detail in Appendix B. First, there was good
agreement between observer and mother in the ratings of
temperament. There was also some evidence that direct observation measures of children's behavior supported the ratings
(Dunn and Kendrick 1980b). It could be argued that since the
same person made both the observations and the ratings of
temperament, this agreement does not mean very much. Yet
the items of behavior recorded during the observations were
very different from those on which the ratings of temperament
were based — which was of course the reason for the initial
decision to include temperament ratings. Second, the mothers
who described their children as being negative, unmalleable,
and intense in response were *not* particularly punitive or
restrictive in their interactions. Both the direct observations
and the interviews showed that some of the mothers who
depicted their children as extremely negative and intractable
were mothers who punished very frequently, and some were
mothers who never used physical castigation at all.

Previous Relation with the Mother and Father

In families where there had been a high level of confrontation
between mother and first child before the birth of the sibling,
with frequent prohibition and restraint during the observations, the first child was more likely to be described as frequently behaving in an irritating or interfering way toward
the new baby. Significantly more confrontation and prohibition took place during the first-month observations in these
families, and indeed there was a greater increase in the conflict
than in other families.

We saw earlier that many of the children were particularly
jealous when the father played with or looked after the baby.

Still, it was also apparent from the observations that in families where the child was reported to have an intense and close relationship with the father, the escalation of conflict and confrontation with the mother, and the decrease in joint attention (focusing together on a common item of interest) after the sibling birth, were much less marked (Table A3.14). We have no evidence for *how* this link might have arisen. It could be an indirect effect: for instance, the children with such close relationships with their fathers may have been less upset by the mothers' involvement with the new baby, or the fathers in such families may have provided more support for their wives, who were in consequence better able to attend to the first children. A more direct link could be that in these families the father was able to care for and distract the first child more effectively and more extensively. Whatever the explanation for the association between the father-child relationship and the changes in the mother-child relationship, its practical implications are obvious and important.

Preparation and Introduction of Child to Baby Sibling

Books of advice for parents often dwell at length on the importance of preparing the first child for the arrival of the second. Ginott (1965), Spock (1969), and Close (1980) all stress that preparation can help the child greatly. They also devote much space to the introduction of the baby to the child. In contrast, Homan in his *Child Sense: A Guide for Parents* writes trenchantly:

Does it help to prepare a child in advance, during the pregnancy, for the fact that he is ultimately to have a rival? Certainly it helps, about tuppence worth, and mostly the mother. (1970, p. 170)

Homan uses the analogy of how the *mother* would feel if her husband brought back a second wife, and comments:

Would it help much if your husband told you about his plans for a second wife in advance? Mostly it would give you a little time to plan the subtlety of your attack. It's rather like preparing the child for his visit to the doctor. It all sounds great until the poor child actually confronts the ogre. Sibling rivalry doesn't begin and end with each homecoming. (ibid.)

Which of these two different views is best supported by research? Sewall's study (1930) found that the degree of preparation did not determine the jealousy reactions to the birth of the baby. In our own study we find we cannot give a precise answer to the question of how differences in preparation affected the child's reaction. All the mothers in the study had discussed the impending birth with the child; many had shown the child books and pictures of babies; and most children had felt the baby kick in their mother's tummy. But the explanations offered and the preparation by the mothers must have had such very different meanings to the different children, ranging in age as they did from 17 to 42 months, that there was no sensible way to compare the "message" the individual children received.

Many mothers had devoted particular thought to the way in which the first child "met" the baby for the first time and had planned their return from the hospital with great care. It is interesting, then, that the initial reaction to the new baby did not relate in any systematic way to the incidence of disturbance. One of the children who over the three postpartum weeks became particularly disturbed, showing first violent anger and tantrums then withdrawal had responded with delight initially to the arrival of his baby sister:

> MOTHER OF ARNOLD H: I gave him her to hold the moment I came in the door. He was delighted and nursed her. He didn't want me to put her in the pram. Just sat and nursed her.

In the Cleveland study by Trause and her colleagues (1978), there was no connection between the initial response to the new baby and the incidence of problems and disturbance over the next few days. Anna Freud gave some wise advice on this issue of preparation and introduction to the baby: she pointed out that however well prepared a child was, and however clearly he seemed to understand what the arrival would mean, he might easily be emotionally overwhelmed by the real event. We should recognize, after all, that even as adults we may be *rationally* prepared for a change in our relationships, yet devastated by the experience of that change.

Breast-Feeding versus Bottle-Feeding the Second Child

Spock in his *Baby and Child Care* (1969, pp. 307–308) advises mothers that it is better "as far as is convenient to take care of her [the new baby] while the older one is not around," and he comments that "many young children feel the greatest jealousy when they see their mother feeding the baby, especially at the breast." The view that breast-feeding is particularly upsetting for the elder child is frequently expressed (see for example Legg, Sherick, and Wadland 1974). However, in our sample the first-born children in families where the mother breast-fed the second were *less* likely to irritate and interfere with the baby. How should we interpret this association? It could be that first children in general are indeed less likely to interfere and irritate their new siblings when their mothers are breast-feeding. Or it is possible that the mothers who breast-fed made more effective attempts to distract the first child before they began feeding. A third possibility is that mothers who breast-feed their babies tend to view their children and interpret their behavior in a less critical fashion.

To examine these various possibilities we compared the observed behavior of the 23 children whose mothers were bottle-feeding with that of the 17 children whose mothers were breast-feeding, both during the feedings and while the mother was not occupied with the baby. In the breast-feeding families we found no significant increase in confrontation and no increase in deliberate naughtiness by the first children during the feedings. (Table A3.15). There was, moreover, significantly more joint play and less confrontation during breast feedings than during bottle feedings, and significantly fewer incidents of deliberate naughtiness by the child (Table A3.16).

Do these differences reflect the impact of the feeding situation in particular, or do they reflect more general differences between the breast-feeding and bottle-feeding families? Since mothers who choose to breast-feed differ from those who choose to bottle-feed in a number of respects (Bernal and Richards 1970), behavior with the first child might well vary in contexts other than during the feedings. However, there were only minor differences between the two groups in the interaction measures during our observations carried out before the sibling was born (the breast-feeding mothers held and touched their first children more during these pregnancy observations), and during contexts other than the feedings in the first-month observations. Breast-feeding mothers played more with their first children when the mother was not occupied with the baby, but no differences in interaction were found between the two groups while the mother was holding, cuddling, or taking care of the new baby.

These findings do then support the mothers' reports that the first children in families where the mothers were bottle-feeding were more likely to interfere with the baby in an irritating way than the children whose mothers were breast-feeding. Why should this be so? The mothers who breast-fed provided better distraction for the first child at the beginning of the feeding; drinks, potty, books, crayons, puzzles all were collected and available before the feeding began. The breast-feeding mothers also were more prepared to interrupt a feeding to help or attend to the first child, and such differences as were found between the two groups in contexts other than the feeding suggest a slightly higher level of positive involvement between the first children and their mothers in the breast-feeding families. What is clear from these findings is that the breast-feeding situation is *not* a situation of particular trauma for first children, as various authorities such as Spock have suggested. Mothers who are expecting a second child need not feel that a decision to breast-feed the second will subject their first child to additional stress.

Age Differences

The only link we found between age of first child and reaction to sibling birth was that the younger children tended to become more clinging. The lack of age-related differences may reflect the relatively narrow age range in the children of the study. However Sturge, in a study parallel to our own which included children of a much wider age range, also found no association between either the disturbance or the positive interest of the firstborn after the sibling birth (Sturge, personal communication).

Home and Hospital: The Effects of Separation

The traumatic effects on young children of even brief separation from the mother have been dramatically and movingly documented in studies by Heinicke and Westheimer (1966), by the Robertsons (1971), and by Bowlby (1973). For many in our sample the mother's departure to the hospital for the delivery of the second child was the first separation from her that the child had experienced. We had expected, then, that the various forms of disturbed behavior would be more marked among the 27 children whose mothers gave birth in the hospital than among the 13 children in families where the second child was born at home. It was a surprise to find that there were relatively slight behavioral differences between the two groups of children during the three weeks following the birth. The first children whose sibling was born in a hospital were in fact significantly more interested in the baby when he finally appeared at home than were the children in the home-delivery families. And the increased behavior problems were just as common among the home-delivered group as in the group of children who had been separated.

Why should there have been so little difference between the two groups? Why did the combination of a separation from the mother and the birth of a sibling not lead to a greater degree of disturbance in the firstborn children whose mothers went to the hospital? First, it is important to bear in mind that there may have been particular features of the lives of the young children we were studying that helped to buffer them against the stress of separation from the mother. Most of the first-born children had close relationships with their grandparents (particularly their grandmothers) and with their fathers. And in most cases it was the grandmother and the father who together looked after the child while the mother was in the hospital. The length of the separation was, for most of the families, not more than 48 hours. In a group of families without these close ties between grandparents or father and child, or with longer separations, the effects of separation might well have been more marked. Most of the children also visited their mothers in the hospital, and it is possible that this too helped to soften the blow of separation. The comments of both the mothers and the fathers on the effects of hospital visits suggest, however, that the value and the length of the visits should be carefully considered by parents. Some children were clearly distressed by the visits. One was described as "very upset after every visit. He cried for an hour after each one." Another was reported not to sleep well on the nights he visited. Others were reported to find the visits tiring (several mothers felt that an hour was too long) or boring; "He's more interested in the presents I've been given than in me or the baby." In a study of the effects of hospital visiting on firstborn children carried out in Cleveland, Trause and her colleagues (1978) compared a group of children who visited their mothers several times with a group who did not visit at all. Whether the child had visited or not did not affect the incidence of disturbed behavior — although the children who had visited frequently were less likely to react to the actual arrival home of the mother by ignoring or hostile behavior.

But there is another set of findings on the children whose

mothers went to hospital that may bear on their reaction to the separation. When we examined the interaction between the first children and their mothers during our observations before and after the sibling birth, we found that there were systematic differences between the home-delivery and hospital-delivery families. In the home-delivery families there was significantly more joint play and physical contact between mother and child before the sibling birth, and the children took a greater role in initiating play and contact than the children in the hospital-delivery families (Table A3.17). After the birth there were differences not only in the measures of play and contact but also in the amount of joint attention and in the initiation of play and attention by the mother and the child. It is possible then that the children in the families where the mother was booked for hospital delivery had slightly less intense relationships with their mothers and were consequently less upset by the change in caregiver and routine than the children whose mothers had insisted on home delivery.

The point that must be emphasized is that even when the mother remained at home to have her second baby, the first child was extremely likely to show signs of disturbance and upset. In these families there had been particularly close relationships between mother and first child; it was clear from the mothers' comments that many of them felt that even though their child had suffered no separation, still the upheaval and change in daily routine that the child experienced were of major importance in accounting for the increased behavior problems. This point has very broad implications for our views on the relations between 2- and 3-year-old children and their parents — implications to which the mothers themselves drew attention, in their comments on why they felt the children had become upset and difficult.

The Mothers' Views

Watching the children and talking to their mothers over the period when the baby was born showed us not only how difficult and tense the relationship with a 2- or 3-year-old frequently is, but also how precarious the balance of that relationship can be. Even when there was no separation from the mother, the events surrounding the birth were enough to distort the relationship and destroy its harmony. And to the mothers, a prime contribution to the child's difficult behavior was the change in his expected routine. The grandparents and fathers who acted as surrogate mothers were described as simply *not knowing* how important the small details of the child's expected routine were to his well-being. A constantly recurring theme was that not only did the substitute mother frequently forget that the child needed his special cup, or his particular bedtime routine, or ritual game, but "she" also disrupted his expectation or understanding of what was *allowed* — either by overindulgence or by overrestriction.

> MOTHER OF HARVEY M: I think he's a bit more defiant. Sometimes he *grins* when I tell him off. He thinks he can get away with it. So he's had a few smacks lately, but I put this down to my parents' being here last week. My dad took him out to the shops every day — spoiling him, in other words.

> MOTHER OF LAURA W: While I was away she was taken out a good deal — a big social whirl. Now she's *got* to get used to having less of that. But my mum wasn't very indulgent with her, in fact she got fed up with her. That didn't help.

> MOTHER OF TIM W: His routine is all messed up. He's upset by the constant visitors.

These comments bring home to us the importance of the expected daily routine to the child, a world in which things happen regularly with comfortable predictability. And they show too how crucial the mother is as the architect of that world, a world that is both intelligible and dependable for the child, and how easily the coordination of mother and child can be disrupted. Some mothers commented on the difficulty they experienced in trying to reestablish the harmonious relationship they had had before the sibling was born, attributing the disruption to both their own *and* the child's behavior:

> MOTHER OF TIM W: He's generally more depressed, more quiet, more touchy. I'm expecting him to play more on his own than he used to—I'm not giving him so much attention. What he finds as occupations tend to be the "come and stop me" ones. I try not to let it escalate, but quite often it does.

Some remarked on how they altered their response to the child's disturbed behavior over the three weeks after the birth, in an attempt to recover the balance of the relationship.

> MOTHER OF DEREK J: He always wants attention during the feeds. At first I got up for him always. Now I've stopped it. The first week was the worst. I think it made it worse that his father was there all the time. He gave in to him more than he usually does—that was a mistake to start off. Next week he wanted sweets and things all the time. I wasn't having that. Now he's no different to what he was before she was born.

> MOTHER OF JOANNE R: She started dirtying for the whole of the first week. I gave her a hiding in the end. We've had no dirtying since.

The comments from the mothers obviously suggest that it may be important to minimize the changes in the child's life that coincide with the birth of the sibling: the mothers' views on the role of these changes in contributing to the disturbed behavior are convincing. But might not these changes also contribute to the sudden increases in independence—the "signs of being more grown up"—reported for more than half the

children in the study? It is certainly plausible that a shift in
the routine of the child, and in what is expected of him by the
care giver, might lead the child to discover for himself that he
can do certain things, and that such achievement is enjoyable,
whether it be mastering a difficult task like putting on a shoe,
or conquering his fear of going to the toilet alone, or
discovering that he has resources for play within himself.

There are three different possibilities here that need to be
distinguished: the first is that with a different care giver
different requirements are placed on the child; the second is
that the new care giver has different expectations and beliefs
concerning the child. He or she attributes intentions and inter-
prets the child's behavior differently than the mother does.
With both these interpretations the explanation for the
changed behavior lies in the molding by the *adults* of the
child's actions. A third possibility is to view the altered
behavior as essentially a response by the *child* to an altered
environment: if you greatly change the world of a child (or
indeed of an adult), the chances are that you will not only
draw his attention to new possibilities in that world, but also
to new possibilities in himself as an actor in that world. It
may be that with a change in care giver both the first two
effects are operative; since we did not observe the children
during the period when they were cared for by grandparents
or father, we cannot explore these possibilities. With either
kind of change in the care giver, though, the consequence is
likely to be a change in the child's feelings, beliefs, and ways
of acting in the world. These changes raise extremely important questions about the processes involved in rapid
developmental advances, in particular the role of emotional
experiences. We shall return to these theoretical issues later in
our discussion.

The birth of a brother or sister must in itself involve a
major shift of a symbolic kind — a change in the child's conception of himself within the family, and indeed of himself as
a person. The presence of the sibling provides a focus for frequent discussion by mother and child of another person; the

baby as a person with wants, intentions, likes, and dislikes; with rights, possessions, and gender; as a rival for the attention, love, approval, and disapproval of the parents. In our sample this frequently led to discussion of the child himself in terms of new dimensions of self-categorization. It is quite possible that this discussion of self and other, which so often centered on the sibling and which involved the child in considerable reflection on the categorization of self and other, contributed to the "great leap forward" reported by the mothers. In the next chapter we look in detail at these conversations between mother and child.

four

Conversations Before and After

Looking at the conversations between the children and their mothers before and after the sibling's birth gives us another perspective on the change in the children's lives, in their interests and feelings, and in their interaction with their mothers. There were two particularly marked changes. One was the increase in confrontation and verbal disputes between child and mother; as we have seen, these were particularly evident when the mother was occupied with the baby. But there was also an interesting change in the quality of discussion about other people. Before the baby was born, most of the discussion of people's feelings, wants, and interests was concerned with the child's own state. This talk reflected both the first child's attempts to draw attention to his own particular desires or needs, and the mother's attempts to clarify and establish exactly what the child wished for (or her attempts to argue against the particular demand). Seventy-two percent of the mothers' conversational turns that included references to people's feelings or wants referred to those of the child. (A conversational turn here denotes the remarks made by one speaker before there is a change in speaker.) The only exceptions to this focus were occasional references by the mother to her own wants, to the wants or feelings of make-believe characters in the child's own fantasy play or of characters in books that child and mother were reading together, or to the feelings of family pets. In the two examples that follow, the first child and mother are discussing the current feelings and interests of the child's teddy bear, and the second child and mother are looking at a book together:

IAN W AND MOTHER:

MOTHER: You can draw Teddy a nice picture. What would Teddy like you to draw him? Mm? Is he watching?

CHILD: Not really.

M: Not really, no. Do you think he's asleep then, really?

C: Yes. Yes.

M: He might be, mightn't he? What are you drawing, a ball?

C: Yes.

M: Ooh, he'll like that . . . Where's Teddy now?

C: On the stool.

M: Is he? Is he hungry?

C: Wants drink.

M: Does he?

C: Yeah.

M: Do you think he'd like a biscuit [cookie]? Do you think Teddy'd like a biscuit?

C: Yeah.

VIRGINIA L AND MOTHER:

C: Great big bonfire.

M: Big bonfire, yes, it is a great big bonfire. What is it burning up in the bonfire?

C: Burning birdies. All hungry.

M: They've got to fly away because they've burned the tree that the birdies used to live in, haven't they? And look at all the little bunny rabbits crying.

C: They sad.

M: That's right, they're sad.

Table 4.1 shows the proportions of these references to the wants and feelings of different people before the birth of the sibling. Overwhelmingly, the discussions were of the emotional state of a person who was present, and in a single-child

Table 4.1   Percentage of references to the wants, feelings, intentions others.

	Child	Mother	Father	Sibling	Pretend character	Book character	Pet	Obse
During pregnancy								
Mother	72	9	1	—	6	5	5	1
Child	65	3	3	—	12	10	3	4
First month after birth								
Mother	52	9	2	29	3	3	3	(
Child	47	1	3	32	8	6	0	3

family this was likely to be the child himself or a figure of his own fantasy. In fact, 96 percent of the mothers' references and 94 percent of the children's references were to the state or feelings of a person who was present. Although the father, grandparents, friends, and relatives of the child were often mentioned, the references were almost without exception either to where these nonpresent people were at the time and what they might be doing, or conversational exchanges in which child and mother recalled in a narrative fashion events in which the other people and the child had all been involved. The frequency of such references by even the children under 2 shows us how important to the child the framework of family members and familiar people can be. Most of these comments were not anxious references — desperate inquiries searching for security; rather, they reflected the interest and absorption of many young children in the placing and naming of the familiar figures in their world. Evident throughout was the enjoyment felt by the children in knowing *where* their friends and family were, and *what* they were doing, as well as in re-counting with the mother the familiar routines these other people go through. Many such references were to the father or to the child's friends. But several children had cousins or neighbors to whom they frequently referred:

Russell S and mother:

C: Aunty Phil?
M: Aunty Phil's at work.
C: Sal?
M: Sal's at school.
C: Sal.
M: Sally's at school.
C: Marie?
M: With Marie, yes.
C: Come school?
M: You can't go to school. You're not big enough, are you? You got to get a bit bigger to go to school.

Since many of the children who engaged in such sequences were not yet very competent linguistically, interpreting precisely what the inquiries referred to presents obvious difficulties. Yet the mothers had no hesitation in answering in terms of *where* the people named were at the time, and *what* they were probably doing. With the children who were linguistically more advanced, the questions were unambiguous:

Martin W and mother:

C: Where's Daddy gone?
M: Daddy's gone to work.

Analysis of these conversations before the birth of the sibling reveals first, then, that feelings and wishes are explored in relation to the people who are present rather than absent and therefore concern primarily the child's own state, and second, that discussion of the actions and whereabouts of the other people in the child's world are of considerable interest, even to children younger than 20 months. The first point we emphasize, because when the baby sibling arrives there is a major change in the discussion of feelings and interests: there is another person, more or less continually present, whose feelings wants, interests, and intentions are a focus of great interest for the mother — and for some of the firstborn children. For the first time in the child's life, another person's wishes and state are extensively discussed.

After the arrival of the sibling there was a significant increase in the frequency with which the mothers referred to the feelings and wants of someone other than the child — an increase from a mean of 2.4 conversational turns to 6.8 turns (per 100 minutes of mother present). The frequency of the children's references to the feelings or wants of others also increased threefold, specifically because of references to the sibling. There was no increase in the frequency of references to the mother's own feelings or those of fantasy characters, pets, and so on. Sixty percent of the references by child and by mother to the wants of people other than the child now related to the sibling. The comments still predominantly concerned the feelings and needs of a person who was present: 97 percent of such references by the child concerned someone present.

The second point, on the references to customary routines of the other people in the child's world who were not present, is interesting in relation to the argument put forward in the last chapter that the routines and the familiarity of the child's world are of much importance, and that disruption of these routines is potentially of great significance for the child. That other people in the child's life are of so much interest and importance, even to a 20-month-old, would not surprise any mother, but again, it should alert psychologists to how far the concept of egocentrism may distort the actual range of cognitive and affective concerns of the child. The children continued, in the conversations after the sibling's birth, to refer very frequently to the whereabouts and the routines of the other people in their world:

SUSAN S AND MOTHER:
C: Where's Ken gone? Where's Ken gone?
M: He's at work.

C: Work. On bike.

M: Yeah. Gone on his bike.

C: Bus and on bike. Where's Grandad?

M: Oh he's at work as well.

C: Where's Uncle Liz?

M: *Aunty* Liz.

C: Aunty Liz?

M: She'll be at work as well.

PENNY D AND MOTHER:

C: Where's Lucy?

M: Lucy's at home with Mummy.

C: Where's Jenny?

M: She's at home with Lucy. I expect they'll be having their dinner soon, don't you?

C: Where's Bob?

M: Bob? He's at work.

C: He's at work.

RUSSELL S AND MOTHER:

C: Car Daddy.

M: Daddy, yes.

C: Car Daddy gone?

M: Daddy's gone, yes.

C: Car Daddy gone?

M: Daddy's gone to work.

C: Tracy Daddy gone?

M: Tracy's Daddy's gone to work.

C: Sally bed.

M: No, Sally's not gone to bed yet. She's gone to school.

In the conversations after the sibling birth there was, then, a dramatic increase in the discussion of the feelings and needs of someone other than the child. But there was also a change in the way in which many children talked about themselves. With the birth of a brother or sister a whole new set of dimensions became directly applicable to the child and was frequently used by the children in referring to themselves. An obvious example was the category of brother and sister:

SUE H AND MOTHER:
C: I sister.
M: Sorry?
C: I sister.
M: Pardon? You scissor?
C: *Sister.*
M: Sister?
C: Mmm.

Other categories began to be used as well. Now the first child was the big one, not the small one; the boy, not the girl; the older, not the younger. Of course we have no evidence that these dimensions had not been used by the children before the sibling birth. Still, it was notable that the presence of the baby meant that explicit discussion and exploration of such dimensions was more common and more extensive after the birth.

GAVIN D AND MOTHER:
C (putting diaper on his head):   Baby nappy [diaper].
     Baby nappy. On baby head. Baby head.
M: You're not a baby, are you?
C: Get baby.
M: Are you a baby?
C: No.
M: What are you then?
C: Gavin. I'm Gavin.
M: You're Gavin, are you?
C: I'm Gavin, not baby. Gavin. Gavin little boy.

The first children often studied the baby with care, and their comments often led to extensive discussion of their *own* attributes in comparison with the sibling. A short example follows:

JOANNE R AND MOTHER:
C (looking at baby in pram):   Got eyes.
M: Are they closed or are they open?
C: Yeah.
M: What are they?
C: Closed.
M: Are they?
C: Yeah. Are my eyes closed?
M: No, they're open. They'll pop out!
C (leaping with excitement):   Will they!
M: Yeah. Ooh, aren't you clever, you can jump.
C: Baby jump.
M: Does she? I don't think so, not yet.

Such discussion often focused on physical differences between the first child and the baby; the potential for such conversations leading to discussion of more general categories such as gender differences is obvious:

BRENDAN F AND MOTHER:
C: Done a wee-wee.
M: Yes she has.
C: Hasn't got a widdly.
M: No she hasn't, has she?
C: Hasn't.

Discussion of the gender of the baby in relation to the gender of the first child was extremely common. Marvin, the little boy talking to his mother in the next example, shows an interest typical of many of the first children in exploring the different possibilities of categorizing the baby, and also some confusion over gender terms. His mother is quick to correct him over the gender terms. This eagerness to correct mistakes over gender was very common, in marked contrast to the rarity with which mothers corrected other errors (syntactic, for instance) in the children's conversation.

MARVIN W AND MOTHER:
C: . . . (inaudible) boy.

M: She's not a boy. She's a little girl.
C: Is she?
M: You're a little boy.
C: Is she a girl?
M: Yes, a little girl.
C: A little girl.
C to baby (B):   You messy. Messy.
M: She's a messy eater 'cause she's only a baby.
C: Hello, little fellow.
M: She's not a fellow.
C: She a little girl. A little girl.
M: Yes, she's a little girl.
C: Brenda good girl, aren't she?
M: Yes, and you're a good boy.
C: Yes, Brenda good boy.
M: No, Brenda's a good *girl.*
C: Brenda Ann, isn't she?
M: Mm. Brenda Ann . . .

In many of the conversations about the differences between the child and the baby, the mothers made didactic comments, drawing the first child's attention to the idea of development, either by commenting on how the baby would grow up (as with Dick C below) or by pointing out that the first child used to be like the baby (as in the Sandra H example).

> MOTHER OF DICK C: He's too small to have cornflakes and weetabix [another cereal], isn't he? 'Cause he hasn't got any teeth yet, has he? You've got teeth, haven't you?

> MOTHER OF SANDRA H (the baby is being sick and Sandra laughs):   You used to do that, Sandra. Don't think that you were any different. You used to be sick all over everybody. I don't know what you're laughing at, Sandra. You were dreadful when you were this age.

Discussing the ways in which the baby was going to grow up was taken by many mothers as an opportunity to stress what an enjoyable playmate the baby would be, almost as if they were promoting the relationship that would develop:

> MOTHER OF SANDRA H: Hello, where's Marcie? Is that your baby sister, is it? . . . Isn't she a nice little girl? You'll be able to play together, won't you? By next summer you and Marcie will be able to go out there and she'll be crawling around and you'll play with her, won't you? Mmm?

"Tutoring" comments about the baby's capabilities occurred, of course, in many other contexts:

> TERENCE K AND MOTHER:
> M to B (who has been crying for a long time): I don't know what we're going to do, do you?
> C: Smack [spank] him.
> M: He's too little to smack.
> C: Smack him.
> M: Can't smack him 'cause he doesn't know any better.

The issue of whether the firstborn was or was not a baby loomed very large in conversations after the sibling's birth. Sometimes the first child switched from asserting that he was *not* a baby to a rather desperate demand to be treated as a baby and to be given exactly what the new baby was being given:

> LAURA W AND MOTHER:
> C (looking at baby's clothes): I want one of those.
> M: Well, you know there aren't any babygros [stretch-suits] for you. What are you doing with those?
> C: I'm a baby. I'm a baby. Another one for me. I want.
> M: There isn't another one for you.
> C: I want one. I'm a baby.
> M: Now look. We've been through this about five times. There are no babygros in the world that would fit you 'cause you're a big girl.

In these comments the combination of pride in new independence and anxious appeal to be treated as a baby mirrored the signs of developmental advance and regression seen in other aspects of the children's behavior. The ambivalence toward the baby that was so evident in some children's behavior toward the baby was also apparent in their comments to the mother:

> LAURA W AND MOTHER:
> C to B: All right, baby (caressing him). (To M.) Smack him.

> FAY G AND MOTHER:
> C: Baby. Baby (caressing her). Monster. Monster.
> M: She's not a monster.
> C: Monster.

And several children were quite explicit about their antagonism to the baby:

> MARVIN W (standing on edge of pram, rocking it) AND MOTHER:
> M: Don't stand on there, there's a good boy, or you'll tip her out.
> C: I want her out.

The dramatic changes in the frequency with which the feelings and wants of another person were discussed, and the extensive discussion of self and other in a range of new dimensions, are surely important transformations in the child's "egocentric" world and could well contribute to the sudden developmental advances reported by the mothers.

Individual Differences in the Discussion of the Baby

There were striking differences between the families in the extent to which the mothers discussed the baby's wants, wishes, and feelings with the elder child in the early weeks after the sibling birth. In some families the mothers commented frequently on whether the baby was feeling hungry or tired and on what his crying might reflect, and they drew the elder child's attention to the baby's interest in him and to what the baby appeared to enjoy. Some examples: "She likes looking at you"; "Is she cross at being woken up?"; "I think he's watching you. Can you see him looking? I think he's watching you"; "He likes you to kiss his face like that"; "He won't smile when you're yelling 'cause it makes him a bit upset"; "He's looking at something there — my dressing gown — he likes the color"; "Listen to little Jamie; he wants his bottle." Other mothers never made such comments about the baby as a person to the first child during the observations. The mothers also differed in the ways in which they discussed caring for the baby. Some discussed what should be done for the baby almost as if it were a matter of joint responsibility for mother and first child together. They would ask the child what *his* views were on why the baby was crying or on what should be done.

TIM W AND MOTHER:

M: Tim, do you reckon he's hungry? Or is he just waiting for his bath? . . . Shall we roll him over and see if he likes going on his tummy? . . . Oh, what shall we do with him? I think we'd better hurry up and bathe him anyway. Lets give him a bath. Can you help me with the bath water?

C to B: Baby! Baby!

M: That's right. You talk to him and cheer him up.

In these families the first children took a real and practical part in caring for the baby. Their pleasure in their own competence was delightful to see, and often very directly expressed by the first child to the baby:

PENNY D AND MOTHER:

C:	Got make his wind [burp].
M:	Got make his wind?
C:	Yeah.
M to B:	Come on, Harry!
C:	(Laughs.)
M:	Are you going to come and help me? I'm not doing very well, am I?
C:	(Pats baby, and baby gives slight grunt.) Ooh!
M:	That was just a grunt.
C to B:	Hello, Harry! Hello, Harry! (Baby looks at her. Child turns to observer in triumph.)
C to O:	Look!
M:	He gave us a smile yesterday, didn't he?
C to B:	Give me a smile.
M to B:	Give us a smile.
C to B:	Whee! (Kisses baby.)
M:	He'll eat your nose if you're not careful, won't he?
C:	He eat nose.
M:	Is he eating your nose? Or giving you a kiss?
C:	Giving a kiss.

JUDY B AND MOTHER:

M:	Do you think she wants to bring up a burp?
C:	No.
M:	No? Oh. Shall we change her nappy instead then?
C:	Mmm. (Takes over with the cream.) I put it on.
M:	Put it on her bottom then.
C:	I can't.
M:	Yes, you can do it. There's a clever girl.
C:	Ugh!
M:	Ugh! Rub it in.

C: Rub it. I done it! I done it! (To B:) I done it, baby!

It was by no means only the girls who were encouraged to discuss the baby's needs and care in this way. Many of the boys took an extremely active part in washing, feeding, dressing, and burping the baby:

HARVEY M AND MOTHER:
M: You pat his back and hold his hand, don't you?
C: Back. (Pats baby, who promptly burps.)
M: That was a good boy. You see you got that up.
C to B: Eeh! More windy!

The child's enjoyment of the baby as a person was very evident in many of these families, where mother and firstborn together delighted in the baby's pleasures and achievements, even in the first three weeks:

IAN W AND MOTHER:
C to B (showing bear to baby. Mother is at other end of room, washing clothes.): Look baby, look! (B looks; C calls to M):   Look Mummy, look!
M to C: What is he doing, Ian? Mmm? What is he doing?
C to M: Look. He's looking. Look. He's looking.
M to C: He likes pretty colors, doesn't he? Not near his face. Look, he likes these, doesn't he? No, he's only interested in his food at the moment. We'll have to put that in his cot, then he can see it, eh?

In the families where the mother encouraged the first child to take part in discussing the care and needs of the baby, she was also likely to describe the baby as a person with likes, interests, and feelings. These differences between the mothers in their discussion of the baby were related also to the way in which the first child talked about the baby as a person. In these families the first child was significantly more likely to refer to the baby's feelings, wants, and interests (Table A4.1). Furthermore, as we followed the children over the next year, we found that these differences in the way the mother discussed the baby were importantly associated with differences in the quality of the relationship that developed between the siblings (see Chapter 8).

Were these differences between the mothers in their conversations about the babies related in any simple way to other aspects of their interaction with the first children? Were such discussions more common in the families with the older firstborn children? And were they related to the first child's reaction to the birth of the baby?

In fact, we found no links between the measures of observed interaction between mother and firstborn child, and these differences in the manner in which the mothers discussed the baby. Mothers who were relatively playful and permissive and those who spent a large proportion of time in confrontation with the first child before the baby was born were equally likely to talk about the baby in this way, and to encourage the elder child to join in decisions about caring for the baby. Nor did we find links between the style of discussion and the disturbance and negative behavior shown by the first child after the baby was born. Among the families where the mother encouraged the first child to help with the baby were children who showed the whole range of different negative reactions to the birth. In addition, we found no association with the mother's state of exhaustion and depression during the postpartum weeks. Some of the mothers who made the greatest effort to include the elder child in looking after and discussing the baby were those coping with the most extreme tiredness and stress. One particularly surprising finding was that there were no links between the nature of the discussion of the new sibling in the first weeks and the age or sex of the first child. We had expected that the firstborn girls in the study might be encouraged to take a more active part in talking about the needs of the baby. Actually, as many of the little boys were encouraged to do so.

There was, however, a link between the extent to which the first child was reported to show positive friendly behavior to the sibling — the frequency with which he offered to help, wished to entertain and cuddle the baby — and the nature of the conversations between mother and child about the baby. Mothers who encouraged their first children to take joint responsibility and who discussed the baby as a person were more likely to have children whom they reported to be particularly interested in and affectionate toward the baby (Table A4.2). We need to be cautious about drawing conclusions concerning the direction of this link. On the one hand, it could be that mothers who notice their first child's interest in and affection for the baby are more likely to talk about the baby's wants and feelings in order to support and encourage this interest, whereas mothers who have noticed aggression, ambivalence, or lack of interest in their firstborn's behavior toward the baby go out of their way *not* to draw attention repeatedly to the baby as a person who has entered the family. On the other hand, it could be that mothers who talk in this way do in fact encourage feelings of affection and interest in the elder child. The fact that the differences between the mothers are evident so soon after the birth, and that they are not related to differences in the negative reactions of the first children, could well be taken as evidence against the first interpretation. When the behavior of the firstborn children to the baby during the observation was compared in the different families, no association was found between the frequency with which the first child showed and gave things to the baby, caressed the baby, or tried to help with the baby, and differences in the mothers' speech about the baby. This evidence strongly suggests that the differences between the mothers did not simply reflect a response to differences in the firstborn child's behavior toward the baby.

There are further reasons for supposing that the differences between mothers were not merely reactions to the behavior of the first children. It seemed extremely unlikely that the marked differences in the ways in which the mothers discussed the baby were unrelated to other differences in their style of talking to their firstborn children. We decided to look at various aspects of their conversational style, including the extent to which the mothers rationalized or justified their attempts to control the children, their involvement in the children's make-believe, the extent to which they explored the motives and intentions of other people (including the child), and the degree to which they used language for relatively complex cognitive purposes. (Here we used the classification of complex cognitive use of language employed by Tizard et al. 1981, derived from Tough 1977. This categorization codes a variety of language uses including comparisons, similarities, differences, conditionals, generalizations and definitions, logical reasoning and inference, and so on. For a full list see Appendix B.)

Since these measures were likely to be affected by the age of the child and since we were also interested in the *child's* use of these aspects of language, we decided to examine the frequency of the features in the transcripts from observations of 20 children who were between 26 and 29 months old at the 8-month visit. The results showed that mothers who referred to the baby as a person in the first-month visits and who encouraged the first child to take part in discussion of care giving were also more likely to give justification for attempting to control the first child, to discuss other people's motives and intentions, and to use language for complex cognitive purposes.

They were also more likely to enter the child's pretend games by making verbal suggestions and comments — although, as we have already seen, these mothers were not more likely than the others to spend time playing with the child in the observations when the measure of "playing with" included more broadly defined types of play: sitting on the floor and joining in with construction toys, jigsaw puzzles, and games, or romping around in physical games. Table A4.3 shows these associations.

We have seen that these aspects of the mothers' language are correlated: that those mothers who discussed other people's motives tended also to use justification when they were controlling the child, to join frequently in make-believe, and to use language for relatively complex intellectual purposes; and, further, that their children tended to use language in these ways more frequently than the children of mothers who did not so use language (Table A4.4).

These differences in language use reflect a particular style of relating to a young child, perhaps similar to the style Light describes in his study (1979) of the development of social sensitivity, which he characterized as reflecting a high degree of "symmetry" in the relationship between mother and child. These mothers were not only tuned in to their children's world in the sense that they enjoyed and entered their fantasies, but they were more likely to treat the child formally as an equal in discussing social rules and control issues. The pattern of these associations suggests that we should not look for simple links between any one aspect of the conversational interactions and later differences between the children. It would be more sensible to regard any connection between the early conversations and the later behavior of the child as reflecting an association between a particular *style* of interacting and the child's behavior. How we should interpret this link between the conversation of mother and first child in the early weeks, and the later sibling relationship is an issue we discuss in Chapter 8, along with individual differences in the siblings' behavior toward each other.

The Mothers' Conversations with the Babies

There were, then, marked differences between the families in the extent to which the first children were directly engaged in conversations about the baby as a person. However, all the firstborn children of course heard their mothers' "conversations" with the baby, and these were very likely to catch the first child's attention, since they were characterized by vivid and dramatic expressions, many questions, and lively intonation patterns. Studies of mothers talking to very young babies have described in great detail how different a mother's speech to her baby is from her speech to an adult or older child (Snow and Ferguson 1977). Lively facial expressions, exaggerated intonation, and a questioning conversational style in which the mother adapts her part to the baby's changing expressions and movements with great sensitivity are characteristics of the interaction of mothers with their babies from birth on (Stern 1977). The baby's grimaces, sounds, and movements are responded to as if they were intentional acts in a communicative exchange, and the mother's comments to the baby in our observations clearly reflected this attribution of intention. Some examples: "Oh good lad — there's all my wind, Mum, he says. There's all my wind"; "Who are you smiling at? Who are you smiling at, cheeky?"; "Are you telling me you're starving?"

Two themes in these mother-baby conversations were common to all the families. One was the baby's state: "Why are you crying?"; "Are you hungry?"; "Are you starving?"; "Oh you're just a big hungry baby, aren't you? Are you a big hungry baby?"; "Oh you're not getting hiccups, are you? Silly fool!"

Another theme was how the baby *should* be behaving: "You should be asleep now; you're naughty"; "That's a good boy. You did it just right."

The point is that even in families where the mother did not address the first child directly on the subject of the baby as a person, the child could not remain unaware of such conversations — and they were conversations, in which the baby was very definitely being addressed as a person with wants, needs, and feelings, and to whom social rules applied. Indeed, some of the older children engaged in conversations with their new

sibling that closely paralleled the mother-baby conversations — in that the children adjusted their questions and comments to the baby to his own noises and grimaces, apparently
taking these expressions as acceptable communications, just as
the mothers did:

> TERENCE K
> C to O: Benjamin's eyes are blue. (B makes a noise.)
>   He says no.
> C to B: Did you say yes? (B makes another noise.)
> C to O: He said no.
> C to B: Are you going to say no, Benjamin? Open
>   your mouth. Say no.

Distress, Dirt, and Fantasy

No account of the conversations between the firstborn
children and their mothers during the first weeks after the sibling birth would be complete without comment on three issues
that were apparently of absorbing interest to the first children.
One concerned signs that the baby was distressed. Many first
children alerted their mothers immediately when the baby
whimpered or cried, and pursued discussions of what should
be done with considerable concern.

> MARVIN W AND MOTHER:
> C: Brenda crying.
> M: Mmm.
> C: Why?
> M: 'Cause you woke her up this morning.

This curiosity about why the baby is crying suggests both a
recognition of the distress expressed by the baby and a view
of the baby as a person who may have *reasons* for crying.

    Secondly, the changing of the baby's nappies provoked
great interest and discussion of bowel movements, and of the

issue of dirt and cleanliness more generally. There was no doubt about either the fascination or in some cases the disgust and distaste expressed by the first children. For several families the matter of toilet training was one that was causing great tension between mother and firstborn. But even where the firstborn child was happily and successfully trained, the drama of this *dirty* baby behaving in a way that was after all well understood to be *naughty* was one of great interest.

In this example Melanie appears both fascinated and disgusted with the baby's bowel movement, and is determined to investigate it:

MELANIE C AND MOTHER:

C: He doing pooh.

M: Yes, I thought that might interest you. Yeah. Well, leave his feet alone. You'll make him uncomfortable.

C: He got pooh.

M: I don't think he's finished yet. We'll have to stand and wait for him.

C: OK. OK. (Peers closely at baby and pulls nappy.)

M: No, don't, Melanie; let him finish first. We'll just stand here while he finishes. No, don't pull it.

C to B (in disgusted tone):   Oh dear, Keith. Have you done a pooh?

M: Well he has to do one sometime, doesn't he? Don't pull his legs off.

C: Keith done a pooh . . . He finished, Mum?

M: I don't know.

C: Do other one?

M: He's done two, hasn't he?

C: Keith done next pooh. Mmm. Mmm. (Starts to investigate nappy.)

M: I'll clean that first, Melanie, thank you. I don't know if he's finished or not. (To B:) Why don't you wait, eh?

C to B:	Why don't you wait?
M:	I suppose he's being cooperative really. (To B:) Have you finished? You're going to be sick now, aren't you?
M to C:	I wouldn't put your hand in it if I were you . . . I shouldn't poke it. Give him a minute longer.

The third feature of the conversations that deserves comment concerns the many episodes of fantasy about babies noted during the post–sibling birth observations. There were not only frequent sequences in which the elder child *became* a baby, but frequent episodes where the first child's games with teddy bear or doll took the form of mother-baby interactions, and these sequences often mirrored very precisely the interactions of the real mother and sibling.

DEREK J AND MOTHER:

C (kicking teddy bear, to which he is very attached):	Mummy!
M:	What?
C:	Teddy bear. Crying.
M:	Well, you're kicking him. He'll cry. You'll have to love him nice and better [a phrase used earlier when she was comforting the baby sibling].
C:	Mummy love him better.
M:	No. Derek love him better. You kicked him.
C:	Derek love nice better teddy bear.
M:	Mmm. Ah. Has he stopped crying?
C:	Stopped crying.
M:	He likes being loved.
C:	(Kisses Teddy.)
M:	Ah. Giving him a kiss?
C:	Pat his back? Wind?
M:	Pat his back; he's got a bit of wind. That's it.
C:	Mummy pat Derek's back.

Whether or not we choose to view these fantasies as expressions of the child's wish to act out inner feelings of ambivalence, concern, or aggression to the baby, we should not ignore the evidence they provide on what aspects of the new baby strike the sibling as being of most pressing significance.

The fantasy games about the baby raise a general issue about the mother's part in fostering the child's understanding of what the baby is "really" like. While many of the mothers did, as we have seen, draw the child's attention to the very real needs of the baby, and discuss both what his expressions might mean and what capabilities he did and did not possess, there were also several exchanges where very *unlikely* capabilities or wishes were ascribed to the baby:

DEBBIE G AND MOTHER:
C to B: Hello, Amanda. Hello.
M to C: Is she a treasure? Oh, she smiled at you. Yes, she just smiled at you. I think she knows you're a little girl just like her. Mmm. She does. She's smiling at you.

FAY G AND MOTHER:
M: There, she's talking to you. She's saying "You're my big sister. Big sister." Isn't she?

SHAMUS S AND MOTHER:
M: He'll scratch your face, he will, look. He'll get your nose. There.
M to B: Kill him, Charlie. Scratch him. Scratch him.

MELANIE C AND MOTHER:
M: What did Keith buy you, Melanie? Did Keith buy you a train set? Uh?
C: Mmm.

How far did the 2- and 3-year-olds distinguish the sensible from the fanciful descriptions of their new sibling's capabilities and wishes? To begin to answer such a question would require experiment rather than simply observation. Where the "fanciful" references to the baby's capabilities took place within the framework of a pretend game, it appeared very likely that the child was clear about the distinction between the baby's real and "pretend" abilities. In the next example the mother made believe that the 2-week-old was hunting the 2-year-old in a hide-and-seek game:

> TERENCE K AND MOTHER:
> M: Are you hiding? Christopher's coming to find you. What are you doing down there?
> C: Hiding.
> M: Eh?
> C: Hiding . . . Is that Christopher come to find me?
> M: Yes, coming to find you.
> C: Here I am. Here I am. Sticking out.

The sensitivity of children of 2 and 3 years of age to the "pretend" mode has been elegantly described in studies of fantasy play, which show how clearly the children enjoy and exploit the distinction between real and pretend (Garvey 1977). It is much less clear what the children understood by the mother's references to, for instance, their baby sibling's having brought presents for them, or to the baby's knowledge that they were sisters. How the firstborn children interpret these comments is of course something we cannot make direct inferences about. But we *can* examine their comments about the baby and their behavior toward the baby at the later observations and use this material as a source of information on their beliefs about the baby. These we discuss in Chapters 6 and 7.

Comment

In this discussion of the conversations after the baby was born, we have touched on a number of issues concerning the children's interests and feelings about the baby. But this focus on the children should not allow us to overlook the extraordinary reserves of humor, patience, and love that the mothers showed in many of these conversations. The discussions often took place in circumstances that were, for the mothers, really desperately difficult. They had to cope with bathing, feeding, or calming a screaming 2- to 3-week-old baby — their hands literally full — while their 2-year-old — often frustrated or miserable, almost always demanding or difficult — tipped over the bath water, opened the safety pins, climbed into dangerous places, knocked over or fingered with soiled hands the baby's bottle, or dabbled in the dirty-nappy pail! Yet the mothers, exhausted after sleepless nights, managed to distract and converse with their firstborn children with good humor and interest, and to see with great sensitivity what might interest or amuse them.

It is, in fact, extremely difficult to have an extended discussion with a 2-year-old, or even with a 3-year-old, without a deep awareness of and concern for his interests. David Wood and his colleagues, studying the conversations between preschool children and their nursery-school teachers or play-group workers, have shown very clearly what these difficulties are, and why such conversations are often extremely limited in nature (Wood, McMahon, and Cranstoun 1980). They have also shown that some practitioners, in spite of the problems of talking to a young child while running a nursery school or play group, did repeatedly become involved in conversations with the children that were both rich and extended. The particular conversational style of these practitioners — one in which the adult offered the child lots of her own personal views, observations, and ideas, and did not control the conversation in an effort to keep it going, but showed a fine tuning to the child's own interests and world — was very similar to the style of the mothers in our study. To hold such discussions under the trying circumstances of these days so soon after the baby's birth reflected a degree of sensitivity and loving patience on the mother's part that was moving and humbling to witness.

In this chapter and the one before it we have seen how dramatically the lives of the firstborn children changed when their sibling was born. It was a period of considerable stress for many children (as well as for their mothers) — yet also a period of excitement and pleasure in the new baby. To what extent were these patterns of response in the early weeks linked to the quality of the relationship that developed between the siblings over the next years? Before we can try to answer that question, we must begin, in the next chapter, with another one. What kind of relationships *do* 2-year-olds and 3-year-olds have with younger children with whom they are very familiar?

five

Affection, Ambivalence, and Jealousy

Young siblings fight with one another. They provoke and irritate one another with devastating lack of inhibition. They amuse and excite one another and engage in uproarious games together. They comfort and care for one another. No psychologist is needed to point out the passion, fury, and jealousy, the range of emotion from gentle sympathy to wild aggression, that is expressed so uninhibitedly by siblings in their first three years. It is clear to anyone who is interested enough to look with care at a few families and to talk with parents and children. But this range of expressive behavior in such very young children raises many questions for psychologists — questions about the kind of social understanding reflected, about the significance the quality of the interaction holds for the later relationship between the two siblings, about the origins of the *differences* between young sibling pairs in their relationships, and about the ways in which the different relationships within the family affect one another.

If we are to begin to answer such questions, we must start from a precise description of the interaction and relationships between young siblings. We therefore have to face the major problems involved in deciding how to describe interactions between young children, in making inferences about the meaning of these interactions to the children we are watching, and in moving from the level of describing interaction to describing relationships. We may feel no hestitation about describing the relationships between some individual children as affectionate, and between others as jealous or hostile. As parents we may be aware of the complexity and ambivalence of the relation between young brothers and sisters, but usually the grounds on which our judgments are based are anything but precisely defined. The subtlety of the relationship between siblings from childhood on has been beautifully caught by novelists—the interplay of affection, jealousy, and ambivalence so powerfully shown in the relationship of Maggie and Tom Tulliver in *The Mill on the Floss*, or Elinor and Marianne Dashwood in *Sense and Sensibility*.

Although the sensitivities of novelists and of clinicians are of central importance in alerting us to the complexities and ambiguities of the relationships of young children, they do not in themselves provide a systematic framework of descriptive categories of the kind we need if we are to begin to address the developmental questions with which psychologists are concerned. To say that we are interested in trying to describe the *relationship* between young siblings implies something far more ambitious than to say that we are trying to describe the *interaction* between young siblings. At the very least, the latter suggests that we wish to capture not only the content, quality, and patterning of interactions in a variety of contexts, but something of the meaning to each individual of the relationship—the feelings, expectations, and understanding of each child. What kind of descriptive language should we use to begin the attempt? No matter how tentative the beginning, it will require description at a number of different analytic levels (Hinde 1979).

One of the challenges posed by the study of the relations between young siblings is that there are no accepted "global" psychological dimensions that are considered to be relevant, beyond those of jealousy and rivalry. After Alfred Adler's (1928) writings on personality and birth order a series of psychoanalytically based studies appeared in the 1930s, in which jealousy was seen as a key dimension in the sibling relationship (see for example Sewall 1930; Smalley 1930; Ross 1930; Levy 1937). MacFarland (1937), by contrast, attempted to develop a range of other global categories, paying particular attention to friendly cooperation and sharing. Bühler

(1939) also stressed the evidence for friendly behavior in older siblings, at the same time drawing attention to the difficulty of describing sibling relationships in broad dimensions. The more recent systematic studies of siblings have focused on the *interactions* between young siblings and have not attempted to relate these observations to sibling relationships on more global terms (Lamb 1978a and b; Abramovitch, Corter, and Lando 1979; Abramovitch, Corter, and Pepler 1980). These studies have not been primarily concerned with the emotional quality of the relationship. When that aspect *is* the focus of interest, there is a strong tendency to describe the relationship in terms of a single continuum, even if the terms are not limited to jealousy and rivalry: "In quality it [the sibling relationship] can range along a continuum from affection, intimacy, and caring, at the one end, to hostility, aggression, and anger, at the other" (Einstein and Moss 1967, p. 550).

In describing the relationship between child and *mother*, the great majority of accounts (at least those focusing on children over 6 months of age) stress the security dimension and use the framework of attachment theory. It is obvious that to assess a relationship as complicated and as rich as that of mother and child solely in terms of the conventional measures of attachment, such as those derived from separating the child from the mother in laboratory experiments (as in the "strange situation" of Ainsworth et al. 1978) would be deeply misleading. Still, there can be no question of the central importance of the security aspects of the relationship, and there is a large body of carefully conducted research that explores this feature of the early mother-child relationship. To describe the relationship between preschool children and their *peers*, a number of different global dimensions have been employed, such as dominance, friendship, and aggression. What kinds of descriptive terms and global dimensions might be appropriate for describing the relationship between a 2-year-old and his baby sibling? Why are jealousy and rivalry so often the only dimensions employed?

The assumption that jealousy is the key dimension surely follows from the focus on the mother-child relationship as the crucial feature of a child's emotional and social development in his first three years, a focus which has meant that the relationship between child and sibling has been seen *only* vis-à-vis the mother-child relationship: that is, in terms of a response to displacement and competition for the mother's affection. The idea that within the nuclear family the relationship with the mother is the only relevant focus for the study of social development in very young children has been challenged and qualified by recent work on the role of fathers. However, for three rather different reasons, this work does not take us very far toward overcoming the difficulties involved in describing the relationship between siblings.

First, much of the previous work has focused on *behavior*—the level of interaction between father and infant—and the terms in which the interaction has been described are those used in the study of mother-infant interaction. There has been little systematic research that has attempted to move beyond this level of description. Second, those attempts that have been made to describe the relationship between father and infant have been in terms of *attachment*: the criteria of attachment used in assessing the mother-infant relationship have been applied to fathers. How appropriate such a dimension might be for describing the sibling-infant relationship we have as yet no way of judging. Yet within the clinical, and particularly the psychoanalytic, literature are observations which suggest that in circumstances when infants are growing up *without* mothers they form relationships with other children for which a wide range of emotional categories may be appropriate. It has been noted, for instance, that when infants are placed in institutional circumstances without their parents, siblings may be a source of considerable security and comfort. Burlingham and Freud have provided a vivid account of the range and elaboration of emotions seen in the relationships between very young children who are brought up together.

In a crowd of toddlers they have to learn unduly early to defend themselves and their property, to stand up for their own rights, and even to consider the rights of others. This means that they have to become social at an age when it is normal to be asocial. Under pressure of these circumstances they develop a surprising range of reactions: love, hate, jealousy, rivalry, competition, protectiveness, pity, generosity, sympathy and even understanding. (1944, p. 23)

Burlingham and Freud argue firmly that under normal family circumstances this variety of relationships and emotions does not develop, and that in a nuclear family the relationship between siblings develops only in response to competition for the parents' love:

Under normal family conditions contact with other children develops only after the child-mother relationship has been firmly established. Brothers and sisters are taken into account for ulterior motives, love and hate towards them are usually not developed directly, but by way of the common relation to the parents. So far as they are rivals for the parents' love, they arouse jealousy and hate; so far as they are under the parents' protection and therefore "belong," they are tolerated, and even loved. (ibid.)

There is, then, no accepted framework for approaching the description of relationships between very young children. Anna Freud considers that the range of emotions she observed would simply not be demonstrated in normal families. But the absence of discussion of such categories of feelings toward other people in the psychological literature reflects a further assumption about the development of young children—the assumption that concepts such as empathy, friendship, concern, and protectiveness are not relevant to children under age 3. Such aspects of social interaction presuppose a far more sophisticated social understanding and ability to make inferences about the state of others than has until very recently been considered possible for children under 3. Our choice of descriptive units is bound to reflect the assumptions we make about the cognitive sophistication of the children whose behavior we are attempting to describe.

And this can be as important an issue for description at the level of social interaction as it (more obviously) is for description at a more global level. Some acts between siblings appear to reflect fairly obvious feelings—snatching a toy, hitting, pinching, pulling hair—but others are far more ambiguous. In one observation an 8-month-old child was crying, and his elder sibling came over and gave him a cracker. We might infer that this act reflected an intention to comfort the younger child. In this particular instance, however, the mother commented later that she thought the elder child performed such acts when the younger cried because he wished to forestall the mother or father's paying attention to the baby. If the mother's interpretation was correct, a description of the act as "comforting" is misleading. How seriously an observer would consider the interpretation the mother was offering would depend largely on the particular theory the observer held: such theories range from a readiness to attribute only the simplest of motives, to an enthusiasm (among some psychoanalysts) for attributing motives of enormous intricacy.

How then did the mothers describe the children's relationship when the babies were 8 and 14 months old, and what kinds of interactions did we as observers record?

Affection, Concern, and Fighting

"He [the younger sibling] loves being with her and her friends; he's very fond of one of her friends. He trails after Laura . . . they play in the sand a lot . . . making pies. She organizes it and whisks away things that are dangerous and gives him something else. They go upstairs and bounce on the bed. Then he'll lie there while she sings to him and reads books to him. And he'll go off in a trance with his hankie [comfort object]. The important thing is they're becoming games that they'll play together. He'll start something by laughing and running toward some toy, turning round to see if she's following. He'll go upstairs and race into the bedroom and shriek, and she joins him."

The mother of 14-month-old Callum did not doubt the warmth and richness of affection between her son and daughter. Indeed, most of the mothers stressed the emotional importance of the relationships between the siblings for the younger child, and gave us accounts of their children's behavior that certainly did not support the view that the relationship with the *mother* is the only one of importance to a baby. But how common was this affection from older to younger sibling? Did most elder siblings show both a concern for their sibling *and* a delight in playing with them? What about jealousy?

First, a brief comment on description. How well did the description of the siblings given us by the mothers accord with our direct observations? For some aspects of the children's behavior, such as the incidence of aggression and fights, we could make a direct comparison between interview and observation and the results showed good agreement (Table A5.1). However, it was clearly not possible for us to observe all the features of the child's behavior about which we inquired—for instance, whether the child reacted, when the baby was very upset, by trying to comfort him or her. For questions where we could not make a direct comparison between interview and observation, we did consider the mother's descriptions of the child's behavior against our simple summary measures; these results too were encouraging (Table A5.1).

The first outstanding feature from both observation and interview was the *salience* of each child's behavior for the other. In the interviews the mothers were asked a number of questions concerned with the elder child's behavior when the younger child interrupted his games, showed signs of being upset, was in a potentially dangerous situation (for instance, if he approached an unguarded fire), behaved in a "naughty" way, and so on. The mothers replied at length, with vivid descriptions of the ways in which the children reacted. It was of course not surprising that it was rare for an older child to do nothing when the baby interrupted a game: only 2 children were described as taking no notice in such circumstances. Yet it was also rare for an older child to ignore a younger sibling's behavior when he did something potentially dangerous (again, only 2 out of 40 children were so described), or when he did something naughty. Figure 5.1 shows that in this situation it was common for the elder child to tell the mother or try to prevent the baby's action, and a few children joined in the forbidden action. Very few did nothing.

If the baby was upset, most elder siblings again showed some reaction: however, the *ways* in which they responded varied a great deal. Figure 5.1 shows the frequency of different reactions ranging from extreme upset at the younger child's distress to deliberately increasing the upset. The majority of children, at least occasionally, made some attempt to comfort the younger when he was upset, and tried to help him when he was frustrated by a toy (Table A5.2).

The *frequency* with which the siblings interacted was emphasized by most mothers: fights were reported to occur daily in 20 families, and games daily in 27 families. Imitation of the baby by the elder child was described as happening occasionally or frequently in 86 percent of families, and it was even more common for the opposite to happen: 89 percent of the babies imitated their sibling occasionally or frequently,

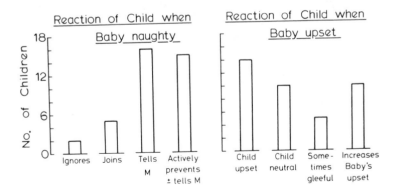

Figure 5.1   Reaction of firstborn when baby is naughty or upset.

and 58 percent were said to imitate the elder child on most days. During the observations most of the siblings did indeed interact very frequently. What stood out in the observations was the striking range of *differences* between the sibling pairs in the quality of these interactions, and in the relative proportion of friendly and more hostile actions. In some families 94 percent of the elder child's social approaches to the baby were friendly – that is, they included giving an object, smiling, helping, touching affectionately, comforting, or taking part in some game or joint physical play. In other families the elder sibling never showed any such actions during the observations. There was a similarly striking range in the frequency and proportion of hostile behavior of the elder to the younger – hitting, pinching, taking toys, and so on. Such actions accounted for 100 percent of the social approaches of one firstborn child and were never shown at all by others.

The saliency of the behavior of the other child to each sibling was also reflected in the immediate and marked reaction by both elder and younger to the behavior of the other sibling with either parent. When asked, for instance, how the first child behaved when the father played with the baby, the mothers described reactions that ranged from the elder child "trying to join in," asking for something immediately, requesting physical attention, or apparently deliberately attempting to disrupt the interaction between father and baby directly. Only 6 children were described as usually continuing their own activities, and 26 children were thought by their mothers to care when their fathers played with the baby, 7 of these children minding very much. With some children the signs of caring were silent: "She just stands there looking envious, as if to say 'please do it to me.' " Some elder children reacted forthrightly, telling the father to put the baby down, and others used more devious strategies: "He says the baby wants to crawl"; "She says it's time for the baby to sleep."

And just as the elder child rarely ignored the interaction between mother of father and younger sibling, so the majority of babies by 14 months were reported to react strongly and immediately to interaction between either parent and the elder sibling. If either parent was playing with the firstborn, few of the second siblings took no notice. The great majority either tried to push the firstborn out of the way or joined in the play in a friendly way (Table A5.3). The importance of the elder child as a focus of attention for the younger was apparent in the frequency of imitation, of games and of fights (which, interestingly, half the younger siblings were reported to "win" usually), and in the response to inteaction between parent and first child. The descriptions that the mothers gave us of the behavior of the baby toward the sibling, and the observations of the babies, certainly did not accord with a picture in which the emotional relationship with the *mother* was the only one of importance to the baby. Many mothers commented vividly on how much they thought the baby missed the elder child when they were apart, and on the warmth of attachment that they considered the baby felt for the elder sibling. Two quotations from families where, interestingly, the elder child was not very warm or friendly toward the baby illustrate the strength of their 8-month-old babies' expressed emotions to the sibling:

> MOTHER OF SIOBHAN F: She thinks he's marvelous. Hero-worships him. If he plays with her foot, she kills herself laughing. She doesn't cry till he goes out of the room.

> MOTHER OF JACKIE E: She misses him a great deal if he isn't there. Shouts till she hears him in the morning. Fusses till she can see him. I'm not enough.

Twenty of the 40 younger siblings were described as missing the elder if he was not there, and 15 of these were said to miss the elder very much. In several cases what the mothers stressed was the importance of the elder sibling as an exciting object of interest and as a potential playmate for the younger:

> MOTHER OF CYNTHIA J: She misses him a lot. She can't
> see what to do when he's not there.

But it would be quite misleading to conclude from the
mothers' accounts that this was all there was to the interest
the younger child felt for the older. By 14 months of age 13 of
the babies went to their older siblings for comfort:

> MOTHER OF IAN AND GRAHAM W: Graham goes to him
> for love and comfort. Saying "ah" and screwing up his
> face as if to say "isn't he sweet!" Ian often comforts him,
> and he's very concerned when he's upset.

Several of the 14-month-olds were described as often attempting to comfort the elder sibling if *he* was upset. The
younger children were more likely to approach the elder for
comfort in those families where the elder frequently attempted
to comfort the younger, where the elder did not mind sharing
his toys, and where fights were relatively infrequent. For some
of the secondborn children, then, it seems appropriate to
describe their relationship with their elder sibling as having
the qualities of an "attachment" in the terms of Bowlby (1969)
and Ainsworth (1973): the elder was *missed* in his absence and
was used as a source of comfort and security in distress.

In contrast to the firstborn children, who showed such a
wide range of individual differences in the friendliness or
hostility of their behavior, the younger siblings were much
more likely to approach their older sibling in a friendly than
in a hostile way. Seventy percent of their approaches were
friendly rather than negative. And they were much less frequently hostile to their older sibling than vice versa, although
it is interesting that the frequency of friendly approaches from
one sibling to the other did not differ significantly between the
firstborn and secondborn children (Table A5.4).

This difference between the friendliness of older and
younger siblings meant that in some families almost every exchange between the siblings—as many as 85 percent of interactions—involved the younger child's acting in a friendly way
and the older child's behaving in a negative fashion. In the

families where these "mismatch" interactions were frequent, there were also fewer games and the elder child rarely helped or looked after the baby (Table A5.5). There were indeed striking differences between the families in the extent to which if one child showed friendly behavior, the other responded in a positive fashion. In some of the families, 85 percent of all interactions were of this "mutually friendly" type; in others, there were none. Similarly, the families varied greatly in the frequency with which aggressive or hostile behavior from one child was followed by hostile behavior from the other. The proportion of these "mutually hostile" interactions ranged from zero in some families to 50 percent in others.

These findings on the mismatch interactions, and the difference in friendliness of firstborn and secondborn, do underline the importance of the differences in the elder child's behavior toward the younger sibling in contributing to the quality of the interaction between them. How clear was the pattern of friendly or hostile behavior in the older children?

Ambivalence, Affection, and Jealousy

Our observations and interviews revealed a dramatically wide range of differences between families in the frequency, quality, and elaboration of games; fights and physical play between the siblings; and reactions of firstborn children to the behavior of the baby. But do the differences in the behavior measures we used suggest that there is a unitary dimension of "warmth" or "affection" between the young siblings? Was the child who initiated frequent games also more likely to comfort his sibling when he was upset? Was he particularly unlikely to be aggressive or to start fights? Or was there more ambivalence in his behavior?

The observations showed that in families where the siblings frequently played games together (such as hide-and-seek or peekaboo) the elder child also frequently helped and looked after the baby, and both children often imitated each other. (Table A5.6 shows the correlations between these measures.)

In these families the elder child was less frequently observed
to hit, push, or pinch the younger. Nevertheless, the negative
correlations between the frequency of the behavior and the
games, helping, and imitation were not large. While some
elder siblings showed very frequent warm, affectionate
behavior toward their sibling, and very rarely showed
physical aggression, and other firstborn children showed frequent physical aggression and little affectionate behavior
toward their sibling, many children showed both friendly
social behavior *and* some physical aggression. Two points apparent in Table A5.6, which will be taken up later, are worth
noting here. First, where the elder child showed frequent
negative physical behavior to the younger, there were few imitative interactions between the children. Second, the frequency with which the children engaged in joint physical play
was not related to either the frequency of the more elaborate
games and imitations, or to the negative interactions.

These findings suggest that it would be misleading to consider the relationship between the siblings in terms of a single
dimension of warmth/hostility: that while there is indeed a
dramatically wide range of individual differences in the emotional coloring of the relationship, there are different aspects
of both positive and negative social behavior that do not form
a simple pattern, and it was quite common for both positive
and unfriendly social behavior to be shown by the same elder
child to his sibling.

Essentially the same picture emerged from our interviews
with the mothers. Take as a starting point the first child's
reaction to the baby's being upset, and his demonstration of
comforting behavior. The children who often comforted their
siblings were less likely to mind when the sibling played with
their toys than those who did not try to comfort the baby,
and they were more likely to help the sibling when frustrated
and less likely to fight frequently. Although the associations
were significant, the links were by no means strong for all
children. Among these "comforting" elder siblings were some
children who also fought frequently with their siblings, while

some "noncomforters" were reported to fight rarely. Fights were also frequent among some sibling pairs where the elder child *did* share toys willingly and helped the younger child when he was frustrated, while in other families the first child *did not* share happily or help, yet rarely started fights. And the relationship between the elder child's demonstration of comforting, and his emotional reaction to the signs that the baby was upset, was not simple. None of the children who responded to the baby's distress with glee, or deliberately increased their upset, ever comforted their siblings. But of the 14 children who themselves became upset when the baby was upset, 8 were also children who never or rarely comforted their sibling.

A reaction of distress or upset at the sibling's upset was in fact linked to the kind of temperament the first child had, rather than reflecting a simple, unipolar dimension of affectionate feeling toward the sibling. Children who reacted with extreme upset at the baby's distress also became very concerned when the baby was in a potentially dangerous situation. These children were described as frequently worrying about the baby. One child, for instance, who according to both his mother's reports and the observation measures, rarely showed affectionate behavior toward the sibling, was described as "always going to check in her room to see if she's all right; he worries about her." This kind of concern was described in detail by the mothers of children who reacted with distress to the baby's upset.

MOTHER OF RUSSELL S: He hates anything to happen to her . . . hates to hear her cry. He moves small toys in case she puts them in her mouth and covers stickle bricks [prickly toy bricks that interlock] with a cloth.

MOTHER OF TIM W: Hes very upset if he thinks he's in danger. He cried yesterday when Graham kept putting his hand near the door.

Some of the children who comforted their baby siblings minded very much when their father or mother played with the sibling—others did not. And among the children who were described as not minding when the father played with the baby were some who never comforted the sibling, others who frequently did.

What these maternal reports revealed was a picture in which some elder children made vigorous efforts to comfort their sibling, frequently helped and played with him, and showed upset when the baby was upset. But for many of the elder siblings, the relationship was a much more ambivalent one. Two other features stand out. First, protective behavior toward the baby was clearly demonstrated by most of the elder children when other people investigated the baby or threatened (jokingly) to take the baby away. This was notably true of some of the firstborns who showed most unambiguous hostility and lack of affection to the sibling in other circumstances.

Second, the complexity and ambivalence of the elder child's reaction to the sibling was especially evident when the mother or father interacted with the baby. The reaction to the parents' playing with the baby has been already mentioned, but quite a different reaction often appeared when the mother scolded or punished the younger sibling. In these circumstances the elder children often sided with the baby:

> MOTHER OF KATHRYN D: She cuddles her, yes, specially if I've told her off.

> MOTHER OF DEREK J: If I tell her off, he says "Oh, you are mean. She doesn't understand," and he goes and loves her.

> MOTHER OF SUSAN S: If I scold him, she says, "You mustn't do that to Alan; he's only a baby."

Such exchanges expose the complexity of the elder child's feelings about the *mother* as well as about the sibling. One

3-year-old girl was very upset when her mother scolded the 14-month-old brother, though her mother said that the child was sometimes quite pleased when he did naughty things, she herself being a compliant child who rarely misbehaved. The behavior (and presumably the feeling of) the elder child toward both the sibling and the mother varied according to the social situation, and how the parents and the sibling were behaving together represented a particularly significant part of that social context, as we saw in Chapter 3.

The ambivalence of the elder child's feelings about the sibling was often vividly and directly expressed, by children who in other respects showed much affectionate concern for and interest in their baby sibling. Brendan F, for instance, commented "I like my sister," within a minute asking for her to be sent back to the hospital. And already by 14 months, the complexity and ambivalence of the sibling relationship was apparent in the *younger* child's behavior to the elder, as well as vice versa. Both MacFarland (1937) and Bühler (1939) comment on the complexity and ambivalence of the behavior of some of the siblings in their studies, and stress that this ambivalence was a characteristic of the relationship of several of the sibling pairs.

Our observations and interviews have shown us the great range of differences in the quality of interaction of sibling pairs by the time the baby reaches 14 months. They have revealed something of the complexity and ambivalence of the relationship between the children. But they provide us also with a very special perspective on the development of social understanding, and present us with information that has implications for a number of major developmental issues: the nature of affective communication, the relation of preverbal to verbal communication, the development of role-taking skills, the beliefs of young children about other children, and the development of empathy—and the role of the mother in all these developments. In the next two chapters we shall consider some of these issues more fully, drawing on our direct observations of the siblings, on our transcripts of family conversations, and on the speech of the first child to the baby.

six

Understanding the Other

The quality of the relationship between the siblings will of course be profoundly affected by the extent to which each child perceives and understands the other's feelings and intentions. Not only sympathetic support and comfort of the other's distress, cooperation in games and play, but also the subtler forms of aggression and provocation will be dramatically affected by the growing sensitivity of each child to the other as a person. At issue is not only the ability of one child to understand the other's emotional state or intentions, but the motivation and capacity to act with effective sympathy or hostility toward his sibling. All of these involve the ability to make inferences about the experience of another person, yet the way in which cognitive ability and emotional response to others are related developmentally is by no means clear.

Our knowledge of the early development of children's understanding of other people's emotional states, wishes, and intentions is very patchy. Psychologists still disagree sharply over just what difficulties very young children experience in taking the perspective of others. Is it correct to see perspective taking as a single capacity? Is it appropriate to assume that empathy is a unitary trait? (See Urberg and Docherty 1976; Hoffman 1981.) Is the extent of the abilities children demonstrate in a perspective-taking task simply an artifact of the task selected? Donaldson (1978), for instance, has argued that many such experiments seriously underestimate the ability of children to perceive the intentions and perspective of others.

Two themes run through the theoretical discussion of the development of empathetic understanding. One relates to the cognitive component: the extent to which one child is able to assimilate the perspective or role of the other, an ability that depends upon a clear sense of the other as separate from itself and upon a capacity to conceive the situation of another as distinct in character and significance from one's own situation. The second theme concerns the emotional response: the child's experience of emotion when witnessing another's emotional state. The relationship between these two components—cognitive and affective—is seen differently by different theorists, just as the concept of "empathy" is defined very differently. In some accounts empathy is taken to refer to "knowledge about, or understanding another's feelings and need not be accompanied by a similar affective experience" (Gore and Keating 1979, p. 594). In others empathy is seen as the shared emotional responses that the child experiences on perceiving another's emotional reaction (Feschbach 1976). In Hoffman's account (1975, p. 613) the emotional response, particularly empathetic distress—"experiencing another's painful emotional state"—develops early, before the infant is capable of differentiating self from other. Hoffman believes that infants are often unclear about who is feeling the distress they witness and may behave as though what is happening to others is happening to them. Similar ideas have of course been elaborated by psychoanalytic writers.

Hoffman gives the example of

a colleague's 11 month old daughter who on seeing another child fall and cry, first stared at the victim, appearing to be about to cry herself, and then put her thumb in her mouth and buried her head in her mother's lap—her typical response when she has hurt herself and seeks comfort. [The child] may only vaguely and momentarily be aware of the other as distinct from self . . . Consequently the child probably reacts to another's distress as though his dimly perceived self-and-other were somehow simultaneously, or alternatively, in distress. As an example consider a child I know whose typical response to his own distress, beginning late in the first year, was to suck his thumb with one hand and pull his ear with the other. At 12 months, on seeing a sad look on his father's face, he proceeded to look sad and suck his thumb, while pulling his *father's* ear. (1975, p. 614)

Hoffman (1981) argues that later, when children become capable of "rudimentary role-taking," they begin to "put themselves in the other's place and find the true source of his distress." Furthermore, "by 2 or 3 years of age they acquire a rudimentary sense of others as having inner states independent of their own, although they cannot yet discern the other's inner states." At this stage they begin to use more appropriate ways to relieve the other's unhappiness. Yet Hoffman maintains that, even as a toddler, the child will use inappropriate means to alleviate the other's distress, since he sees the world only from his own viewpoint. The examples quoted above do not, however, demonstrate that 11- and 12-month-old children cannot distinguish another from themselves. It is perfectly possible, for example, that the 11-month-old child above, witnessing the other's distress, felt distress himself, and that his initial action to comfort himself was not therefore inappropriate.

We have here a number of questions, questions that our observations of siblings may well help us to address. How do very young children respond to the emotional state of others with whom they have close relationships? Is there any evidence that they *can* discern the other's inner state? Is it reasonable to infer from their response that young children have difficulty in distinguishing the emotional reaction of others from that of themselves? Or that young children respond simply by projecting their own feelings onto the situation of others, as some would predict? (See for example Flavell 1968; Rothenburg 1970; Chandler and Greenspan 1972.) Or is there evidence that children under 3 can ascribe to other people a perspective that is not their own? If young children have such difficulty in understanding the distinction between their own perspective and that of others, what is the nature of their hypotheses or beliefs about their baby sibling as another person, as distinct from the mother or father? How do these beliefs change as the children grow up?

Our observations of the siblings, and the transcripts of their conversations with each other, with their parents, and with us as observers provide us with a number of different kinds of information. First, there are the *comments* made by the elder child about the baby's actions, wants, and intentions; his remarks about the baby's state, his interpretation of signs of emotional upset, and his observations about the baby's capabilities. Second, there are the *actions* of each child in relation to the other, as recorded in our observations. Third, there is the elder child's *speech* to the baby. This differs in a number of respects from his speech to the other adults present, or to his peers: whether this shift in speech register can be taken as evidence from which we can make inferences about the elder child's understanding of the baby's cognitive and linguistic capabilities will be discussed in the next chapter.

Comments about the Baby

Interpretation of the Baby's Wants and Wishes

The majority of the children commented during our observations on the wants and intentions of the baby. Such comments were as frequent when the firstborn child was under 3 years old as they were when the firstborn was older, and usually were made to the mother or to the observer. Some, for instance, followed actions, expressions, or noises by the baby which the mother had not noticed or responded to.

> SUE H: He wants go out.
>
> JOANNE R: Donna wants cakey, Mum.
>
> JILL J: Kenny want bit meat.

Often such comments were accurate predictions of the baby's actions. Some were comments on particularly expressive behavior of the baby.

HARVEY M: Ronnie's happy.

Some were remarks in which the child apparently took pleasure in "explaining" the baby's actions or wishes to the observer.

JUDY B: She wants to come to you.

BRUCE S: He likes that. He a silly boy.

HARVEY M: He likes me.

JIM E: Jackie not like monkey (after Jackie had thrown down toy monkey).

LAURA W: Callum's laughing for his dinner isn't he? He sometimes gets Bonzo's dinner [the dog's] 'cause he likes his dinner quick.

JILL J (showing O a toy):   He likes this. He likes it squeaky.

LAURA W: Callum's crying 'cause he wants his food cold.

Sometimes such comments on the baby's desires reflected what was perhaps wishful thinking on the elder child's part, rather than a particularly sensitive interpretation of an ambiguous act.

BRUCE S (when M suggests putting the baby to sleep in the elder child's bunk): He doesn't *want* to sleep in my bunk.

IAN W (in a rough physical game between the siblings):
M: I don't think that he likes that.
C: He do. He do.

LAURA W (to O): He loves it when I smack him.

SUSAN S (when father picks up baby): Baby wants to
crawl.

There were also many incidents in which the elder child read the baby's behavior in a way that appeared to be "detached" in the sense that it did not reflect the *elder child's* interests in any direct way, but was finely tuned to the baby's range of wishes. Several of the more general comments on the baby made to the observer reflected this broad sense of what the baby liked or disliked, rather than the baby's immediate wants in the here and now. Both the following remarks were made in the absence of the baby:

JUDY B: Carole likes these monkeys.

DEREK J: She likes my ted.

There were also many incidents where the elder child took issue with the mother over the baby's wishes, protesting on the baby's behalf against the mother's interpretation. These examples suggested that the elder child observed and interpreted the sibling's wishes with considerable accuracy:

ANDREW W:
M to B: You don't want to go in there (as B tries to
get into cupboard).
C to M: He does.

MARVIN W (M trying to get B out of kitchen into sitting
room):
M to B: You go and play with your toys.
C to M: She wants to go in the kitchen. She's allowed
to go in the kitchen.

And there were numerous examples where the mother asked the baby a question, and the elder child provided an answer:

PAUL G:
M to B: What are you doing?
C to M: He just doing a funny noise to you.

SABRINA D:
M to B: Do you want to go to bed?
C to M: No, he doesn't.

There are of course many possible interpretations of the *motives* of the elder children in making such comments to their mothers or to us as observers. But it surely seems justifiable to conclude that children under 3 notice how the baby apparently feels in a particular situation, and comment on it in a way that certainly does not always represent a projection of their own feelings. For instance, when an elder child commented with apparent glee on the baby's crying and offered an explanation of why the baby was upset, he was certainly attributing to the baby a perspective not his own. Sometimes this difference in perspective was quite explicit:

BRUCE S (B playing with a balloon): He going to pop it in a minute. And he'll cry. And he'll be frightened of me too. I *like* the pop.

Such observations fit much more closely with the interpretation put forward by Borke (1972), on the basis of her experimental findings, that children as young as 3 understand how other children feel in familiar situations, than with the interpretation put forward by Chandler and Greenspan (1972), who argue that children of this age can merely project their own feelings onto others. Our observations support the thesis put forward by Bretherton, McNew, and Beeghley-Smith (1981), that very young children do have a "fairly sophisticated model of others and of themselves as psychological beings." Bretherton and her colleagues base their argument on a systematic examination of children's explicit verbal comments on internal states imputed to themselves and to others. They show that by 20 months children do make references to the following states—happy, hungry, tired, sad, mad, scared, cold—both in relation to themselves and to others. They note that *causal* utterances about internal states of self and other appear almost as early as internal state labeling itself. Hood and Bloom (1979), analyzing causal utterances produced by children in their second and third years, found that the majority were concerned with the internal states of people. *Psychological* causality was apparently more salient to these young children than *physical* causality, and the children were, moreover, as interested in explaining the internal states of others as they were in explaining their own.

What is particularly striking in our own study is that there were very marked individual differences between the elder children in how often they made such comments on the baby's affective state or intentions. These differences in sensitivity relate to other individual differences in the children's behavior with their siblings, and in their mothers' behavior. The origins and implications of these differences are discussed in Chapters 8 and 9.

Capabilities of the Baby

This study was not designed to explore systematically the beliefs of 2- or 3-year-olds about their baby siblings; it provides only suggestive examples rather than a coherent or conclusive account. But before exploring the speech of the elder child to the baby, which can give us some systematic data bearing on the issue, we should comment on some of the remarks made by the elder child about the baby's capabilities.

The remarks reflect a fairly accurate sense of the baby's current skills, whether in manipulating objects, in mobility, in language, or in understanding and memory.

JILL J (to O):   He doesn't know you.

LAURA W (to B): You don't remember Judy. I do.

JOANNE R:
C to M (who is encouraging B to post shapes into a
postball [sphere with variously shaped slots]):
Donna can't put 'em in the ball.
M to C: Why not? She can learn.

SUE H (to another child who has told B to find his bike):
He can't find his. And he doesn't know where it is.

SYLVIA C (to O; B has just made an excited noise when
Sylvia appears with a tube of Smarties [candies]): He
knows Smarties.

The ability to infer that another may have different thoughts
or knowledge than the child himself appears, then, to develop
in relation to the sibling *far* earlier than the age of 6 years, as
has been suggested by previous work (see Shantz 1975).

A commonly discussed theme in some of the families was
the ways in which the baby was developing.

RUSSELL S:
C: Baby can't walk.
M: No, she can't walk yet, can she?
C: When she gets bigger she can.
M: When she gets a bit bigger she can, yes.

This kind of discussion often centered on the way in which
the elder child *used* to be like the baby. A triumphant sense of
always being ahead was sometimes evident:

LAURA W:
C to M (after M comments to B about cutting teeth):
I was cutting teeth. I was walking before he
was. I walked before him.

C to O: He's a walloper. He'll smack me when he's
bigger. I'm going to be huge when he's a bit
bigger. Up to the ceiling. Like you.

O to C: I'm not up to the ceiling.
C to O: Well, I'll be up there. I'll grow so much. Up to
the ceiling. So high.

On the other hand, many children expressed real delight in
the baby's accomplishments. The mothers of 15 out of the 40
children reported that the elder child frequently noted new
achievements, and a further 18 were reported to comment occasionally on these achievements. Several of these children did
remark in the course of the observation on the baby's new
developments.

JUDY B (to M):   She called you Mum.

The interest of the firstborn children (particularly the older
ones) in the concept of growing up and changing was often
reflected in persistent questioning, which sometimes exposed
their mother's logic rather mercilessly:

DIANNE H (M has been discussing how C had played in
the back garden when she was 14 months old):
M: *You* used to talk to Lucy through the fence.
C: Mmm. I didn't know I could talk when I was
one.
M: Well you didn't *talk* talk. You didn't talk like
you do now. But you used to make noises to
each other. Like Marion and Dawn do.
C: Like "loos loos loos"?
M: I suppose!

C to B: You're not to bite. (Then to M): Mum, when she
was a baby she had one at the top and one at
the bottom.
M: Mmm.
C: Why?
M: Oh, 'cause she hadn't any teeth in her gums,
had she?
C: Why?

M: 'Cause they hadn't come through.

C: Why?

M: 'Cause they don't when they're babies.

C: This one at the top and one at the bottom had
    come out.

M: Yes.

C: Why not more?

M: Well, because they take a long time to come
    through, don't they? Same as second teeth. You
    didn't have any when you were first born. And
    Marion didn't have any.

C: Why?

M: No babies . . . well, very few babies are born . . .
    (M fails to finish.)

Categorization of the Self and the Baby

It is notable that the presence of the baby, and the discussion
between the mother and firstborn about the baby, often led to
comments by the elder child that were concerned with categorization of himself as well as of the baby. These remarks,
particularly those that involved *playing* with dimensions of
self/identity, demonstrate particularly forcefully the confidence with which the elder child applied dimensions such as
gender, age, size, or good/naughty to himself and to the baby
sibling. In the next example, the little girl *plays* with the
father about the gender identity of herself and of her brother.

SALLY C:

C (playing with her teddy) to father, F: Teddy's a man.

F: What are you?

C: You're a boy.

F: Yeah. What are you?

C: A menace.

F: Yeah, a menace. Apart from that are you a boy or
    a girl?

C: Boy (laughs).

F:	Are you? What's Trevor?
C:	A girl (laughs).
F:	You're silly.

The next conversation, which took place between a mother and a 26-month-old, illustrates that the children in the sample seemed very clear about gender identity even when not verbally advanced:

WARREN D (throwing comic book at B):	
M:	You giving Joyce your comic, are you?
C:	No.
M:	Are you a monkey?
C:	No. Me not monkey. Me boy. Joyce girl. Joyce baby.
M:	Is she?
C:	Joyce baby.
M:	She's not a baby now, is she?

Many of the self-categorizing comments made in the context of conversation about the sibling were, unsurprisingly, about the big/small, or big/baby dimension:

JANE B:	
C to M:	I'm a pudding.
M:	Are you a pudding? And who is Robert?
C:	Robert is a pudding too. He's a baby pudding.

The boy in the next example corrected the observer when she referred to his 8-month-old sibling as a "big brother":

IAN W (to O): *Little* brother.

There was in some cases, as we saw in the quotation from Laura W, some uncertainty about the constancy of the size difference. The hope was expressed by several firstborn children that they would always be bigger than their sibling.

The possibilities of playing with the well-understood categories of identity were endlessly exploited in pretend games. These make-believe games gave the elder child, for instance, opportunities for capricious refusal to comply with the mother's requests. In the next example the 3-year-old shifted from being himself to being his baby brother, and then to being himself *as a baby*, in order to avoid doing what his mother wanted. The claim to be a "baby" was one that recurred frequently in our observations of other families too, particularly in response to requests for help from a parent.

HARVEY M (making pretend crying noises):

M: Now what are you crying for?

C: I want my drink.

M: You want your drink? You Ronnie? You pretending you're Ronnie? (M turns to B—Ronnie, 14 months—and comments on his game, then says to B:) Now Harvey can do it for you.

M to C: Can't you, Harvey?

C: No. I'm Ronnie.

M: Well, pretend you're Harvey for a little while.

C: Pretend I'm Harvey *baby*.

M: Harvey baby?

C: Mammammamma gagaga gagaga. Bababa.

M: You'd better not leave that Plasticine on the floor. You know what Ronnie'll do with it.

C: I'm a little baby boy.

M: I don't care what you are.

C: I'm a *little* boy.

SUE H (to M, refusing to get off seat): 'Cause I'm a baby.

The enthusiasm and adroitness with which the children played with the categorization of their *own* identity leaves little room for doubt about the confidence and certainty with which they understood the dimensions of age and gender as applied to themselves and to their parents.

The spontaneous comments of the first children and our observations of their behavior indicate, then, that the children had little doubt about the gender of the secondborn, had good understanding of his present capabilities, likes and dislikes, and intentions to act, and had some notion of the way in which the baby's capabilities had changed and would continue to change. In these ways the baby was apparently understood to be "like" the first child, in the sense that the same categories and dimensions were applied to both selves. There were several aspects in which the baby was apparently regarded as different, however. Not only were the baby's limited capabilities often discussed, but it was abundantly clear that the elder also regarded the sibling as a person/thing who needed *protection* in many circumstances — who would harm himself without the vigilance of other people. And while the baby was seen as a person to whom *rules* of behavior applied, there were many instances where the first child suggested that the rules that applied to the baby were different from those that applied to the firstborn, the parents, visitors, or others. An extreme example was the following comment from a 3-year-old about her 14-month-old brother who was trying to follow his mother into the street:

> PENNY D (to O): He can't go out. No. 'Cause only people can go out.

Almost every observation included some discussion of the issue of whether B was allowed to do X. It was also clear from every observation that B was regarded as an individual who potentially threatened C's interests, in the literal sense that he was likely to spoil the game C was playing, was intending to take the drink C was enjoying, or would take and destroy a precious possession unless C took preventive action. The firstborn's peers were never discussed in this way; in fact, there were much clearer parallels with the way in which family pets were discussed. In such conversations there was considerable agreement between firstborn and parent: there was a strong flavor of conspiracy between them in controlling the younger child, or frustrating his intentions. We shall return to such conspiratorial discussions in Chapter 8.

Observations of Empathy and Antipathetic Actions

At some point during the observations made at 8 months and again at 14 months, most of the elder children in the sample did act toward the baby in a way that suggested that they were concerned about or understood well the other's state. Since it is obviously important not to read too much into such incidents, we were extremely conservative in categorizing them as showing concern or understanding of the other's state. For instance, several of the sequences where the elder child gave the younger a toy could have indicated some interest in his or her welfare. Such incidents were, however, not included in the group we have classified as showing empathy, unless the elder child gave the toy (unsolicited) after the younger had hurt himself, or for some other reason was distressed or was clearly frustrated.

In 65 percent of the families observed when the younger child was 14 months old, there were incidents we classified as showing empathetic concern for the younger child. These included helping the younger with a toy when he or she was frustrated by it, offering toys or food when the sibling was crying, going to ask the younger child if he or she wanted a drink and then fetching it, showing concern that the younger child should be included in games, and some incidents that reflected quite subtle readings of the younger child's expression.

No parent of a child aged between 2 and 3 years would be surprised by the finding that the elder children showed such "prosocial" behavior toward their baby sibling. But it is important to note, first, that 13 out of 16 children showing empathetic behavior to their 8-month-old siblings were under 30 months at the time. Second, there were a number of incidents which suggest that the *younger* sibling was, by the second year, becoming capable of some degree of understanding the other's wishes. These incidents were more commonly observed where the younger child was 15 months than at 14 months; they were also noted in a study of 14- and 15-month-old kibbutz children where the prosocial acts were directed toward age-mates. For instance, when one 15-month-old fell over, a 14-month-old watched and then approached and attempted to pick her up. Such actions do not imply any elaborate understanding of the other's state. In some cases it is evident that the younger child behaves in a way that is more appropriate as comfort for *himself* when distressed than for the other (sibling or parent). For instance, one child who had reduced his mother to tears, ran to fetch his security blanket, which he habitually sucked when upset or tired, and tried to stuff it in *her* mouth. It would be quite justifiable to infer from this example that the child was at a stage of development where he recognized the mother's state of distress but was still operating on the belief that "what will assuage my distress will assuage hers."

But there are three important qualifiers that should be noted before any general conclusion is drawn on the limited ability of 2- or 3-year-olds to comprehend others' feeling states or to act in a nonegocentric way toward them.

(1) Several incidents suggested that during the second year children begin to recognize that the distress of others can be relieved by the provision of comfort, but that what constitutes comfort for the other is not necessarily identical to that which would constitute comfort for the child himself. There appears to be an awareness as early as 14 to 15 months that some of the acts within the child's power can provide some comfort for others, but the child may well overgeneralize the types of occasion or person for whom the action can be expected to provide comfort. Take for instance the following incident, which occurred when a 15-month-old was in the garden with his brother. The 15-month-old, Len, was a stocky boy with a fine round tummy, and he played at this time a particular game with his parents which always made them laugh. His

game was to come toward them, walking in an odd way, pulling up his T-shirt and showing his big stomach. One day his elder brother fell off the climbing frame in the garden and cried vigorously. Len watched solemnly. Then he approached his brother, pulling up his T-shirt and showing his tummy, vocalizing, and looking at his brother.

(2) Some incidents reflected the *opposite* of empathy and suggested that even by 14 months the children had considerable powers of understanding how to annoy the other sibling:

> Laura W:
> Callum repeatedly reaches for and manipulates the magnetic letters Laura is playing with. Laura repeatedly says no gently. Callum continues trying to reach the letters. Finally, Laura picks up the tray containing the letters and carries it to a high table that Callum cannot reach. Callum is furious and starts to cry. He turns and goes straight to the sofa where Laura's comfort objects, a rag doll and a pacifier, are lying. He takes the doll and holds tight, looking at Laura. Laura for the first time is very upset, starts crying, and runs to take the doll.

Note that even though this particular child did use his own pacifier when he was upset, he took his sister's doll — a source of comfort to *her*, not to him — when frustrated by her.

(3) The third point concerns interpretation of the egocentric responses of children to others' emotional states — the "self-referential" acts like that of the little boy who gave his security blanket to his mother. Rather than dismissing these incidents as reflecting an ability to take the viewpoint of others, perhaps we should consider them in a slightly different way. Yarrow and Waxler (1975) have made the interesting point that such acts may have quite an important function: they may represent "active attempts to *comprehend* (to form hypotheses about) others' affects by 'trying them on,' in this way trying to master (act positively on) the feelings in themselves which are aroused by others' affects. Support for such an idea is found

in our data where it is not uncommon to observe self-referential responses follwed by compassionate responses"
(p. 79).

There are two questions that must be separated in considering the issues of egocentrism and empathetic understanding: Does the child recognize that the other's affective state is different from his own? What does the child think that he is doing in carrying out the remedial act?

In relation to the second question, it is not unusual for even an adult to recognize that another person is in a particular affective state, and yet have no idea what to do about it; it is, in fact, a rather common feature of adult life. And as we have suggested before, even if a child's hypotheses about what constitutes comfort for the other appear to be comically self-centered, this does not show that the child is confused about the self/other distinction. If a child responds to another's affective state in a way that would be appropriate remedially if the affective state were the child's own, we cannot infer either that the child cannot tell the difference between the other's affective state and his own, or that the child presumes that anything that remedies his own affective state will remedy others—that he or she assumes uniformity about sources of comfort. We *can* infer that small children do not have very good theories about what will comfort human beings, particularly adult human beings. Since what a child has to do, to succeed in finding the appropriate remedy, is to "model" the situation of the other, it should not surprise us if children are better at "understanding" (in a pragmatic, remedial way) family pets and siblings. Our observations (and those of Yarrow and Waxler 1975) suggest that in their second year children understand the affective tone of adults, but do not yet have the experience to comprehend what constitutes an adequate remedy for an adult's distress or anxiety. They are, in contrast, in a position to generate very good theories about the life-world of the infant: so many of the situations in which the baby sibling shows distress, excitement, fear, or joy are situations extremely familiar to the elder child.

These naturalistic observations do not provide *measures* or tests of the extent to which children understand others' states of mind or are motivated to act empathetically toward others. They do show unequivocally that before 3 years of age elder siblings can and do recognize their baby sibling's emotional states and intentions, and that this understanding does not reflect a simple projection of the elder's own current emotional state onto the baby. They show that the children respond to the baby's state in a way that is often appropriate to the *baby's* state, and not simply to the way the child would expect or want to be treated himself. Finally, they show that there are marked individual differences in this sensitivity to the baby; it is clearly important to pursue the origins of these differences.

Furthermore, both our observations of the younger siblings and the reports by the mothers of their babies' responses to other people support the conclusion of Yarrow and Waxler from their own study that children of around a year are very sensitive to others' need states, and that they show comfort to others in distress:

Our infant subjects supplied very provocative data on sensitivity to affective states of others. Responses were by no means universal. However very young children were often finely discriminative and responsive to others' need states. Children in the youngest cohort showed distress to parental arguments and anger with each other. Responses were sometimes marked: crying, holding hands over ears, comforting a distraught parent, or (punitively) hitting the parent perceived as the guilty one. Parental affection toward each other was equally arousing: Children of 1 to 2½ years tried to join in or to separate the parents—even kicking the mother's leg. One child, from 15 months to 2 years showed consistently different responses depending on whether mother or father initiated the affectionate hug or kiss. Initiation by the mother aroused no affect in the child, whereas with the father's (or grandfather's) initiation toward the mother, the child would "fall apart" (hitting, glaring, sucking her thumb).

Around one year most of the youngest cohort first showed comfort to a person crying or in pain by patting, hugging, or presenting an object. Among 1½ and 2-year-olds comforting was sometimes sophisticated and elaborate, e.g., fixing the hurt by trying to put a Band-aid on, covering mother with a blanket when she was resting, trying to locate the source of the difficulty. Children also began to express concern verbally, and sometimes gave suggestions about how to deal with the problem. Such precocity on the part of the very young gives one pause. The capabilities for compassion, for various kinds of reaching out to others in a giving sense are viable and effective responses early in life. (1975, pp. 78–79)

Burlingham and Freud (1944) also give some vivid examples of children in the second year helping, consoling, soothing, and comforting each other.

There is really very little work with which these observations can be compared: systematic studies of the beginnings of empathy other than those of Yarrow and Waxler have focused on children from 3 years upward. However, a few anecdotes have been reported that describe incidents very similar to our observations, such as the examples given by Borke (1972). The discrepancy between the powers of understanding shown by the young siblings, and those which would be attributed to them on a classic Piagetian model underline the point that the kinds of conclusions we draw about children's ability to react on an empathetic basis depend crucially on the situation in which they are studied. If we observe children in contexts that have emotional significance for them, then Borke's conclusion seems very reasonable: we cannot characterize their reaction to the distress of others as egocentric, in the sense of an inability to perceive that the other has a perspective different from their own. Borke's claim is that conscious awareness that another person's emotional experience is different from one's own is the first step in developing empathy, and our observations suggest that many 14-month-old children demonstrate such an awareness in response to the emotions expressed by sibling and by parent. Naturally, this empathetic awareness differs greatly from the increasingly complex perspective-taking abilities shown by the child in the third and fourth years.

To stress that children demonstrate empathetic understand-

ing toward familiar others far earlier than they do toward unfamiliar others is not new (see for example Shantz 1975). But
the observations of the siblings, the findings of Bretherton and
her colleagues, and those of Yarrow and Zahn-Waxler surely
show that it is not appropriate to conclude that because
preschool children are not accurate in judging the emotions of
an unfamiliar person in an artificial setting, their accuracy in
relation to a familiar person in a familiar situation "may be no
more than self description" (Shantz 1975, p. 281). It simply
does not follow that when a child is accurate in his judgment
about the emotions of those he cares about he is necessarily
only accurate because of self-projection.

If we examine the sensitive and careful studies of perspective taking carried out by Donaldson's group (1978) in Edinburgh, we find a striking theme emphasized repeatedly, which
recurs like a Wagnerian motif in our own observations.
Donaldson and her students, notably Hughes, examined very
carefully the Piagetian claim that children under the age of 6
had difficulty in "decentering"—in understanding what another
person knows, sees, or feels. They carried out a series of experiments in which children were required to perform tasks
very like the perspective-taking tasks on which Piaget had
based his views of children's egocentrism, yet different in one
important respect. The original task had required the child to
decide what a model mountain would look like to someone in
a different position from himself; the Edinburgh experiments
required the child to play with a boy doll and a policeman,
and to place the doll in such a position that he would be effectively hidden from the policeman. The results were dramatically different from the original perspective-taking experiments,
and 90 percent of the 3-year-olds were successful. A series of
more elaborate tasks followed, in which the experimenter took
great care to establish that the children had understood the
task fully, and again there was a high level of success among
the 3-year-olds. In discussing the differences between her
findings and the original Piagetian results, Donaldson comments:

In the course of trying to reconcile Hughes' findings with Piaget's I suggested that Hughes' task is easy for the child to grasp because it makes human sense. It rests on an understanding of the interaction of two complementary intentions of a very basic kind: the intention to escape and the intention to pursue and capture. Now it is worth observing that the appreciation of such a complementary pair of intentions, however simple and elementary, calls already for an ability to decentre that is not concerned with the literal understanding of another point of view: not with what another person *sees* from a given standpoint, but with what he is feeling or planning to do. Hughes' task, though designed primarily to test the former, also rests upon the latter. And what I have been suggesting is that the latter is a very fundamental human skill. (1978, p. 25)

What stands out from our observations of the siblings, and from the comments made by the children themselves, is that well before age 3, children are unequivocally skillful at reading, anticipating, and responding to the feelings and plans of their baby siblings.

seven

Communication between the Siblings

The children's comments about their siblings, and their actions toward them, have shown us something of the beliefs they hold about the baby as a person like or unlike themselves. Concern for the baby, and some pragmatic understanding of how to annoy and how to console, are demonstrated in their behavior and in their comments to their mothers and to us. In this chapter we examine the communication between the siblings themselves, beginning with two general questions. How does a child of age 2 or 3 communicate with a baby — linguistically and cognitively immature — with whom he or she has a close and important emotional relationship? Can an analysis of the speech of the children give us any insight into the extent to which such youngsters can respond effectively to the difficulties of communicating with the sibling? The baby is, after all, someone whose powers of understanding and expression are so very different both from their own powers, and from those of the parents in conversation with whom their own linguistic skills have developed. We examine first how the children *talk* to their siblings.

Elder Talking to Younger

There has been enormous interest in the ways in which mothers talk to babies, interest that stems from the attempt to elucidate and clarify the part played by the mother's speech in the child's acquisition of language (see for example Snow 1972; Snow and Ferguson 1977). When adults talk to young children, their speech differs in several distinctive ways from their speech to other adults, and these features of "baby talk" change as the child becomes able to understand and use language with increasing skill himself. Mothers' speech to infants has a high pitch and exaggerated intonation. It is repetitive and has a distinctive "conversational" style, with a high frequency of questions. To 1-year-olds and 2-year-olds, adults' speech consists largely of simple, grammatically correct, short sentences, many of which refer directly to physical objects that are present. Just how important these features of baby talk may be for the acquisition of language is a controversial matter. It has not been easy to show conclusively that these features of "mother-ese" are *necessary* for the child to acquire language, or to demonstrate which modifications are most important. But it is clear that many features of baby talk are responses to the level of the child's comprehension of the speech: signs of noncomprehension lead to further shortening of the utterances, for instance, and parallel changes are found in the speech of adults to foreigners. Other features of baby talk, such as the use of endearments, diminutives, and pet names, parallel the way in which people address lovers or pets, and reflect the intimacy and affection of the mother-child relationship (Brown 1977).

It is not just adults who adjust their speech when talking to babies. It has been shown that 4-year-olds talking to 2-year-olds (Shatz and Gelman 1973), or even talking to a doll designated as a baby (Sachs and Devin 1976), show many of the same "clarification" changes in their speech: short, simple utterances, many repetitions and much use of names, exclamations or exhortations such as "Now," "No," "Hey," "Look," and "Watch," which draw the attention of the younger child (Sachs and Devin 1976). Shatz and Gelman (1977) argue that these changes can be explained in terms of what the 4-year-olds are trying to achieve in the particular communicative context in which they are addressing the 2-year-olds. They argue convincingly that both the simpler and the more complicated grammatical utterances used by the 4-year-olds reflect their selection of utterances that the younger child can be expected to understand in that particular situation.

This evidence that 4-year-olds adjust their speech with such delicacy is difficult to reconcile with a view of children of this age as egocentric, and it raises the question of when and how such sensitivity to the comprehension of the listener develops. How do our 2- and 3-year-olds respond to the problems of communicating with their baby siblings?

In practice all the children, even those as young as 2½ years, changed their speech dramatically when talking to their baby siblings. Their speech to the baby consisted of much shorter utterances than their speech to their mothers, and it contained a high frequency of repetitions and of attention-getting utterances.

> PENNY D: Harry! Harry! Have my camera! Have my camera! Naughty boy. You . . . aah! Aah! No!

> JUDY B: Watch me. Do it on the settee. Watch. Watch . . . Oh look, Carole! Can you do it, Carole? You do it.

Figure 7.1 compares the frequency of utterances with repetitions and with attention-getting devices in the children's speech to the babies and to their mothers, and in the mothers' speech to the babies. These features, which made the child's message to the baby simple, clear, and difficult to ignore, were even more marked in the speech of the children to the babies than they were in the mothers' speech to the babies. Forty percent of the children's utterances to the babies contained attention-getting devices and 31 percent included repetitions, as compared with 18 percent and 16 percent in the mothers' utterances.

But it would be misleading to suggest that the ways in which the children spoke to the babies closely paralleled the mothers'

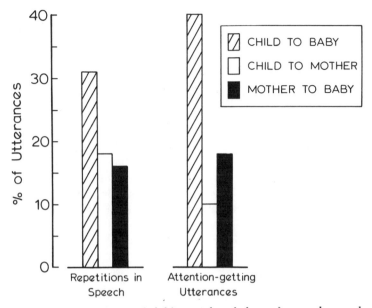

Figure 7.1   Comparison of child's speech to baby and to mother, and mother's speech to baby.

baby talk. The first difference is in the context in which the babies were addressed. Most of the speech of the child to the baby sibling occurred in two types of situations: when the child was trying to prohibit, dissuade, or restrain the baby (49 percent of utterances), or when he was trying to direct the baby in joint play (25 percent of utterances). For instance, the proportion of the child's repetitions, in speaking to the baby, that took place when he was trying to prohibit the baby was very high — 60 percent. In contrast, only 18 percent of the mother's repetitions occurred in such a situation. Now these differences between children and mothers in the frequency of repetitions and attention-getting devices may well reflect a difference in the practical problem facing them — the greater difficulty experienced by the children in getting and holding the attention of the babies. What is important is the nature of their response to these problems: the children, even the 2½-year-olds, *were* adjusting their speech in the face of the particular pressures of communicating with a baby.

Consider for example the case of Duncan, aged 31 months, whose baby brother (Robin) has picked up a sweet from the floor and is licking it. Duncan, who often shows concern for his brother's welfare, attempts to prevent this. He tells him that the dog (Scottie) will eat the candy, then attempts to distract him by urging him to go into the kitchen. The attempt fails and he is finally driven to push him through the door with a gentle kick; however, in his efforts to direct the baby we can see a typical example of the use of repetitions, attentional devices, and progressive shortening of the utterances:

> DUNCAN K: No, don't you eat it. Scottie will eat it. Scottie will eat it. No, not you. Scottie will eat it. Not you. Scottie. Not you. Shall we go in door? Right. Come on. Come on. In door, Robin. In door.

In considering why it was that such young children changed their speech when they talked to their baby siblings, it is important to note that a very high proportion of the children's utterances occurred in a context of trying to prohibit, or trying to control, the baby's actions in joint play. In each of these contexts it clearly mattered a great deal to the child that he should "get the message across" and make himself understood. Most interactions between the young siblings did not in fact involve words; as we shall see in the next section, their communication could be varied and rich, but it was largely nonverbal. The firstborn child only used words to the sibling in a small proportion of his interactions, namely those where the child was *especially* concerned to influence the baby's actions. Words were the weapons of last resort. The proportion of the mother's speech to the baby that was concerned with prohibition or control of the baby was in contrast much lower, since the mother frequently engaged the baby in verbal play, attempted to distract him with "conversation" while caring for or comforting him, or simply chatted to him about her own actions while continuing with household activities.

The second major differences between the speech of the children to the babies and that of the mothers concerned the frequency of questions. When mothers talk to babies, they use a great many questions. In our study the mean frequency was 26 percent of the mothers' utterances, which parallels the findings of other studies. On the other hand, 23 of our 40 children did not pose a single question to their baby sibling at the 14-month visits. Why is it that mothers use so many questions in talking to their babies? And what do these differences between mother and child in questioning style imply for the quality of communicative interaction between mother and baby and between child and baby?

Catherine Snow (1977) has argued that the frequency of questions in mothers' speech to babies reflects their desire to communicate reciprocally with their babies. She comments that "questions, especially tag-questions and post-completers like 'hmm?' are devices for passing the turn to the partner, which is precisely what mothers are trying hardest to do." She and others (for example Schaffer 1979) have suggested that the frequent use of questions is linked in an important way to the development of turn-taking skills in babies. In our own data it is certainly the case that many of the exchanges between mother and 14-month-old fitted a conversational model, and that questions played an important part in many of these turn-taking sequences. In 39 of the 40 families sequences of vocal turn taking occurred between mother and baby, and many of these included questions from the mother:

MOTHER OF DONNA R:
M: Go on. You terror.

B: Aah.
M: What?
B: Aah.
M: Come on then, show me. You want a drink?
B: Aah.
M: All right, I'm getting it. Come on then.

Very often the questions that formed part of the turn-taking sequence involved inquiries of this sort by the mother about the baby's wishes. They reflected a concern on the mother's part to understand more fully the baby's intentions or needs. There were also several other types of turn-taking sequence, such as imitative interactions, and often the conversation involved both questions and imitations.

MOTHER OF JOYCE D:
M: What do you want? Oh dear, we are miserable.
     Come on. What's the matter, eh? What do you
     want? (Offers cup.)
B: (Pushes cup away.)
M: You don't want that, do you?
B: (Reaches for spoon.)
M: Do you want a spoon? There's nothing on it.
     Nothing to eat. Can you see Joyce in it? Look.
     You're upside down. There's Joyce, look. Joyce.
B: Mmm.
M: Mmm.
B: Mmm.
M: Mmm.
B: Mmm.

The striking differences between mothers and children in the frequency of questions in their speech to the infant reflects, in fact, a more general distinction, which is that the conversational model is not really appropriate to describe the speech of the child to the baby. Vocal turn-taking sequences were rare between child and sibling. But it was, in fact, only the *vocal* turn-taking sequences that were infrequent. Other forms of reciprocal turn-taking interactions, such as cooperation in games or sequences of nonverbal imitation, were often observed between the children. What distinguished the mother-infant interaction from the child-sibling interaction was not only the desire of the mother to engage the baby in such conversations, to understand his wishes, and to play vocal games, but the behavior of the *infant* toward his hearers. By 14 months the baby was initiating many of the vocal turn-taking sequences with the mother, and also playing a central part in maintaining the conversation. Sometimes this involved considerable perseverance in holding the attention of the mother:

JOYCE D (age 14 months) AND MOTHER:
B: Aaah (pointing).
M: Oh yeah. What is it?
B: Aaah (pointing).
M: No, he's not there.
B: Aaah (pointing).
M: What? What is it?
B: Aah.
M: Oh yeah.
B: Adaah.
M: Yeah.
B: Adaah.
M: Yeah.
B: Adaah (pointing).

DONNA R (age 14 months) AND MOTHER:
B (pointing to something; M pays little attention and apparently does not see what B is pointing at): Look.
M: Yeah, flies. Horrible things.
B: Look.
M: Yeah, that's a light.

B: Look (increasingly agitated).
M: Yeah, lovely.
B: Look (increasingly agitated).
M: You getting frustrated?

The babies seldom behaved this way with the children. How these differences between baby-mother and baby-sibling communication develop is a topic we shall examine a little later.

The frequent use of questions by the mothers can, as we have seen, be plausibly linked to their interest in engaging the baby in reciprocal interaction. Now, the analysis of the observations (Chapter 5) had shown that there were striking individual differences among the children in the extent to which they tried to engage the babies in reciprocal interaction, and it appeared likely that the variation in the use of questions might be linked to these more general differences in the firstborns' affectionate interest in the babies.

We examined the issue by grouping the children according to whether or not they used questions in speaking to the baby and also according to whether or not they used diminutives or playful repetitions. There were in fact strong associations between these aspects of speech to the baby. Children who used questions to the baby were also likely to use diminutives and repetitive verbal play. And when the relationship between these aspects of the children's speech and their behavior to the babies was examined, the results showed that the children who talked to the baby with questions, diminutives, and repetitive verbal play were children whose *nonverbal* behavior showed them to be far more affectionately interested in the baby than the children who did not talk to their siblings in this way. Children who asked questions of their siblings averaged 26.6 friendly approaches during the same time period that those who never asked questions made only 17.0 friendly approaches (Table A7.1).

The contexts in which the children spoke to their siblings with diminutives and playful repetitions were in almost all instances situations where the elder child was inviting the baby to come and play.

Ian W (trying to get brother, Graham, to come and play in the next room with him): Come on, Gramie. Come on, tinkerwinker!

Eve D (showing sister, Kate, toys in a box): There, Kay-Kay, look! Kay-Kay, Kay-Kay, look! Kay-Kay! Kay-Kay! Look! Look, baby-baby.

The two utterances that were exceptions to this pattern occurred when the elder child was trying to comfort the younger, who was in a state of distress. When children were trying to prohibit or restrain their baby siblings, they never used such diminutives.

It could be argued that the adjustments in speech made by such young children in talking to their infant siblings reflect imitation of the *mothers'* style of speech to the baby, rather than adjustments made by the children in direct response to the constraints of communicating with a linguistically and cognitively immature infant in a particular range of social contexts. But frequency of imitation of the mother's speech as it occurred during the observations was in fact very low. Only 32 of 877 child-to-baby utterances (3.6 percent) were full or partial imitations of the mother's comments to the baby. What makes this level of imitations surprisingly low is that the mother's speech to the baby is characterized by features that we could reasonably expect to catch the elder child's attention (exaggeration of intonation, vividness of expression, and the like), and also that interaction between mother and baby, nonverbal as well as verbal, is in most families a very potent source of interest and of emotional significance to the elder child.

Which particular mother-to-baby comments get imitated is also interesting. Most of them are not utterances where the elder child is directly engaged in prohibiting, in playing with, or in comforting the younger. Rather, they frequently are vivid expostulations by the mother — often used in greeting the baby, and often also pejorative in tone — which are immediately repeated by the child.

WARREN D AND MOTHER:
M (to B):   You're a little monkey.
C (to B):   Monk.

SYLVIE A AND MOTHER:
M (to B):   Bad boy.
C (to B):   Bad boy.

LAURA W AND MOTHER:
M (to B):   Hello, you rat bag.
C (to B):   Hello, you hairy rat bag.
M (to B):   You're a clever clogs.
C (to B):   Clever clogs.

From observations such as these we cannot arrive at any general conclusions about the importance of the parents' style of speech to the baby as an influence on the child's style of speech to the baby. But the observations do suggest that in interactions where it is important for the child to make himself understood by the baby, he seems to adapt his speech by clarifications and/or by endearments and diminutives of his own, *in his own way*, rather than by simple repetitions of the mother's speech.

All the 2- and 3-year-olds in the study did, then, make obvious adjustments in their speech when they talked to their siblings. In the context of prohibiting or directing the baby, they made appropriate and in most cases effective use of communicative devices: shortening and repeating their utterances, drawing the baby's attention with emphasis and exhortation. Some of the children also used diminutives, endearments, and questions when attempting to comfort, to distract, or to engage the baby in play. What the findings show is that these very young children adapt their speech in ways that are rational if and only if they believe the baby sibling is different—linguistically and cognitively—from their mothers and the other adults they speak to. This result seems unsurprising in light of the fact that the children do, as we saw in

the previous chapter, frequently *assert* beliefs about the properties of the baby sibling, which show that they have a fine
grasp of the differences between the baby's properties and
those of either adults or children of their own age, and that
they *act* toward the baby in a way that shows a complex
pragmatic grasp of such disparities.

Communication between the siblings involved so much
more, however, than just the speech of the first child to the
baby. It clearly differed from the communication between
baby and mother, or between first child and mother, in a
number of striking respects. Observations of the siblings not
only revealed the great range of expressed emotion and excitement in the relationship; they suggested a richness, variety,
and elaboration of communication and social understanding
between the children that current approaches to the study of
early communication hardly begin to consider. We need to
look at the quality of the communication between the young
siblings within this wider framework, drawing not only on the
observations made in our main study, but on those made by
Greenwood in a study of 8 families with secondborn infants
aged between 6 and 13 months (Greenwood and Dunn 1982).

Nonverbal Communication

Studies of communication in young children have focused
primarily on the development of linguistic skills. Attempts to
understand the growth of communicative abilities have
centered on tracing the early use of gestures, and the transition from preverbal to verbal interaction between infant and
parent. The focus on language is hardly surprising: quite apart
from the profound significance of the development of
language for a child's understanding and social behavior,
theories of adult discourse provide a powerful tool, a model
that gives the investigator beliefs to test, questions to be
asked, a scientific paradigm, a grid that imposes order on an
otherwise confusing stream of behavior.

Still, to use a linguistic model to describe and analyze the early communicative behavior of a baby in his family, and to concentrate on the development of language, means that the development of a vast range of human capabilities may be ignored. It is important that humans communicate their own moods, desires, sense of amusement or absurdity, and not simply cue each other in to propositional exchanges. The use of language is, after all, subordinate to human desires. By concentrating on the development of linguistic skills, and by using a linguistic model to describe early interaction, we may be failing to capture not just a range of nonverbal skills that are intrinsically interesting facets of human communicative capabilities, but also the growth of the child's understanding of the intentions of others, his ability to recognize and share emotional states, to interpret and anticipate the reactions of others, to emphasize, deliberately to irritate and annoy, and to manipulate others.

We know very little about the growth of these kinds of communicative skills, or about how it relates to the development of gestural communication and the acquisition of language. Observing a young child with his sibling as well as with his parents offers a useful perspective on the development of these different aspects of social communication, because the interaction between infants and their siblings reveals a richness of communication skills (Lichtenberger 1965), because these interactions are often emotionally charged, and because they frequently do not involve the use of words. Look, for instance, at communication between siblings in play and games.

Communication in Play

The importance of "ritualized," repeated routines between mother and infant to the development of the infant's communicative skills has been repeatedly emphasized, and play routines have received particular attention (see for example Bruner and Sherwood 1976; Bruner 1977; Ratner and Bruner

1979). In most of the families in our study, role-taking games such as hide-and-seek, chaser-chased, and peekaboo were frequent features of the interaction not only between mother and infant, but between sibling and infant.

> Carole B (14 months) is being held by her mother; she has a piece of paper, which three minutes ago was the focus of a chasing game between the siblings. Judy (3 years) starts running around and around her mother. Carole watches and laughs at Judy, leans over her mother's shoulder, and offers the paper to Judy as she runs behind her mother. Judy laughing, looks (mutual) at Carole, takes the paper, and continues to run around her mother. As she passes in front of her mother, she offers the paper back to Carole, who takes it, then as Judy passes to the back of her mother on the next circuit, Carole again leans over her mother's shoulder and offers the paper to Judy. Judy again takes it, laughing, and continues to run around her mother. The whole pattern of passing the paper back and forth, first over the mother's shoulder and then in front of her, is repeated three times, with both children laughing and vocalizing together.

In the families where such games are observed, they develop an elaboration and an excitement that is quite remarkable. The theme may be varied by one of the participants, and the new variation is often greeted with delight by the other. The younger child can, and does, frequently take each role in the course of one observation. For instance, in the same observation in which Carole and Judy played the paper-passing game, the younger chased the elder in one sequence, then a couple of minutes later "invited" the elder (with a look over her shoulder, vocalization, and a "funny" gait) to chase her. The elaboration and reversal of roles in these sequences suggest that by 14 months the babies have considerable skill in cooperating with and anticipating the actions of the other. In these families there is a long history of joint activities of the siblings; this history, the frequency, and the positive affect expressed suggest that such interactions have considerable potential for the development not only of role-taking skills, but of understanding the mood and intention of the other.

Bruner (Bruner 1977; Ratner and Bruner 1979) has argued that it is in the context of such highly familiar, "conventionalized," playful interactions with the mother that the child develops an understanding of the notion of a prediction, a "pragmatic base structure" from which linguistic discourse features such as "comment on a topic" can develop. He cites four features of such playful interactions as important for the development of language:

(1) In playful exchanges the semantic domain and structure of the routine are highly restricted and well understood by the child.
(2) The role structure is reversible.
(3) The play routines ("tasks") are amenable to having their constituents varied, and the variations can be marked with vocalizations.
(4) The playful atmosphere of such interactions permits the child to "distance" himself, in a way that sustains the child's readiness to innovate without erring.

The data from our comparatively large sample of 40 families are in good agreement with Bruner's emphasis that verbal "marking" by the mother in ritualized playful exchanges features prominently in the child's developing use of verbal communicative signals.

Play with the sibling, by contrast, may be elaborate and varied; it may involve give-and-take of objects, joint attention to objects, and reversing of roles, but these interactions are not in the majority of cases marked vocally, either by the sibling or by the baby. This difference between mothers and children in their interactions with the baby is, as we have seen, particularly striking in the occurrence of vocal turn-taking episodes — not only in play sequences but in other contexts. At each of the monthly observations in Greenwood's study when the 8 families were visited, vocal turn-taking episodes were more commonly observed between infant and parent than between infant and sibling. At the 7-month visits, for instance, such episodes were observed between infant and parent in 6 families, and between infant and sibling in only 1; whereas at 9, 11, and 13 months they were observed between infant and mother in all families, and between infant and sibling in only 1 family at 9 and 13 months, and in 2 families at 11 months.

These observations in themselves do not provide grounds for making inferences about the special importance of either conventionalized play routines with the mother, or of vocal turn-taking sequences in the development of communicative understanding. However, it is worth noting that the differences in the quality of communicative behavior shown by the baby to parents and to the sibling are clearly brought out by Greenwood's analysis of the development of communicative gestures in the 8 babies in her study. She found (Fig. 7.2) that between 7 months and 13 months there was an increase in the frequency of communicative gestures; such gestures were frequently made toward the mother, much less often toward the sibling.

These data on gestural communication and the differences between the dyads in the occurrence of vocal turn-taking and vocal marking of play perhaps suggest that the interactions between infant and adult are more important in the child's acquisition of language than those between infant and sibling, but the findings do not imply that the latter are unimportant in the growth of communication. If the development of the skills of cooperating with others, of understanding how to combine actions with objects and with people, and the routines of playful games are as important in the development of children's capacities to predict the actions of others and to understand other-as-agent as has been claimed, then the interactions between baby and sibling must be considered as seriously as those with the mother.

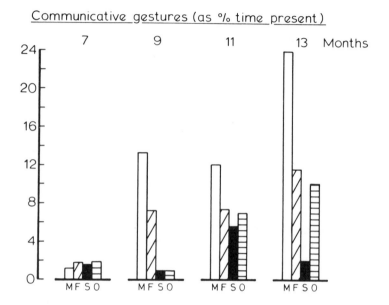

Figure 7.2   Frequency of communicative gestures of baby to mother (M), father (F), sibling (S), and observer (O), as percentage of time present.

We cannot *know*, from these naturalistic observations, what the younger sibling may be learning about the elder during the interactions in the first year. (Nor, of course, can we know what a baby is learning in the interaction sequences with the mother, episodes that are assumed to be so significant in the acquistion of language.) But the sibling interactions are clearly opportunities for the baby to learn about the elder and to develop beliefs about the elder. The frequency and emotional loading of the interactions, and the baby's interest in the elder, all suggest that as potentially important social experiences such interactions should not be ignored by the psychologist. Over time the interactions provide learning opportunities; *at* the time, they demonstrate acquired powers.

When the babies are observed at 14 months, it certainly appears that their skills of cooperation, anticipation, and even manipulation of the sibling are well developed.

On "Turn Taking" and "Coaction"

Many of the interactions between the siblings, both when the baby was 8 months of age and when he was 14 months, involved sequences where one child replicated the sound or action of the other.

> Brendan F bounces up and down, looking at Siobhan (8 months). Mutual gaze. Siobhan bounces up and down, while Brendan continues to bounce. Both bounce together, laughing.

> Judy B puts her hand on the high chair where Carole (8 months) is sitting. Judy wiggles her fingers on the tray on the high chair. Carole watches. Judy wiggles her fingers; both continue to wiggle their fingers together, with mutual gaze and laughter. Three minutes later Carole, still in high chair, wiggles her fingers on the tray, looks at Judy and vocalizes.

Such sequences of "doing things together" are distinctive features of the interaction with the sibling rather than with the mother during the second half of the first year. The data from Greenwood's study show, for example, that of 49 bouts of joint play where the same actions were performed by the infant and another, bouts where the actions were performed simultaneously were much more common with the sibling: 19 out of 21 of simultaneous same-action bouts were with the sibling and only 2 with the mother—and all of the 28 *successive* same-action sequences were with the adult. In our own study the observations made when the second child was 14 months old included 67 bouts in which the 14-month-old engaged in simultaneous same-action sequences with the elder sibling, and only 10 bouts in which the 14-month-old engaged in successive same-action sequences.

It is a characteristic of these simultaneous same-action sequences that both children express positive emotion and excitement when the other joins in the activity. It is particularly interesting, then, to note that Stern and colleagues, in a fine-grain study of interaction between mothers, and 3-month-old infants, describe two "structurally separate communication modes"—one of them turn taking, the other "coactional." They report that the "coactional pattern is mainly manifest during the highest levels of arousal . . . At moments when the infant (and almost invariably the mother also) are at a high level of affectively positive arousal, they will vocalize together and appear to derive much enjoyment from it" (1975, p. 97).

Further support for this emphasis on the emotional significance of acting together comes when we look at the individual differences in the frequency of such sequences in the interaction between siblings. There were marked individual differences between the sibling pairs in the frequency with which they engaged in the coaction sequences. The pairs who engaged in relatively frequent sequences of such joint activity were the pairs who engaged in relatively frequent games and directed a good deal of affectionate behavior toward each other. For instance, the correlation between the rank order of the frequency of "same-role" simultaneous sequences and other aspects of positive socially directed behavior by the elder child was 0.51 ($p < 0.01$). A linguistic model that emphasizes the importance of early interaction in terms of the development of turn-taking skills as a route to the acquisition of dialogue would miss the significance of this synchrony. Indeed, the frequency of sequences of interaction between the siblings in which one child replicated the action of the other—either simultaneously or successively—and the excitement expressed in such sequences raise a number of questions on the nature and significance of these replications or imitations, which must be explored more fully.

Replication Sequences

WARREN D: Joyce (8 months) vocalizes while playing. Warren looks at her, she looks at him; mutual gaze. Warren "imitates" her vocalization. Joyce repeats her vocalization. Both laugh.

This example, and those already quoted, drawn from observations when the baby was 8 months old, illustrate the pleasure and interest expressed by both children in many of the exchanges when one child replicated the action of the other. Why should it be so interesting and pleasurable for both children when one joins in or imitates the action of the other? How do these observations relate to the different theoretical views of the developmental significance of imitation in young children?

First, which children imitated their siblings? At the 14-month visit the firstborn children who frequently imitated their siblings were much more friendly to the baby than those who rarely imitated the baby. They started games and helped the baby more often, cared for the baby more frequently by brushing hair, dressing, washing, feeding, and they showed the baby toys and objects of interest. The patterns of these correlations were described in Chapter 5 (and Table A5.6), where we noted too that the children who behaved in this friendly way were unlikely to be physically aggressive. By the 14-month visit the babies whose elder siblings had behaved in this friendly fashion were much more likely to imitate the elder siblings and be friendly to them. Imitations by the younger siblings showed the same pattern of correlation with friendly social behavior as imitation by the firstborn. Thus both sorts of imitation were significantly correlated.

How do individual differences in the babies' imitative behavior develop? We cannot begin to answer this question with any precision, for we have data from only the 8-month and 14-month visits. But the results do show an interesting parallel with a much more detailed and fine-grain study, carried out by Pawlby (1977), of the development of imitation between infant and mother. Pawlby's study suggested that the process by which a baby comes to imitate his mother intentionally begins with the readiness with which the mother imitates the baby. Mothers apparently select for imitation those acts to which they can attribute communicative significance, such as gestures and grimaces. Babies were found to pay special attention when their mothers imitated an act they had just performed. This means that the act is "highlighted," and it is argued that the act is then produced on another occasion in order that the mother will imitate again. The study found that initially the number of imitations by the mother of infant acts was greater than the number of infant imitations of acts by the mother, but that with age the number of the latter increased.

Our observations show a parallel progression:

8 months	14 months
Baby acts; child imitates	Baby acts; child imitates
69 instances	74 instances
23 families	27 families
Child acts; baby imitates	Child acts; baby imitates
36 instances	104 instances
19 families	30 families

At 8 months most of the replication sequences were imitations by the sibling of the baby; by the 14-month observations the number of imitations of the elder child by the baby had markedly increased. These findings demonstrate both the interest of the elder child in the baby, and the importance of his behavior as a model for the younger sibling. They also suggest that the developmental course of the communicative sequence follows a pattern similar to that described by Pawlby.

We are not proposing that the *motivation* of the elder child in imitating the baby is necessarily the same as that of a mother engaged in playing with her baby. Indeed, it seems likely that some of the incidents when the elder child replicated the actions of the younger reflected attempts to draw the attention of the mother, rather than an interest in communicating with the baby. We should certainly be cautious about considering all sequences of imitative behavior as a group, as if they had similar significance for the course of social interaction or reflected similar motives. Just as Keenan (1975) has shown that repetition in children's dialogue may play many different roles in discourse, so—if we examine the imitative sequences—we find that according to the context and the details of the interaction, imitations by either child may have very different consequences for the course of interaction among the family members. In some sequences, such as that involving Warren and Joyce, the replication of acts apparently plays an important part in "making it last" (compare Keenan 1975). These interactions should be distinguished from the sequences (which were far less frequent) where one child imitated the other without apparently seeking his attention and immediately attracted the attention of the mother.

One possible interpretation of these particular examples of replication by the elder child might be in terms of Whiting's status-envy theory (Whiting 1959, 1960). In the original formulation, imitation and identification were seen as the outcome of a rivalrous interaction between the child and the envied parent. Where Freud considered the child to be competing with the father for the mother's sex and affectionate attention, Whiting proposed that *any* form of reward, maternal or social, could be a valued resource around which rivalry might develop.

The Whiting theory predicts that the more strongly a child envies the status of another person in relation to desired resources, the more he will enact the role of that person in fantasy. However, experiments that were carried out to distinguish between the prediction of this theory, and the theory that the child would identify with the source of power rather than with the desired envied competitor, showed that at least in the circumstances of the experiment, children identified with the source, not the competitor. Certainly the pattern of imitation in the present study does not support a status-envy theory, in that such a theory would presumably predict more imitation by the older child in families where the first child was particularly jealous of the younger. As we have seen, no such pattern of association was found; the individual differences in frequency of imitation showed exactly the opposite trend—that A imitated B more in families where there was a particularly warm sibling relationship. (Even in those sequences where it seems most reasonable to infer that the elder child was imitating the baby in order to gain the attention of the mother, there is no reason to assume that the imitation involved the elder child fantasizing that he *was* the baby.)

An alternative interpretation of the pattern of imitation by the firstborn children would be simply to suggest that if the elder child A is interested in and affectionately concerned about the younger child B, then it is rewarding for A that B is interested in and amused by him; and that B is particularly amused by A's behavior when it is contingent upon and matches B's own. It could also be argued that the pleasure expressed by A when B laughs at or enjoys his imitations reflects the satisfaction the elder child feels to have such power over the baby.

While 2-year-olds and 3-year-olds do of course have influence over their parents and often manipulate them very effectively, the *degree* of attention and interest of the younger sibling in the elder's actions, particularly when he imitates him, is in many families very striking and of a different order from the interest shown in the elder's behavior by the parent. For most older siblings the baby is a readily attentive and easily moved audience, responding with flattering enthusiasm to jokes and clowning, and particularly appreciative when his *own* actions are imitated. And once the baby begins to imitate the elder sibling, then presumably the rewards for the elder child as a powerful model for the younger increase.

The baby's interest in imitating the elder child could be interpreted in terms of the arguments put forward by Bandura,

Ross, and Ross (1963), that children imitate individuals who are particularly powerful or particularly nurturant. We know that from the earliest weeks babies are particularly responsive to behavior that is contingent upon their own (Papousek and Papousek 1975), and we know that the elder siblings in our study who displayed this kind of behavior were also in other respects the most nurturant and affectionate (see Table A5.6). It is not surprising then that such elder siblings become particularly powerful models.

There is, however, a different line of argument about the pleasure expressed in the imitative sequences that must be considered, an interpretation that involves the issue of self-recognition. It is possible that for both children the pleasure expressed in the sequences where both replicate each other's actions reflects a recognition of the other as in some sense "like me." The notion that "like me" attracts, while "not like me" repels, is one that has been extensively explored in the social psychological research on older children, adolescents, and adults (Kohlberg 1973). These findings may seem very remote from the world of 2- or 3-year-olds, and even more remote from that of their baby siblings; it may, in fact, seem quite inappropriate to consider them in relation to such cognitively immature children. The idea that "like me" attracts depends, obviously, upon a comparison between self and other, and such a principle presupposes not only a recognition of the distinction between self and other but a fairly elaborate categorization of self. Nevertheless, there are now some intriguing experimental findings which suggest that it may not be inappropriate to consider this general notion as applicable to the young siblings.

First, Lewis and Brooks-Gunn have shown in a series of studies using experimental settings that infants and young children prefer to attend to and approach other *children* rather than adults. These results can be interpreted in a number of different ways, but Lewis and his colleagues put forward a plausible argument in favor of the idea that the child's recognition of the other as "like me" is important in explaining the attraction. In a further series of experiments with children between 3 and 5 years, the children were asked

to decide with which of three persons (as represented by pictures) they would like to do the following things: play with, learn from, share, and receive help. The three pictures were of a 3-, 7-, and 20-year-old. Of interest here are their responses when asked, "With whom would you like to play?" In general, the children 3 to 5 years of age preferred to play with a child of like age, approximately 3 years old. There were, however, children who preferred to play with the 7-year-old. When the children were asked which picture they were most like, it was found that those children who wished to play with the 7-year-old were those who were more likely to have reported that they were like the 7-year-old, whereas those who reported they wished to play with the 3-year-old were more likely to have reported they were like the 3-year-old. The child's choice was a function of the similarity of self to B or C. (1979, p. 265)

The findings of the studies of very young children reviewed by Lewis and Brooks-Gunn (1979) suggest that even by 14 months the baby sibling may be attracted to the elder because he recognizes the sibling as "like me." And there is one particular set of findings in our own observations that supports such an interpretation. The frequency of imitation was much higher in same-sex pairs than in different-sex pairs (Table A7.2), not only for imitations by the elder but also by the younger.

These results are open to a number of interpretations. Since it seems that most elder siblings do recognize the gender of their baby siblings, it is possible that the elder sibling is more drawn to imitate and play with the younger if he is of the same gender, and that this interest from the elder child promotes a continuing pattern of affectionate interest from the baby. As we shall see, same-sex pairs do show much more positive social behavior toward each other than different-sex pairs. The frequent imitations by the younger sibling in same-sex pairs could then be explained in terms of the warm relationship promoted by the elder sibling. An alternative, or additional, interpretation might be that the younger child is during the second year already becoming conscious of his gender (see Money and Ehrhardt 1972) and is more interested in social encounters, such as imitative exchanges, with the sibling if they share the same sex. In other words, she or he recognizes the elder sibling as "like me" in the dimension of gender and is attracted because of this similarity.

A quite different interpretation would be that the high frequency of replication arises because children of the same gender enjoy the same kinds of activities, and that two boys would tend to imitate each other's activities more than a boy and a girl because of this common interest and not because of any recognition of gender of self and other on the part of the younger child. Support for this thesis would require significant sex differentiation in the types of activity and play that were imitated; as we shall see in Chapter 8, we found no sex differences in these activities.

Assessing Understanding and Communicative Intention

It is clear that our interpretation of the pleasure expressed by the siblings in the sequences of coaction and imitation depends on what kind of cognitive sophistication we attribute to the children. Very often our assumptions about the communicative intention and understanding of young children are built into the categories we use to describe their interaction. Our observations of the siblings highlight both the importance of precision in our inferences about what is intended and what is understood by the younger child, and the difficulties involved in making such inferences. Take the following examples from observations made when the second child was 8 months old:

> Duncan K (3 years) and Robin (8 months), playing at opposite ends of the room, look at each other and laugh.

Penny D (2½ years) is banging bricks together. Harry (8 months) watches, crawls over to her. Penny looks at him; mutual look; both smile while Penny continues to bang the bricks.

Brendan F (3 years) falls off his tricycle, then deliberately repeats the fall with an exaggerated rolling over. Siobhan (8 months), watching, laughs. Brendan repeats the fall and roll.

What precisely can we infer from such examples and from others quoted earlier? At a very general level we can say that A (the elder child) is interested in B (the younger child) and his acts, and vice versa, and that the sibling interactions are powerfully loaded emotionally. What can we say about "sharing"?

(1) We can say that some siblings have a history of joint activities, which are characterized by the expression of pleasure and excitement by both children.
(2) The pleasure and excitement are expressed by each child when the other joins in the activity.
(3) In some cases there is evidence that the two siblings have the same expectations for the course of the activity or game.
(4) The younger child, as well as the elder child, attempts to initiate joint activities. (These are different sorts of joint activity from those he starts with the mother.)
(5) The younger child is sensitive to the mood of the elder in the sense that he laughs at clowning or playful acts, and sobers when the elder is upset.

In the sequences where A repeats the action of B, then B repeats the imitated action, laughing, and A imitates the act again, it seems reasonable to infer that it is A's imitation of B's acts that amuses B. However, it is clear that other actions by A also amuse B, and in making such inferences we must be very careful about the detail and sensitivity of observation on which the inference is based. The conclusion, from observing similar imitative sequences between mother and infant, that "a great deal of mutual understanding obviously comes about well before even the passive understanding of words" (Pawlby 1977, p. 218) is surely too vague and generous an inference. Mutual understanding of what?

In much of the observational work on early social behavior between mother and infant there is a slide from careful accounts of the behavior to a discussion of its significance for communication and understanding in much more ambiguous terms such as "shared understanding" or "intersubjectivity" (Newson 1979).

The term "intersubjectivity" is often used with the direct implication that mother and infant are "sharing" an experience. But to say this can imply that the experiences the partners are undergoing are indeed in relevant respects identical, and that each believes that the other is undergoing an experience identical to his own. It is clearly not appropriate to use the term "share" in this sense for a 2-month-old infant. If what we are trying to describe and understand is in fact the *development of sharing* in this sense of understanding, then it becomes all the more important to be careful about what inferences we draw from observations of such joint activities, and about what our descriptive categories should be. Several observations, as we commented in the last chapter, suggested that the younger child has some pragmatic understanding of how to upset the elder; other observations are more ambiguous:

> Dianne H and Marion (14 months). Marion has been repeatedly prohibited from touching the glass balls on the Christmas tree. She pushes a chair over to the tree, climbs on it, and as she starts touching the balls looks across to her sister (3 years); mutual look; both laugh.

What can we conclude is shared here?

Describing the interaction between the baby and the older sibling presents a problem common to studies of the develop-

ment of communicative skills in both animals and humans.
The intimacy and shared history of two individuals means
that the signals between them to which each responds may
become increasingly subtle and fleeting. In his leader-follower
experiments with young chimpanzees, Menzel (1974) found
that at the beginning the chimpanzee who was given information about a hidden food source engaged in obvious and
dramatic signals to get his companions to follow him —
gestures, tapping on the shoulder, pulling and tugging in a
very excited manner. After two years together the signals between the adolescent chimps were so subtle that to an
observer it appeared that all the chimps set off together
simultaneously toward the food source, the direction of which
only one of them knew.

It may well be that even at 8 months the younger child's
sensitivity to the communicative signals of the elder is so
much greater than that of the observer that the nature of the
exchange is completely misunderstood by the observer. We
were baffled by several of the sibling interactions, such as incidents where there was simply a mutual gaze across the room
and both siblings laughed. One interpretation (of the
Christmas tree balls, for example) might simply be that the
elder sibling is associated by the younger with rewarding
experiences, and vice versa, and that the sight of the other
evokes feelings of pleasures linked to these previous experiences. It is also possible that such an exchange of looking
and laughing is an allusion to something the observer does not
and cannot understand. Shared expectations and routines can
become grounds for allusions and jokes, and neither a parent
nor still less an observer can be party to all such shared expectations and jokes.

In these examples from the 8-month observations, interpretation of the significance of the interaction depended very
strongly on the younger child's *looking* at the elder, and vice
versa. Our information on the development of the child's
capacity to notice and respond to the reactions of other
people to his acts, and his interest in and anticipation of the

behavior of other people, is sparse. It has been well argued, and widely accepted, that it is the mother's interpretations of the child's communicative intentions that play a central role in the development of the child's understanding of the meaning of his acts for other people, and this implies that the child must be paying close attention to the mother's reactions to his acts. How well has this response to the mother's interpretations been described?

One possible medium for such communicative checks is through visual behavior. For the early months of infancy there are elegant studies describing and analyzing the coordination of visual behavior between mother and infant; there is evidence too that babies are extremely sensitive to changes in the mother's mood and in the deployment of her attention (Stern 1977; Tronick et al. 1978). Trevarthen, working with 7- to 12-week-old babies, commented that "very slight temporary and subtle changes in the mother's actions made experimentally produced strong but entirely reversible changes in the infant's communication" (1977, p. 267).

For the second half of the first year, when we might expect significant developments in the baby's interest in the reactions of others to his behavior, we unfortunately have very little evidence. Experimental work by Emde and Campos and their colleagues now in progress, shows that 12-month-old babies, when in a situation of uncertainty, immediately monitor their mothers' faces. The babies' behavior is then dramatically affected by whether their mothers' faces are expressing fear, interest, anger, or sadness (Emde, personal communication). Further study of the development of this "referencing" of emotional expression in other people over the first year of life will clearly be of very great interest.

In the research on the transition from preverbal to verbal communication, the focus has been on the child's expression of intention and demands, on the development of demanding or referential gesture, and the linking of gesture to vocal signal and finally to words. The child's response to the behavior and intentions of others has been less sensitively described. Incidents of "showing off" by the baby, which involve the child's looking at the adult and repeating an act that has received attention, are reported by Bates, Camaioni, and Volterra (1975) and by Trevarthen and Hubley (1978) to appear around 7 months. However, such incidents are dismissed rather cursorily by both sets of authors, who devote most attention to the development of the child's capacity to combine his acts with objects and with people, which they see as reflecting his understanding of adults as agents. Thus in the study by Bates and her colleagues of the transition from preverbal to verbal communication, the focus is on the preverbal development of imperatives and declaratives; these are defined as "protoimperatives" – the child's intentional use of the adult, as a *means to a desired object* – and proto-declaratives – the child's preverbal effort to direct the adult's attention to *some event or object in the world.*

The descriptive analysis of the child's visual behavior over the second half of the first year is, in several developmental accounts, primarily in terms of a linguistic model. Thus the child's glances at the mother when he is playing with an object are described as "referential" looks (Jones 1977), or as "comments on a topic" (Bruner 1977). Built into this description is an assumption about the content/meaning of the child's look and about its relevance for the development of language. One can say with confidence that the mothers in many of these examples do treat the child's look, in this context, as referring to the object and reply by commenting on the object themselves. Their interpretation of the glance may indeed be crucially important in influencing the child's future use of glance. But inferences about what the child's glance means at the time to the child are much more questionable.

eight

Individual Differences in Sibling Relationships

MOTHER OF JILL AND KENNY (14 MONTHS) J: It's worse now he's on the go. He annoys her. They fight a lot—more than four or five big fights a day, and *every* day. They're very *bad tempered* with each other. He makes her cry such a lot.

MOTHER OF DUNCAN AND ROBIN (14 MONTHS) K: They rarely fight. If Robin has something, Duncan may take it, but he always gives him something else. Duncan's always been interested in him—fetched and carried for him; now it's on the other foot—Robin gets things for *him*. Duncan always holds his hand, walks him up the road. The last month or so they've really played; the latest thing is these chasing games—quite complicated ones. And they do comfort each other.

Here were two very different pairs of siblings at the 14-month visits. In some families, as we saw in Chapter 5, the siblings fought continually by this stage; in other families almost every exchange between the siblings was warm and affectionate. What could account for the development of such a wide range of individual differences among the families? Books of advice for parents emphasize the part parents can play in minimizing conflict, and some attribute much of the responsibility for the quality of the sibling relationship to the way the parents handle issues of jealousy and conflict. Clinicians caring for children who show more extreme disturbance have taken a rather different perspective. They have attempted to discover retrospectively whether the quality of the relationship between mother and child before the sibling was born contributed to the disturbed behavior and have suggested that overprotection by mothers, and overdependence in children, were both linked to extreme jealousy (Levy 1937; Stendler 1954). The approach of developmental psychologists has been to concentrate on the more easily quantifiable differences, such as age gap and sex of sibling, and to ask how these might relate to differences in the siblings' social behavior (Lamb 1978a and b; Abramovitch, Corter, and Lando 1979; Abramovitch, Corter, and Pepler 1980).

How important, in our families, were differences in the relationship between mother and firstborn before the arrival of the second? How significant were individual differences in temperament, or differences in the way in which the first child responded to the birth of the second? Did the mothers' strategies for coping with the two children affect the way in which the siblings behaved toward each other? How far did the age gap between the siblings, or their sexes, matter? In this chapter and the next we consider these questions, looking first at the significance of the first child's reaction to the baby's birth, at age differences and sex differences, and at one particular aspect of the mother's behavior.

It is, unsurprisingly, a complicated picture. In order to present its main outlines as clearly as possible, we shall describe the associations between these different "independent" variables and the sibling interaction chiefly in terms of two indexes of the behavior of each sibling toward the other—the summary measures of friendly social behavior and hostile social behavior. First, we consider each of the independent factors and the summary measures of the children's behavior in turn. Second, we examine the relative importance of these factors when they are considered together.

Individual Differences before Sibling Birth

In families where the firstborn children had been described in the first interview as worrying frequently, the interactions between the siblings were less friendly at 14 months than in families with nonworrying children. In contrast, the children who had been described as having frequent temper tantrums were very friendly to their siblings (Table A8.1). This finding, with its suggestion that the children who acted out and expressed their frustrations and anger freely on the whole got along better with their siblings than the more withdrawn, worrying children, is echoed in findings from a number of points in the study, for instance in the pattern of the first child's reaction to the arrival of the baby.

The Arrival of the Second Child

Were the marked differences between the first children in their responses to the birth of the baby associated with differences in the sibling relationship 14 months later? Three issues stand out from our analysis of the interview carried out in the early weeks after the birth.

The first concerns the first child's interest in the baby. Not only were those children who were reported to show interest and affection to the baby in the second and third week after the birth more friendly to their siblings 14 months later (Table A8.2), but most strikingly their baby siblings were significantly more friendly to them than the younger siblings in the rest of the sample. Table 8.1 shows that in families where the first child imitated the baby sibling frequently in the first three weeks, both siblings were particularly friendly to each other 14 months later.

This continuity in the friendly behavior of first child to second was demonstrated in the consistency of individual difference in the observational measures of friendly social approaches at 8 months and 14 months ($rs = 0.42$, $p < 0.05$). The children were also consistent in the frequency with which they showed unfriendly behavior at the 8-month and 14-month observations ($rs = 0.35$, $p < 0.05$).

This pattern of association between the interview measures of the first child's interest in the baby at three weeks after the

Table 8.1   Frequency of friendly and hostile social approaches to sibling in 14-month observations: comparison of families in which first child frequently imitated newborn sibling and those in which first child rarely or never imitated newborn sibling.

Approaches at 14 months	C's imitation of B in first month		p level (Mann-Whitney U test)
	Frequent	Rare/Absent	
Friendly			
Child	24	12	0.01
Baby	26	13	0.01
Hostile			
Child	13	21	0.01
Baby	9	11	

sibling's birth and the behavior of the siblings 14 months later was markedly stronger for firstborn boys than for firstborn girls. In families where the firstborn boys had frequently entertained their newborn baby siblings—showing them pictures, rattles, or toys; playing with them; or trying to engage them in games or make them laugh—the siblings were much more friendly than in families where the firstborn boys had shown no such interest in the early weeks. The firstborn boys who had entertained their newborn siblings made an average of 30 friendly approaches to their siblings per two hours' observation when they were 14 months old, and the 14-month-olds made an average of 25 friendly approaches. In the families where the firstborn boys had not shown this interest in the postpartum weeks, the friendly approaches were significantly less frequent: 12 and 15 per two hours from the firstborn and baby respectively.

It could well be that the sex differences in these links over time reflect differences in the ways mothers view and report on the behavior of boys versus girls toward young babies. It could be argued that friendly interest in the baby, and imitation of the baby, would be seen by the mother as a natural and socially approved behavior for a girl, but less so for a boy. It is possible then that the mothers' reports of the first child's interest in the baby reflect the application of different criteria for girls than for boys. However, if this were the case, one might expect that there would be sex differences in the frequency with which such friendly interest in the baby was reported. No significant sex differences in the various indexes of friendly interest were found.

Another possibility is that the interest of a young boy in a baby reflects a different kind of concern for the sibling, or sensitivity to others, than that reflected by the interest in the new baby shown by a girl. For a boy to show either much or little interest and physical affection for his new sibling may reflect a more enduring aspect of his personality than a parallel interest shown by a girl, for whom such an interest is so much more socially approved.

The second point concerns the reaction of withdrawal shown by several children in the early weeks after the birth. In these families the siblings were significantly more unfriendly to each other than in families where the first children had shown no signs of withdrawal after the birth (Table A8.3).

The third point involves the mother's state during the early weeks after the baby's birth. It is a finding that at first sight appears counterintuitive: in those families where the mother was in the first weeks very tired and/or depressed the siblings were, 14 months later, getting along better than the siblings in the other families (Table A8.4). It is a pattern that was reflected both in the fine-grain measures of aggressive behavior (first child hits younger) and of friendly behavior (first child gives toy to younger), and in the summary measure as illustrated.

Age Differences

The age gap between the siblings was not found to be related to any of the measures of sibling interaction. Here our results match those of Abramovitch and her colleagues, who in two studies found that the interval between siblings did not affect levels of aggressive, cooperative, or imitative behavior for either same-sex or different-sex sibling pairs (Abramovitch, Corter, and Lando 1979; Abramovitch, Corter, and Pepler 1980).

Same-Sex and Different-Sex Siblings

Dramatic differences between same-sex and different-sex sibling pairs were apparent for all the measures of sibling interaction, not just the frequency of imitations noted in Chapter 7. These differences, though significant for the whole sample, were most striking for the families with firstborn boys. Table A8.5 shows that elder boys with a younger brother were far more frequently friendly and less frequently negative toward their sibling than the boys with a younger sister.

At the 14-month visits both first child and infant showed much more friendly behavior to their sibling if he or she shared the same sex. There was a marked increase in the frequency with which the first child showed friendly behavior to the baby between the 8-month visit and the 14-month visit if they were of the same sex, and no increase in hostile behavior. In sharp contrast, the first children in different-sex pairs became much more frequently aggressive and hostile to the baby between the 8-month and the 14-month visits. And the *babies* who had an elder sibling of the same sex also became much more friendly to their sibling between the 8-month and 14-month visits, unlike the babies with an elder sibling of the opposite sex (Table A8.6). There are some interesting findings from cross-cultural work, which parallel these results. The Whitings and their colleagues (Whiting and Whiting 1975; Whiting and Edwards 1977) studied children in a number of widely differing cultures, and in three African communities observed sibling interaction in special detail. They found that friendly behavior occurred far more frequently, and aggressive hostile behavior less frequently, in same-sex pairs than in different-sex pairs.

In Chapter 7 we discussed some of the possible interpretations of these differences between same-sex and different-sex pairs. It is perhaps worth noting that clinicians with a psychoanalytic perspective on the sibling relationship have suggested that, as a result of the oedipal situation, same-sex pairs would be *more* jealous and hostile than different-sex pairs, since they would both be competing for the love of the same parent—the parent of the opposite sex (Obendorf 1929).

Discussing the Baby as a Person

During the first weeks after the birth of the baby there were, as we have seen, notable differences among the mothers in the ways they talked about the baby. Some mothers often referred to the baby as a person with needs, wants, likes, and dislikes; they explained what they thought the baby wanted and frequently drew attention to the baby's interest in the elder child. These mothers discussed the care of the baby with the first child, almost as if it were a matter of joint responsibility, and accompanied such consultation with a very real encouragement of the elder child's attempts to help.

Already by the third and fourth weeks after the sibling's birth, the firstborn children in these families were much more likely to comment on the baby as a person with needs and wants than were the children whose mothers did not discuss the baby with them in this manner. By the time the baby was 14 months old, friendly behavior from both elder child to younger and vice versa was much more frequent in the families where the mother had discussed the baby in this way (Fig. 8.1).

The Combined Effect of These Influences

So far we have considered the separate effects of a number of different variables on the behavior of the siblings toward each other. What was the *relative* effect of these variables? What *separate* contributions did they make to the differences in the children's behavior? To examine the relative contribution of different variables, we used a regression technique. This gives an estimate of the amount of variation in a measure that is due to different independent measures; it can also be used to discover whether particular combinations of measures have an extra additive effect on the variation of the dependent measure.

When we considered the effects of the various factors such as the first child's reaction to the birth of the sibling and the quality of the mother/firstborn relationship at the time of the birth, the results (given in detail in Appendix C, note 1) confirmed the findings described above and showed that the

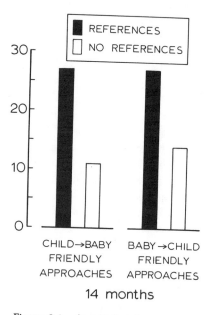

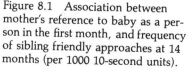

Figure 8.1   Association between mother's reference to baby as a person in the first month, and frequency of sibling friendly approaches at 14 months (per 1000 10-second units).

following all contributed significantly to the variance in the measure of the first child's friendly behavior:

(1) Whether or not the mother had talked about the baby as a person during the first-month observations;
(2) Whether the siblings were of the same sex or not;
(3) How positively the first child had reacted to the birth of the baby.

There was also an interaction effect: in families where the siblings were of the same sex *and* the mother had talked about the baby as a person in the early weeks, the likelihood of the first child's behaving in a friendly fashion to the baby was greatly increased. However, these variables did not account for a high proportion of the variation in the positive social behavior of the children: the remaining variation was accounted for almost entirely by the behavior of the younger child toward the older during the 14-month observations. There was also considerable overlap of (1), (2), and (3) in the variance that they accounted for. And the analysis showed that the effect of some of the variables, such as the mother's state in the postpartum weeks and the reaction of withdrawing, did not make a significant contribution to the variation when analyzed in this way.

The behavior of the *baby* to the elder child was analyzed in the same way, and the results paralleled those for the first child's behavior. Separate significant contributions to the variance were made by (1) whether or not the children were of the same sex and (2) whether or not the mother had talked about the baby as a person, and there was again an interaction effect between these two variables. They accounted for 42 percent of the variation, and a further 30 percent resulted from the first child's behavior (Appendix Table C1).

Comment

We have discussed earlier what may explain the differences in the relationship between same-sex and different-sex siblings.

Here we wish particularly to emphasize the importance of considering the *mother's* contribution to these differences. The following remark was made by one mother to her daughter when the baby sibling, a girl, was only 2 weeks old.

> MOTHER OF DEBBIE G: Oh she smiled at you, yes. She just smiled at you. (To B: Didn't you?) I think she knows you're a little girl like her. Mmm? She does. Yes, she's smiling at you.

The findings we have reported in this chapter demonstrate just how closely the mother's construction, in her comments to the elder child, of the baby as a person is associated with the quality of the developing relationship between the siblings. It may well be the case that the mother's comments on *this* particular dimension—that of sharing gender—are of special significance. But whatever the mother's contribution to the child's sense of sharing gender, the importance of her discussion of the baby as a person with wants, likes, and intentions is striking. This third theme running through the results has a number of different implications for psychologists and parents.

First, it suggests that even with a child as young as 2½ years, the discussion of a person's intentions and wants may influence how the child behaves toward, and presumably feels about, that individual. We stressed in Chapter 4 that we should not interpret the association as a simple link between one single aspect of the early mother/firstborn conversations and the later behavior of the children toward each other: rather, we should regard it as reflecting an association between a *style* of interaction between mother and firstborn and the children's behavior later. Nevertheless, we must take very seriously the implication that our 2-year-olds were capable of a far higher degree of reflection about the baby as a person than would have been presumed likely in such young children—an implication supported by the finding that the elder children whose mothers discussed the baby in this way *themselves* were much more likely to comment on the baby's intentions and wants. The ways in which mothers' interpretations of and beliefs about the behavior of their babies influences their own behavior, and indeed that of the baby, have been extensively discussed from a theoretical point of view (Newson 1978; Shotter and Newson 1980). Our results suggest that the articulation of these beliefs may have a direct influence on the behavior of the elder child extremely early in its life, and thus affect the most intimate of family relationships.

Second, the findings have a more practical implication. They suggest that what the mother says about the baby — an aspect of her behavior that is, at least sometimes, well under her control — may influence the quality of the relationship that develops between the children.

A third implication concerns the appropriate way in which to study development. As the findings have made clear, any account of causal influences on the development of sibling relationships that ignores the role of the mother's perceptions and explicit verbal comments in molding the long-term patterns of interaction between the siblings may simply misstate the causal basis of those differences which it has identified.

Finally, a comment on the clinical implications of the findings. The particular patterns of association between the child's immediate reaction to the sibling birth and the later relationship between the siblings are of some relevance to clinicians. Signs of withdrawal in the early weeks were associated with a difficult relationship later between the siblings (see Winnicott 1977). On the other hand, children who were reported to imitate frequently their new sister or brother were significantly more likely to show a warm, affectionate interest in their sibling over the next months, and by 14 months their young siblings were showing remarkably friendly and affectionate behavior toward the elder siblings. Imitation of this sort, particularly in the weeks immediately after the birth should not be taken as a sign of "regression" (if this is assumed to reflect disturbance and a poor prognosis for the child's family relationships).

These analyses have shown that the reaction of the first children to the sibling birth, the sex of the dyad, and the way in which the mothers talk about the baby were all associated with differences in the quality of the relationship that developed between the siblings. But how important were differences in the mother's relationship with each child? And how do these relationships interact and influence each other? It is to the patterning of the different relationships within the family that we turn next.

nine

Mothers, Brothers, and Sisters

In the first weeks after the baby was born, demands and naughtiness from the first child increased dramatically at times when the mother was caring for the baby—feeding, bathing, or simply cuddling him. By the time the baby was 14 months old, his demands on his mother, and her pleasure in playing with him and talking to him, were of course of a very different quality. How did the firstborn child respond to the interaction between mother and secondborn at this stage—a period when mother and 14-month-old shared an elaborate and complex relationship, and when the baby took an assertive and demanding part in family interactions?

For many mothers the stage when the baby was 14 months old was a particularly rewarding and pleasurable one, and the delight that both mother and second child took in each other was obvious to all. We have seen that games and play, and long "conversations" between mother and baby, were often initiated by the baby, and the baby frequently showed great persistence in keeping the conversation going:

SEAN R:
B: Bye-bye.
M: Bye-bye.
B: Bye-bye.
M: Bye-bye. Cuckoo.
B: Bye-bye.
M: Cuckoo, Sean!

B: Bye-bye.
M: Bye-bye. Bye-bye.
B: Bye-bye.
M: Got your big tummy! I got your big tummy!
     Where's that big tummy? Where's that big tummy?
B: Bye-bye.
M: Bye-bye. Where's Daddy?
B: Papa.
M: Papa. Papa. Where's Papa?

B: Peepbo.
M: Peepbo.
B: Peepbo.
M: Peepbo.
B: Peepbo.

There was also, of course, quite frequent "trouble" between the 14-month-olds and their parents, trouble caused by the babies' exploits (actively exploring kitchen cupboards, dropping toys down the toilet, trying out the cat's food), by their persistent and assertive demands for help or attention when frustrated, or by their distress when exhausted or ill. Many mothers were kept very busy not only caretaking, but restraining their irrepressibly inquisitive 14-month-olds. What were the reactions of the firstborn children to the games and to the incidents of confrontation between their mothers and siblings?

In many families the interaction between mother and baby had a marked effect on the behavior of the first child. Some of the first children reacted clearly and directly to an extremely high proportion — as high as three out of four — of the exchanges between mother and sibling (Table A9.1). The most common direct response was a protest, or a demand for precisely the same attention that the sibling was getting:

JOANNE R AND DONNA:
M to B: You play with that one.

C: It's mine! It's mine!
M to B: Well, have a look at the book then. Where's
            the book?
C: It's mine!
M to B (looking at book): Pretty!
C: Donna will tear it.

FAY G AND RUBY:
M to B (commenting on her playing): Are you enjoy-
            ing yourself, Ruby?
C: She can't have that any more.

VIRGINIA L AND MALCOLM:
M to B (playing with Lego): I'll make you a little car,
            Malcolm.
C: Well, I want one.
M to B: Shall I make you a car? Mmm?
C: Don't let him have the red pieces.

                       .   .   .

M to B (picking him up and imitating his noises):
            Wawwaw! Wawwaw!
C: Can I sit beside you? Can I sit on knee?
M to C: Is that just because Malcolm's up here?
C: Yes.
M: Come on then.

ALISTAIR M AND SHIRLEY:
M to B (exclaiming playfully at B's muddy hands):
            Hullo Shirley, what's that? Guess? Mud! Look
            at you! Poofy! Dirty.
C promptly runs to flower bed and covers his hands
with mud, then runs to M showing his dirty hands.

This mirroring of those actions by the baby which had
drawn the mother's attention usually followed incidents in
which the mother was playing with the baby or cuddling him,
but several children also copied the baby's "naughty" acts, if

such acts drew attention from the mother — as in the example
that follows:

> DUNCAN K AND ROBBIE:
> B is pulling papers and magazines out of bookcase.
> M to B: No! Stop!
> C immediately runs over and starts pulling out papers
> too, looking at M.
> M to C: No, Duncan, there's no need for you! You
>   know better — or don't you?
> C: No!

It was also quite common for the first child to join the
mother and baby in a very friendly way, especially when the
two were involved in a game:

> SUSAN S AND ALAN:
> B is engaged in "running away" from Mother (crawling
> fast, with an excited noise).
> M to B: Bye-bye! Bye-bye!
> C (joins in by chasing B, to his great excitement):
>   I going catch him! I am!

The first children were in fact particularly likely to react to
play between mother and sibling: they ignored far more of the
incidents when the mothers were caretaking, restraining, or
simply talking to the sibling. Not only did play between
mother and baby arouse much more interest in the first
children; the proportion of *friendly* responses to playful exchanges was also much higher than the proportion of friendly
responses to other interactions (Table A9.2).

However, some children were also eager to join in when
their mothers were attempting to console, soothe or help the
baby. They either made suggestions to the mother or directly
helped the baby:

> SUSAN S AND ALAN:
> B is crying, after hurting himself.

M to B: Oh dear, you're not going to cheer up, are
          you?
C: He's not going to cheer up. Perhaps he wants
          some chocolate.
M to B: Oh dear, oh dear! It wasn't all that bad. I'm
          sure it wasn't. Eh?
C: Give him some chocolate.

LAURA W AND CALLUM:
B requests help from M by noise and gesture:
M to B: You want it undoing?
C to B: I'll undo it for you, Cally!

Other children watched the interaction between mother and
sibling without comment, often sucking their thumbs or comfort objects. The children rarely made direct aggressive attacks
on the baby while mother and baby were involved together,
except when a mother punished or scolded the baby. On these
occasions the firstborn sometimes scolded or attacked the
baby too.

Which children responded in a friendly way, and which
were hostile? The pattern of very marked individual
differences in the responses followed closely the patterns of
individual differences in the sibling relationship. For instance
there were again striking differences between families with
same-sex and with different-sex siblings. The firstborn children
with siblings of the same sex were much more likely to join
mother and baby in a friendly fashion than the children in
families with different-sex siblings. Those with same-sex siblings joined an average of 18 percent in a friendly way, compared with only 8 percent in different-sex pairs. The sex of the
elder or of the younger child did not affect the way in which
the first child behaved.

The first child's behavior was also related to his reaction to
the birth of the baby 14 months earlier. Children who had
shown a positive interest in the baby, who had offered to help
frequently, and who had wanted to play with the new baby in

the first three weeks were more likely to join mother and baby in a friendly way at 14 months (Spearman rank correlation *rs* = 0.60). They were less likely to ignore the interaction than the children who had not been interested in the first three weeks (*rs* = 0.54). Protest was more common from those children who had reacted to the birth by becoming more demanding and difficult, and these children were also less likely to ignore mother and sibling 14 months later. Finally, direct aggression to the baby when the mother was involved with him was more common from children who had never, during the first three weeks, imitated the new baby (Table A9.3).

Temperamental differences between the firstborn children, assessed before the birth of the baby, were also important. Children who were in the "extreme" group on the traits of unmalleability and intensity of emotional response protested more than the other children and were less likely to ignore an exchange between mother and baby. And children who were relatively extreme on the traits of emotional intensity more often watched the interaction between mother and sibling, sucking their thumb or holding their comfort object, than those who were average or below average in the intensity of their emotional responses (Table A9.4).

The association between temperamental differences and these variations in the responses of children to the involvement of mother and sibling raises again the question of whether temperamental differences should be viewed as differences between children, or as differences in the relationships of children with particular individuals. Temperamental differences were not found to be related to differences in the interaction between *siblings* in this study, nor in the study of Thomas and Chess (1977). But they were associated with differences in the mothers' behavior toward their children, both before and after the sibling birth. These links may not illuminate the origins of differences in temperament, but they do show us again how closely the quality of the child's relationship with the mother, rather than with the father or sibling, is associated with "temperament."

The response of the first children to the involvement of mother and baby at the 14-month visits was also related to the way in which mother and baby had behaved toward each other at the earlier visits. In those families where mother and baby had spent much time involved together during the 8-month visits, the elder child was, six months later, more likely to be aggressive to the baby when mother and baby were relating to each other, than the first child in families where mother and baby had spent less time together six months earlier ($rs = 0.52$, $p < 0.01$).

And finally, in families in which the mother had talked about the baby as a person and had discussed his needs with the first child as a matter of joint responsibility in the first weeks after his birth, the first children were significantly more likely to respond in a friendly way to the interaction between mother and baby. They joined, on average, 19 percent of the mother-baby interactions in a friendly fashion, while the firstborn in families where the mother had not discussed the baby in this way only joined 8 percent of the interactions in a friendly way.

Was the age gap between the siblings important? The younger firstborn children watched their mother and baby siblings more, but otherwise no differences were found.

Patterns over Time

Many of the children, then, responded directly to the involvement of mother and sibling; and their response was linked to the quality of the relationship between mother and baby that had developed over the previous months. It is a familiar claim that the different relationships within a family affect one another. Yet we still know little about exactly how these influences operate, or about how extensive or how durable these effects are. In what ways is the quality of the relationship between two young siblings linked to the relationship each child has with the mother? When two children quarrel violently, their mother is likely to react immediately; but the form her reaction takes is likely to be influenced by the kind of relationship that has grown up between the siblings over the previous months or years. The children's propensity to quarrel, in turn, may well be influenced by the way in which she has related to each of them over the previous months. Levy (1937) found in his clinical studies that sibling rivalry was greater if the first child had a very close relationship with an oversolicitous mother. And many parent manuals imply that the responsibility for a successful sibling relationship rests with the mother and depends on the quality of her relationship with each child: "The difference in the quality of the sibling relationship is a result of the parenting offered" (Calladine and Calladine 1979, p. 11).

How far were these views confirmed by the patterns of family relationships revealed in our study?

Mother and Firstborn Child

We saw in Chapter 3 that the families differed markedly in the quality of the relationship between mother and first child both before and immediately after the baby was born. The differences were particularly marked in two aspects of the relationship: in the amount of play and joint attention between mother and first child, and in the frequency of confrontation and prohibition. Did these differences relate in any systematic way to the quality of the *sibling* interaction 14 months later?

For the firstborn *girls* in the sample the answer was, most strikingly, yes.

In families where there had been a relatively high frequency of joint play and attention between mother and daughter before and immediately after the birth of the baby, the firstborn daughter was more likely to behave in a hostile and unfriendly way to the sibling 14 months later (Table A9.5). In these families, moreover, the younger sibling was much less friendly to the elder than in the other families (Table A9.6). In families where there had been frequent incidents of prohibition and much confrontation between mother and daughter in the first month after the baby was born, the firstborn girls were particularly friendly to their siblings. For the firstborn boys there was no such clear pattern linking the sibling interaction with the earlier relationship between mother and son.[1]

The interview questions about the first child's relationship with the father before the sibling birth present a very similar pattern. Those first children who had shown intense affection for their fathers were significantly less friendly toward their siblings at 14 months than those who were less affectionate, while the 14-month-olds were much less friendly to their older siblings (Table A9.7). Since we do not have sufficiently systematic observations on the behavior of the fathers and firstborn children throughout the study, we cannot explore these relations in any detail. But we can consider the striking findings on *mothers* and their firstborn girls; one possible explanation lies in the behavior of the mother with the baby sibling.

The Relationship between Mother and Baby

What requires explanation is the fact that in families where there was an intense playful relationship between a mother and her firstborn daughter, a relatively poor relationship frequently developed between the siblings. And for both girls and boys, a pattern of very friendly interaction between the siblings developed in families where there had been a high level of spanking and confrontation (Table A9.8). Now if the mothers who had been relatively playful with their first

---

1. The measures of observed behavior examined here reflect, of course, only limited aspects of the relationship between the children and their parents. The lack of a demonstrated association between the sibling interaction and these particular measures of mother-child interaction for firstborn boys obviously does not exclude the possibility that there may be associations with other aspects of their family relationships.

children were also particularly playful with their second, it is possible that the first children reacted to this high level of mother-baby play by behaving in a hostile way to the baby. The link between the mother's relation to her first child and the relation between the siblings 14 months later might then lie in the association between each of these and the behavior of the mother with the baby.

The mothers differed markedly in how much time they spent in playing with, caring for, or restraining their babies, or simply in talking to them, and it was in the frequency of play between mother and baby that these differences were most dramatic. The proportion of the exchanges that included play ranged from 0 to 88 percent in the different families. (It is, of course, precisely these sequences of play between mother and babies of this age that psychologists have singled out as being of key developmental significance for the beginnings of communication and understanding between mother and baby; see Chapter 7). Were the differences in playfulness with the baby related to the mother's style of behavior with her first child? If so, could this link explain the striking association between the hostile behavior of the firstborn girls to their siblings and their earlier relationship with their mothers?

There certainly was consistency in the mothers' playful and attentive behavior with their first and their second children. In families where the mother and first child had played a lot together and had spent much time looking at things together, the mother—one year later—was also relatively attentive and playful with her second child (correlations of $rs = 0.64$, $p < 0.001$ and $rs = 0.44$, $p < 0.05$ for joint attention and joint play respectively). But the differences in playfulness of mother and baby in themselves did not fully account for the differences in hostility of the elder girls toward their baby siblings. When the effect of "mother-and-baby play" was controlled for by the use of partial correlations, there was still a significant correlation between the quality of the sibling interaction and the mother-firstborn relationship 14 months earlier (Table A9.9).

We have here evidence which suggests that in families with girls there are long-term associations between the relationship of mother and first child before the birth of the sibling, and the relationship between the siblings 14 months later.

But it would be misleading to suggest that the quality of the relationship between mother and baby had *no* effect upon the relationship between the siblings. We have two quite different sources of evidence that in fact it was important. The first is the immediate response of the firstborns to the involvement of their mothers and siblings (the reaction we described earlier in this chapter). The second source is the longer-term pattern of correlation between the different relationships. In families where mother and baby spent a relatively high proportion of the observations at 8 months involved with each other, the elder sibling was less friendly to the baby six months later ($rs = 0.41$, $p < 0.05$). We cannot assume from this correlation that the differences in the time that mother and baby spent together *caused* the differences in the first children's behavior to their siblings. Still, the correlation over time was not accounted for by the amount of time mother and baby spent together at 14 months (Table A9.10), a result which does support the suggestion that the elder children were reacting negatively over time to a particularly warm involvement between mother and younger sibling.

In the same way the *babies'* behavior to their siblings at 14 months was linked to the quality of the mother-baby relationship earlier in the year. In families where mother and 8-month-old had played together more, the younger child was relatively unfriendly to the elder six months later, removing toys more frequently and attacking the elder child physically ($rs = 0.56$, $p < 0.01$). Again, this association was still strong when the effects of the other correlations over time were held constant (Table A9.11).

What these results show is that where the relationship between mother and baby was intense and playful, *both* children six months later were particularly hostile to each other. These links between the relationship of mother and baby at 8 months and the sibling relationship six months later were strong both for families with elder boys, and for those with elder girls. They show us how important it is, if we are trying to understand the siblings' behavior toward each other, to take account of the mother's behavior with the baby over the previous months.

Interpreting the Patterns over Time

The kind of relationship the mother and father have with their firstborn girl before the sibling is born is related to the ways in which the first child behaves toward the second and, most strikingly, to the way in which the baby behaves toward the first child. One obvious interpretation of this pattern is to see the hostile behavior of those girls who had enjoyed a close and intense relationship with their mother as a response to the displacement—hostile behavior directed at a usurper. There is another way to see the pattern, though, and that is to focus on the high level of warm and friendly behavior toward the sibling of those children who had had a more detached relationship, or a relationship with a high degree of conflict and confrontation, with their parents. In such families the developing relationship with the sibling can contribute greatly to the emotional life of the first child. Fitting well with this perspective are the findings, given in the previous chapter, that in families where the mothers were depressed and tired during the first three weeks after the birth, the sibling relationship developed in a particularly friendly fashion.

Our information on the father-child relationship is less reliable than that on the relationship between mother and first child. However, it is interesting that the pattern it reveals parallels that found for the mother: where the first child was particularly closely attached to the father, the sibling relationship one year later was relatively hostile and unfriendly.

A second theme running through the findings concerns sex differences. Why should there be such different patterns of association for firstborn boys and firstborn girls? How can we explain the *lack* of a correlation between the mother-child interaction and the sibling interaction in boys, when we have demonstrated its presence in families with girls?

One possible explanation is that the arrival of a sibling, and the consequent dramatic decrease in maternal attention, could have rather different significance for a girl and a boy. It may be the case, for example, that mothers are more effective in their influence on girls at this age and that boys are more autonomous or independent of their influence. In several longitudinal studies, clearer patterns of association between the mother's behavior and the child's behavior are found in families with girls than in families with boys.[2] (While statistical effects may have contributed to some of these results—see Yarrow, Rubenstein, and Pedersen 1975—it is extremely unlikely that they provide the sole explanation.) This interpretation of the sex differences, in terms of the different significance that the changes in maternal attentiveness have for boys and for girls, would certainly fit with Chodorow's (1978) view that for girls the developing sense of self is closely bound up with *identification with* the mother, while for boys it is linked to *difference from* the mother.

A second possible explanation of the sex differences in the present study is a statistical one. There may have been more variability from day to day in the measures of mother-firstborn interaction for the *boys*, with the procedures failing to sample a sufficiently large proportion of interactions to give a reliable picture of the differences in the mother-child interaction and the behavior of the first child in families with boys. When we examined this possibility (Appendix C, note 2), the results suggested that the lack of association between the

---

2. A number of different studies of parent-child interaction have reported different patterns over time for girls and for boys (see for example Moss 1967; Kagan 1971; Yarrow, Rubenstein, and Pedersen 1975; Kagan, Kearsley, and Zelazo 1978; Pawlby and Hall 1980). Both Moss (1967) and Kagan (1971) suggest on the basis of their longitudinal data that girls are more susceptible to maternal or environmental influence.

parent-child interaction measures and the sibling interaction measures for the boys is not simply the result of inadequate sampling, though other statistical explanations cannot be ruled out.

Even where we can demonstrate an association between a particular pattern of parent-child interaction at one time point and later differences between children, we are very far from understanding the basis of such continuities. It may be that an association between the ways in which children react to a change in their environment and later differences in behavior reflects a pattern of *parental* behavior that is consistent from the change point to the next time point studied. In the association between the extent of the reported interest of boys in their newborn sibling and the observed interaction between siblings 14 months later, for instance, it is clear that parental support for such an affectionate sibling relationship may be of great significance.

Mothers' Reactions to Sibling Quarrels

How a mother behaves with her two children is obviously likely to be influenced in turn by the way they behave together. Perhaps the most striking effect of the siblings' behavior on their mothers concerned quarrels between the children. When we examined the mothers' reactions when the first child told off or hit the younger child, some intriguing patterns over time were revealed, and these patterns were strikingly different for firstborn boys and firstborn girls.

Quarrels between the siblings were quite frequent in many families, even when the baby was only 8 months old, especially when the younger sibling was mobile and interfered with the first child's games. At this stage it was the elder child who was more often aggressive and hostile—taking away toys, punching or hitting the baby, or shouting at him. Many mothers found these quarrels upsetting and irritating, and they reacted to the first child's hostility in a variety of ways.

Some attempted to distract the elder child, or the baby; some scolded the elder child or punished him; and some simply ignored both children. To examine these differences in the mother's reactions we separated the instances of hostile behavior of the firstborn into two groups: on the one hand, "scolding" — where the elder child simply told off the younger, or took away whatever the baby was playing with — and on the other hand, "negative actions" — where the elder child actually hit, pushed, or physically attacked the younger. Unsurprisingly, mothers were significantly more likely to prohibit the elder if he *hit* the younger than if he simply shouted at the younger, and they were more likely to distract the children in instances where the first child scolded than in instances where he hit the younger (Table A9.12).

Patterns in Families with Firstborn Boys

In families where the mothers reacted to their firstborn boys' scolding the younger sibling by themselves telling off or restraining the firstborn, the first child was, six months later, behaving much more frequently in a hostile way to the baby than in families where the mother reacted less frequently in this way ($rs = 0.60$, $p < 0.05$). And in families where the mothers were particularly likely to have scolded their firstborn boys if they hit the baby sibling at 8 months, these firstborn boys were significantly less friendly to the baby six months later ($rs = -0.64$, $p < 0.01$). The analysis showed that differences between mothers in their response to aggressive behavior by their sons were extremely stable over time. Those mothers who frequently reacted to physical aggression toward the sibling by scolding or punishing at the 8-month visit were highly likely to react in the same way six months later: they were still the most punitive mothers ($rs = 0.88$, $p < 0.01$).

In families with girls, the patterns over time were quite different. There was little consistency between 8 and 14 months in individual differences in the way mothers responded to aggressive behavior in their daughters. The *daughters*, on the other hand, were consistent: those who were frequently hostile at the 8-month visits were still relatively hostile six months later (*rs* = 0.66, *p* < 0.01). And in these families where the daughters were frequently aggressive to the sibling, many of the mothers became more punitive, over the next six months, in their response to their daughters' aggression than the mothers whose daughters had not been so aggressive. Frequent hostile behavior from daughter to baby at 8 months was correlated with a punitive response by the mother six months later (*rs* = 0.49, *p* < 0.05). (The possibility that these effects over time were the result of associations between the 14-month measures was ruled out by the results of partial correlations, as shown in Tables A9.13 and A9.14.)

What can we conclude from these differences in the patterns over time in the families with firstborn boys and with firstborn girls? The mothers were not only more consistent in their response to aggressive behavior from boy to baby than from girl to baby, but in their prohibitive and punitive behavior to their *sons* more generally (Table A9.15). It is unlikely that this consistency was a response to consistent individual differences in the boys themselves, since there was little stability in the boys' aggressive behavior. Some of the boys who had been least aggressive to their sibling at 8 months were the most aggressive at 14 months.

What the data suggest is that mothers' behavior in response to aggression may have a stronger effect on the boys, perhaps because it is more consistent over time. As we have indicated, it is possible that this difference in the consistency of response reflects attitudes to aggression in boys that are more clearly articulated and more deeply felt about *boys* than about *girls*.

Of course there are other possible interpretations of the pattern of correlations. It could be that boys respond with hostile behavior to rather different actions by their 14-month-old siblings than girls do. The mobility and the new assertiveness of the 14-month-old baby might arouse specific aggressive behavior from some boys who had previously been tolerant of their (relatively) passive 8-month-old sibling. But the striking consistency in maternal behavior in response to boys' aggression remains evident, and it certainly seems plausible to interpret the pattern of correlations as showing the effects of some aspect of the mothers' behavior (not necessarily the response we have measured here, of course, but quite possibly some other aspect of their behavior correlated with this response).

How should the differences in the patterns of consistency for families with firstborn girls be interpreted?

The data for girls suggest that a major influence on the mother's response to her daughter's aggressive behavior to the sibling may in fact be the daughter's behavior toward the sibling over the previous months. The individual differences in the hostile behavior of girls to their siblings *were* consistent between 8 and 14 months (unlike those of the boys), and this consistency in itself may have contributed to the apparent influence of the girls' behavior on their mothers six months later.

Comment

There obviously is an elaborate relationship between the behavior of the siblings toward each other, the response of the mother to their interaction, and the relation of mother and baby. To understand the behavior of any one of these dyads, we must therefore take account of what is happening between the other family members, both at the time and over the previous months. The link between frequent play of mother and baby and later aggression between the siblings is relatively easy to interpret. The pattern of influences involved in the aggressive behavior between the siblings is more complex: the drama of aggression and hostility is just beginning with these 2- and 3-year-olds and their siblings. By the time the firstborn children were 6 years old, their discussion of their feelings about the sibling and their views on what kind of person the sibling was were dominated by descriptions of fighting and aggression, as we shall see in Chapter 11. What we have tried to show here is how closely the development of particular patterns of hostility between the siblings was bound up with the mother's response. To begin to understand these developments more fully, we need to study all three family members, to look separately at families with boys and those with girls, and probably to analyze the interactions at a far more detailed level than we have attempted here. Since quarrels dominate the sibling relationship in so many families for so many years, and since their impact on the mothers is so great, it is obviously important both theoretically and practically to understand the development of this hostility more fully. As the Newsons comment in their illuminating book on 4-year-olds in Nottingham, England, "The control of aggression is in fact for most mothers the central problem of children's social play, whatever attitude they take" (Newson and Newson 1968, p. 113).

ten

Patterns of Change

MOTHER OF BRENDAN F: I'm at my wits' end. It's his demanding, whining, and *misery*. His anxiety . . . he won't play with children . . . he won't let me alone. It's his crying, moaning, and whining that are driving me spare [crazy]. It's two or three tantrums a day. I've never hit him so much as in the last week. It's getting to the point I'm at screaming point all the time. There was a time when I never smacked.

For the mother of this boy, the difficulties of coping with an unhappy 3-year-old, 14 months after the sibling was born, were tremendous. His problems had certainly not decreased in the year following his sister's birth. How common were such difficulties at the 14-month visits? Did the marked increases in demanding and negative behavior, in clinging, and in tearfulness—which had become evident in so many children at the birth of the baby—persist over the next year? For the mothers, did life get easier as the children grew up? In this chapter we examine the changes in the first children's behavior and in their interactions with their mothers and fathers over the year following the sibling's birth.

The first issue we address is whether or not problems persisted over the year following the sibling's birth. By comparing the answers to interview questions at each of the four time-point stages of the study, we can examine changes in the incidence of problems that the mothers reported for the sample as a whole, and also changes in the scores of individual children. We see that some problems decreased markedly between the first and the eighth months after the sibling's birth, but that other problems increased.

The second issue we consider concerns individual differences in the persistence of problems, and the question of which children appeared to be most vulnerable; individual differences in temperament do seem to be associated with differences in the persistence and the increase of difficulties during the year following the sibling's birth. Comparison of the interview material at each time point shows not only changes in the incidence of problems, but changes in the children's expression of affection for their parents and in the fathers' feelings for their children.

These findings are based on the mothers' reports of the children's behavior. How well do such descriptions compare with our own observations of the children? And do the changes in mother-firstborn interaction that we observed after the birth of the sibling persist over the next year? The third issue considered in this chapter is the extent of agreement between interview and observational information on the changes over the first year, and on the pattern of mother-firstborn interaction when the baby reached 14 months.

What these findings on changes over the year indicate is that in some respects living with the two young children presents new problems and difficulties for the mother, and that in other respects life with the siblings gets easier. In the last section of the chapter we examine the mothers' comments on what the changes meant for them—the stress, the irritations, but also the pleasures of living with their two growing children, and we consider again the issue of *which* families seem most at risk of difficulty.

The Pattern of Problems

Figure 10.1 shows the changes in the incidence of problems among the whole group of 40 families. The marked increase in demanding behavior after the birth shows a sharp decline: by the 14-month visit only 6 children were described as being frequently or constantly demanding. Sleep problems, which had increased sharply after the sibling birth, also declined over the next 14 months. Table A10.1 shows that the incidence of *marked* misery (those children who were described as being frequently miserable most days, or unhappy for long periods on more than three days a week, in contrast to those who had "miserable moods," see below, or who were rarely miserable) decreased very sharply over the 8 months following the sibling's birth. The changes over this 8-month period in the probability of these problems were all significant.

In contrast, Fig. 10.1 shows the number of children who were described by their mothers as having "miserable or grumpy moods" on most days for short periods (less than an hour), or for long periods once or twice a week, had *increased*

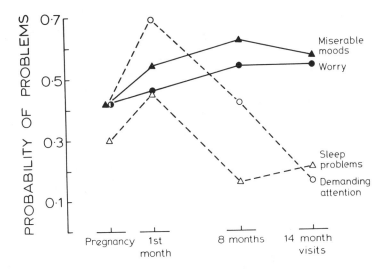

Figure 10.1   Changes over time in the incidence of problems of the firstborn.

between the first interview and the interview at 8 months from 43 to 62 percent of the sample. The number of children reported to have several marked specific fears also increased. Children of this age often have particular fears, and in some children these fears were marked—so strong that they interfered in a very real way with the children's lives. One 3-year-old would not go into the street if he saw a cat; another was terrified by the vacuum cleaner, by the dark, and by water in the bathtub. We categorized children with "marked fears" as those who had more than three marked fears. Thirty-eight percent of the children increased in marked fears, and only 7 percent decreased. Marked ritualistic behavior also tended to increase between the first interview and the 8-month visits. Bedtime, bathtime, and mealtime rituals were particularly strong, as were rituals for saying goodbye to parents. One child would not go to sleep unless all his teddies had been kissed, his mother had kissed him between each bar of the cot, and the door was left open at a specific angle. Another insisted at meals that her mother put her food in a certain dish, that each member of the family have a particular placemat, and that her mother blow on her food three times. Thirty-five percent of the sample increased in *ritualistic* behavior of this kind, and only 8 percent decreased.

These different kinds of "neurotic" behavior tended to go together: children who were frequently moody and had marked fears tended also to have frequent tantrums and to worry (Table A10.2). As Fig. 10.1 shows, the numbers of children who were described as frequently worrying did not decrease. The mothers had been asked, "Is X a worrier? Does he get anxious about something that might happen, about plans, changes in routine . . . things changed? If he loses something? Does he brood over things, like accidents or monsters?" The children who were described as being anxious in this way would, for instance, constantly refer to incidents that had upset them, would become preoccupied with the possibility that something precious to them would be broken or lost, and they were frequently upset by particular television programs.

MOTHER OF BRUCE S: He's very concerned about losing things, and about me hurting myself. Or about dangers. He "reports" to his dad about me, or to me about his dad, if we've done dangerous things — "naughty things," he calls it.

There was also an increase in dependent behavior by the first children — insisting on their mothers' dressing them, taking them to the toilet, feeding them — between the time when the baby was 8 months and when he was 14 months old.

Since the sample of children we have studied is comparatively small, it is clear that we should be cautious about generalizing these findings. However, our confidence in the *grouping* of problems, the association between the different aspects of so-called neurotic behavior, is increased by the parallel findings of the large-scale study of 3- and 4-year-olds by Richman, Graham, and Stevenson (1982).

We argued earlier that the sudden increase in demanding behavior, sleep problems, and unhappiness at the time of the sibling birth is unlikely to be attributable *solely* to age changes in the children. The decrease in these problems during the eight months following the sibling's birth certainly supports this argument. But how should we interpret the increase in fears, moodiness, worrying, and ritualistic behavior? Is this an age effect, or has the arrival of the sibling contributed to the increase in this type of behavior?

Since we do not have a control group of children followed over this age range without the birth of a sibling, we cannot provide a definite answer. We can, nevertheless, ask whether the incidence of these particular aspects of the children's behavior is related to their relative age within the sample. That is, are the older children more likely to have marked fears, to worry, and to be moody? The answer is that age is not related to the incidence of these behavioral items at any of the four time points of the study.

It is also possible that the age of the children at the time of the sibling birth influenced the likelihood that they would develop particular problems. Again we found no association between the age of the children and the increase or decrease in problems. The only change with age was an improvement in the establishment of toilet training, which was strongly related to age (Table A10.3).

Since the age range of the children in the study was comparatively narrow, we should be very cautious about coming to any general conclusions about the lack of relevance of age to the increase of these problems. This is particularly important since in their large-scale study of the behavior of children followed from 1¾ to 14 years of age Macfarlane, Allen, and Honzik (1954) did find a sharp increase in fears between the ages of 1¾ and 4 years, an increase that peaked at 3 years for the girls and 3½ years for the boys. This evidence suggests that the increase in fears among our 40 children could well have been a developmental change. The Macfarlane study unfortunately does not provide information on worrying or miserable moods, with which we might compare our data.

Whatever the origins of the increase in fearful and miserable behavior, we know from the carefully conducted large-scale study by Richman, Graham, and Stevenson (1982) that "neurotic" behavior—particularly fearful behavior—in 3-year-old and 4-year-old children is associated with a pattern of persisting difficulties over the next five years. In our group of families there was also evidence for the persistence of worrying, fearful, or miserable behavior over the period in which the children were studied. Children who were reported to be frequently miserable at the pregnancy interview were significantly more likely to be still miserable at 14 months than to be *not* miserable. In contrast, children who were described as not frequently miserable at the pregnancy interview were equally likely to be similarly described at the 14-month interview or to have become miserable by 14 months. (Table A10.4).

Similarly, children who were notably fearful at the first interview were significantly more likely to be described as fearful at the 14-month interview than to be described as not suffering from marked fears. But children who were *not* reported to have marked fears at the first interview were equally likely to be similarly described at the 14-month interview or to be reported to suffer from marked fears.

The persistence of these aspects of mildly anxious or moody behavior over time can be expressed another way. The probability that a child who was a nonworrier at the pregnancy interview would have become a worrier by the 14-month interview, was significantly lower than the probability a worrier would remain a worrier. In like manner, the probability that a child who did not have marked fears at the pregnancy interview would have developed marked fears by 14 months was significantly lower than the probability that a fearful child would have remained fearful, and the probability that a child who did not have frequent miserable moods would become a miserable child by the 14-month interview was significantly lower than the probability that a miserable child would remain miserable. Finally, the probability of sleep problems emerging between the pregnancy and 14-month interviews was significantly lower than the probability that a sleep problem would persist (Table A10.4).

In summary, there are two points to be emphasized. The first is that fears, worries, and miserable moods increased over the period from the pregnancy interview to the 14-month interview, with some children who had not been so described at the pregnancy interview becoming miserable, fearful, or worrying, and some who had been mildly fearful or worried increasing in the frequency or intensity with which they showed such behavior. The second point is that individual differences in such behavior persisted: children who were reported to be fearful or miserable at the pregnancy interview were significantly more likely to continue to be so described than to "improve," whereas children who had not been fearful or miserable or worriers were equally likely to develop fears or worries or to remain free from such anxieties. It is important that we understand the degree to which the increase or persistence of this kind of behavior is associated with

temperamental differences between children, with differences
in patterns of family interaction, with sex differences, or with
the reaction to the birth of the sibling. It is to these issues we
turn next.

Temperamental Differences

Differences between the children in temperamental characteristics were associated with the persistence and with the increase
of the neurotic aspects of behavior between the first interview
and the 8-month interview. Children who had been described
by their mothers in the pregnancy interview as negative in
mood and intense in emotional reaction were more likely to
have increased in fears, worries, and ritualistic behavior
(Table A10.5). Thus, by the time the baby was 8 months old,
there were strong links between the children's temperamental
assessment before the sibling birth and the incidence of a
variety of problems—not only worries, fears, miserable
moods, and rituals, but sleep problems and feeding problems
too (Table A10.6). The pattern of association showed that
children rated as high in intensity on the first visit were at the
8-month visit more likely to use comfort objects, have marked
intense fears, worry frequently, and show marked ritualistic
behavior. Children described as negative in mood were more
likely to have sleep problems. Those who had been withdrawn were now less likely to have tantrums than the rest of
the sample. The "unmalleable" children were more likely to
have feeding problems and to demand more attention.

The First Child's Reaction to the Birth

Analysis of the different reactions of the firstborn children to
the arrival of the sibling showed that children who had increased in withdrawal at the time of the baby's arrival were
more likely to have sleeping difficulties at the 8-month interview. Fears, rituals, and frequent use of comfort objects were

also more common 14 months later among children who had reacted by becoming more tearful (Table A10.7). This evidence suggests that the events surrounding the birth were influencing the increase in unhappiness over the year following the sibling's birth.

Frequent worrying was more commonly reported at the 14-month interview for those children who had become increasingly withdrawn or more clinging at the birth of the sibling, and miserable moods and tantrums were more common among the children who had reacted to the birth by becoming increasingly negative toward their mothers. These changes had taken place between the first interview and the 8-month interview. However, the fact that these children were not likely to have become even more worried, fearful, or ritualistic between the 8-month and the 14-month interviews lends some support to the argument that it was the *arrival of the baby* between the first and the 8-month interviews that contributed to the increase in neurotic behavior in these children.

Affection for Mother and Father

Not only did the first children become in many ways less difficult for the parents by the time the baby was 8 months old, but many of them were also seen by their mothers as having become more affectionate toward their mother and, particularly, toward their father (Fig. 10.2). The change was often described by the mothers as an increased wish for cuddling:

> MOTHER OF PATRICIA R: She never did want cuddling . . . Now she does; she's become more interested in people, more affectionate to me, and most of all to her daddy . . . It's because of Sean.

> MOTHER OF LAURA W: Recently she likes a lot of cuddling — the last four months. It's quite new.

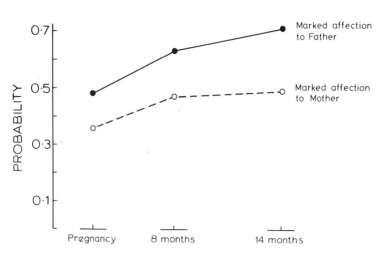

Figure 10.2   Probability of first child showing marked affection to parents.

The increase in this marked expression of affection for both parents between the first interview and the later visits was significant (Table A10.1). Does it represent a developmental change, a change that is related to the increasing age of the children? There are no epidemiological data on children followed between 2 and 4 years of age, with which our findings can be compared. But it is striking that at no point in the study was the demonstration of marked affection for either parent related to the age of the child, nor was the *increase* in affection related to age.

Individual differences in this expression of affection were, on the other hand, related to temperamental differences between the children (Table A10.6). Children described as intense in emotional response were by 8 months significantly more likely to be markedly affectionate to the mother, and there was a tendency for them to be more affectionate to the father. Individual differences in the expression of affection were also related to the way in which the first child had reacted to the birth of the second. Children who had reacted by an increase in withdrawal behavior were more likely to express marked affection to the father at 8 months.

We should not assume that the changes in the children's expression of affection for their parents were unrelated to their parents' behavior toward them. It was obvious from the interviews that many of the fathers in the study became increasingly interested in their firstborn children between the first and the 14-month interviews. The mothers often attributed this change to the child's growing up—to an interest in *children* as opposed to *babies*.

> He prefers older children. He's more of a *child-lover* than a *baby-lover*.

> He isn't really interested in babies; more interested as they grow up.

In 53 percent of the families the mothers thought that the elder child's growing up had made a difference in how involved and interested the father felt in the child. And in 40 percent of the families the mothers said that the father now unquestionably spent more time with the older child.

> There's definitely a difference now. He enjoys her coming with him fishing or to the garage. He *makes* more time to be with her now.

It is also possible that the firstborn child's increased expression of affection and wish for cuddling was a response to the parent's interest in and involvement with the baby sibling. The importance of this *immediate* reaction to the interaction between parent and baby as an influence on the relationship between mother and firstborn child was explored in Chapter 9. Here we wish to emphasize four points about the fathers. The first is that the majority of them—71 percent—were reported to be interested in the baby sibling. When the baby was 8 months old, 34 percent were said to be very interested and involved, and a further 37 percent were reported to show quite a bit of interest. The second point is that when father and secondborn were playing together, very few of the first children ignored the interaction. The third point concerns jealousy. Specifically, overt jealousy of the baby was more often apparent when the *father* interacted with the baby than when the mother was involved. And the fourth point is that the fathers were, in a number of families, seen by their wives as rather insensitive to the first child when they were involved with the baby. Several mothers commented that they had to point out to the father that the first child was particularly upset when the father played with the baby, and that the father apparently just did not notice this reaction.

It was common, then, for the children to express particularly strong affection for their fathers in the year following the sibling's birth, and to react very noticeably when the father played with the sibling. These emotional responses were also evident in the children's reaction when their fathers expressed anger or irritation with them. Many children in the study (58 percent at the 14-month interview) were far more upset if the father was angry with them than if the mother lost her temper, and they were far more compliant with the father than with the mother. The descriptions the mothers gave of these reactions were strikingly similiar:

MOTHER OF VIRGINIA L: Her father doesn't have to smack. If he just speaks to her, she'll do what he says. She's very upset if he's cross.

MOTHER OF WARREN D: His father only has to *speak*. I threaten, and he ignores me.

MOTHER OF RUSSELL S: He doesn't have to do more than raise his voice. I shout and they take no notice.

MOTHER OF EVE D: She's less tearful when I shout than when her father does. He never smacks, or very rarely. Just has to say "don't do it."

MOTHER OF SUSAN S: Sometimes he'll shout. She gets very upset. Not if *I* shout.

This compliance was not related to the relative patience of the two parents (the families were equally divided into those where the mother thought the father was *more* patient than she was and those where the father was considered less patient). Yet it certainly was reflected in a difference in the frequency with which the two parents were driven to spank the children. At each time point in the study the mother was far more likely to be the parent who punished (Table A10.8).

The differences in emotional reaction to mother and to father could be interpreted in a variety of ways. They could, for instance, be seen simply as a response to the greater familiarity of the mother. Since most of the mothers spent all day every day with their children, their anger and their pleasure, their punishments and their demonstrations of affection were routine everyday experiences for the children. Most of the fathers, on the other hand, were not able to spend much time with their children. Not only was the time when they were at home often *different* for the children, but many fathers took their first children off with them—to work, to fish, to visit grandparents. To be with the father was, in many families, to do exciting things, to do different things, and, often, it was to be away from the sibling. More elaborate psychoanalytic interpretations of the differences in the children's responses to their fathers and their mothers could of course be suggested. What is clear from the findings is that the relationship with the father was a powerful, growing one, which in many families could provide emotional support for the children. And because it was so important, it was also a relationship in which the child was particularly vulnerable.

Evidence from the Observations

These results have shown that some of the changes in the
children's behavior following the sibling's birth were comparatively short-lived, but that many children continued to be
unhappy, fearful, or worried. How well does this picture,
from the mothers' descriptions of the children, agree with our
direct observations? For many of the problems — such as sleeping difficulties, or fearful responses to specific TV programs — we, as observers visiting the home during the day,
simply did not have enough information to be able to make
useful and systematic comparisons. However, we were able to
examine the time the children spent using comfort objects,
wandering aimlessly, or sitting without playing or focusing on
any activity during the observations. We compared the frequency of these items in the group of children who were
described as having increased in miserable moods, and in
those reported to have increased in marked fears, with the rest
of the sample. The results showed that there were significant
differences between the groups (A10.9). The children who
were reported to have *increased* in marked fears had increased
the time during which they used comfort objects, and had not
decreased the time spent in aimless wandering or sitting
without playing. The rest of the sample had *decreased* the
time during which they used comfort objects, wandered
aimlessly, or sat without playing.

Further evidence of the reliability of the mothers' replies to
interview questions about the children's behavior came in the
agreement between (*a*) their reports of frequency of punish-
ment and the observed confrontation between mother and
child, and (*b*) their reports of the frequency with which they
turned the child's activity to a game, and the observed frequency of joint play and highlighting suggestions.

Change in Interaction between Child and Mother

Our observations of the children before and after the birth
had shown that there were very dramatic changes also in the

interaction between child and mother — with increased confrontation and decreased joint play and maternal attentiveness. How persistent were these changes?

Figure 10.3 shows that the dramatic increase in confrontation between mother and child after the birth did not continue over the following 14 months. However, the levels of joint play and maternal attention, which had dropped immediately after the sibling birth, did not rise again. In fact, the frequency of highlighting suggestions — where the mother commented in a "child-centered" and supportive way on what the child was doing or playing with — dropped significantly from the postbirth observations to the 14-month observations (from 5.7 to 3.9 per 1000 10-second units; not shown on Fig. 10.3).

There were interesting changes in the *looking* behavior of mother and child (Fig. 10.4). At the observations before the sibling birth very few of the child's glances at the mother went unreturned. Mothers seemed to catch their children's glances

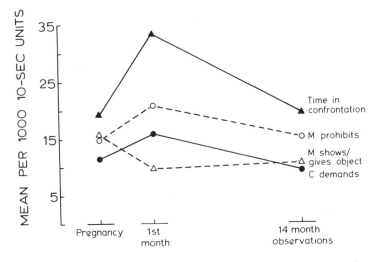

Figure 10.3 Changes over time in interaction between mother and firstborn.

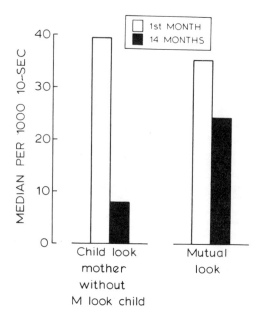

Figure 10.4 Changes over time in the way mother and firstborn look at each other.

with great sensitivity. At the observations immediately following the sibling birth, this had changed: the children now frequently looked at their mothers *without* the mothers' returning the glance. By the 14-month observations the frequency of these unreturned glances was again very low. But the frequency of mutual looks between mother and child – where the mother did catch the child's glance, and vice versa – was also significantly lower. It is possible that this general decrease in the frequency of mutual gaze between mother and child reflects the attention that by 14 months both mother and child paid to the sibling. It is also possible that mother and child kept contact, to an increasing extent, by talking without necessarily looking at each other.

While the interaction between child and mother showed these general changes over the 14 months following the sibling birth, the relative differences *between* the families remained very stable, at least for some aspects of the interaction. The families where there had been relatively frequent play and maternal attention before the sibling's birth were still the families in which there was most frequent play at 14 months, and the families where there had been most confrontation and prohibition were still the families with the most conflict (Table A10.10). In contrast, some of the measures of child behavior, such as the frequency of wandering aimlessly or sitting without playing, showed no consistency over the period of study. Others, such as the frequency of fussing and verbal demands, showed consistency from the observations made *before* the sibling birth to the 14-month observations, rather than from the observations made in the three weeks following the sibling birth. The marked alterations in these particular aspects of the children's behavior immediately after the sibling birth seem to reflect *transient* changes — differences between the children — which did not continue.

The Mothers' Point of View

MOTHER OF HARVEY AND RONNIE M: This is a pretty good patch [time]. I used to get stroppy [cross] when I had so much to do. I felt as though I wasn't giving Harvey enough attention, I was so busy when I first had Ronnie. I seemed always to be doing Ronnie. Now Harvey's got play school and his friends, and Ronnie doesn't need me so much. I feel as though I've got some of my independence back. I can get out more. On the bus. My mother-in-law meets me at the bus station and we look round the shops. When they're first born, you can't do nothing. I wasn't, you know, right on the edge. But looking back on it, I'm a lot happier now.

For this mother, as for several others, life was much less strained when the baby was 14 months old. Many found that it was easier to get out, and to enjoy both the children.

> MOTHER OF IAN AND GRAHAM W: I think things are a lot better now. Sometimes things get on top of me, but not very often. I can overcome it myself. I do go out quite a bit. I used to think I *must* get it all done—now I think, "well, just blow it," if it isn't done. Since having Graham—from having the two of them—I feel more content somehow.

For other mothers the stage when the baby was 14 months old was particularly difficult. They had the strain of coping with a mobile and demanding baby, frequent strife between the siblings, and often the exhaustion from broken nights and a miserable or difficult 3-year-old. Several mothers commented on how near the edge they felt:

> MOTHER OF VIRGINIA L: I'm very tired. The baby wakes two or three times a night, and then they are both awake at 5:30. Some days I get very edgy. I have to watch myself.

> MOTHER OF JUDY B: It's the baby who drives me mad. She screams when she can't get her own way . . . and I get so tired with the broken nights, and my husband's away.

Others had felt very desperate earlier in the year:

> MOTHER OF DEREK AND CYNTHIA J: When she was about 6 months daily I felt over the top. I stayed in bed because I felt I might hit her.

During the interviews the mothers talked about how often they felt really irritated with the first child—snappy and liable to fly off the handle over quite trivial incidents. The probability that the mothers would report feeling extremely irritable and snappy with the child *every day* did not change over the period of study for the sample as a whole, although there was a marginally significant increase between the first interview and the time when the baby was 8 months old. At least the extreme exhaustion and depression felt by several mothers in the first three weeks after the baby was born did not continue very long for most of these mothers.

In one respect, the figures are encouraging. The probability that a mother who had reported feeling extremely exhausted and depressed in the first three weeks after the baby was born would describe feeling extremely irritated every day with the first child at 8 months was only 0.28. On the other hand, the probability that a mother would describe this frequent irritation with the first child at 8 months if she had *also* been frequently irritated at the first interview was 0.50, a difference in probabilities that is significant. In another respect, of course, the figures are disheartening, since they reflect a persisting pattern of extreme maternal irritation in some families. The effects on women's mental health of living under difficult financial or social conditions with several small children has been graphically documented by the studies of Brown and Harris (1978). Their results leave us in no doubt about the grave vulnerability of women in this situation.

The group figures on the probabilities of frequent irritation do mask some marked changes experienced by several mothers, changes illustrated by the quotations given earlier. The mothers were asked at the interviews at 8 months and at 14 months which period they had found the most trying, and the answers revealed a variety of patterns. For 29 percent of the mothers, the early weeks after the sibling was born were the worst. Fourteen percent found the 6- to 8-month period particularly trying:

MOTHER OF SUE AND RONNIE H: I was so tired . . . Ronnie was waking five or six times a night. I was *very* miserable. I smacked Sue all the time. I was screaming and shouting at her. *He's* very easy in the day, very undemanding. Quite unlike her. If he'd been like her, I'd be in hospital.

For 37 percent of the mothers, the period when the baby was between 9 and 14 months old was the most trying.

It was clear from the interviews that the mothers attributed their exhaustion and irritation to a variety of factors. Very few of them referred to the elder child's behavior as the sole cause. For most who described themselves as on the edge, it was a combination of difficulties: illness or unemployment of the husband, loneliness, being housebound, in *addition* to broken nights and difficult and demanding children. (It is worth noting that a smaller proportion of the fathers were reported to have helped with the first child at mealtimes and bathtimes, or with dressing or getting up at night, at 14 months than at the first visits. However, the number of fathers who were reported to have played with the child remained high, and the number who had looked at books with the firstborn had increased. There was no particular change in the proportion of fathers who had gone to the store, cleaned the house, cooked, or helped with the laundry.)

Given the combination of difficulties that many mothers described, it is perhaps not surprising that our simple measures of "extreme tiredness/depression" or "frequency of irritation" were not linked in any unambiguous way to the temperamental differences between the children, or to their reaction to the birth of the sibling. The only links found were that mothers whose children had reacted to the birth by becoming very tearful reported being more frequently irritated when the baby was 8 months old than the rest of the sample, and those whose children had reacted by withdrawing were less frequently irritated (Table A10.11).

The frequency with which mothers reported punishing or spanking the children also did not show any simple links with the children's temperament or reaction, or with their age or sex, though mothers whose children were withdrawn reported spanking their children less frequently. (While such reports might be regarded as unreliable, we found good agreement between the frequency with which mothers reported spanking and the observed confrontations between mother and child during our visits.)

Comment

A number of themes run through these findings — themes that have implications for both psychologists and parents. One concerns our ignorance about developmental changes in many aspects of children's emotional behavior. There is so little solid, systematic information about the development and the prevalence of fears and anxieties, or about changes in children's affectionate behavior toward their parents, over the second, third, and fourth years of life that we cannot come to any real conclusions about how much the birth of a sibling has contributed to the changes in the children we have studied. What we do know from the large-scale longitudinal studies of Richman, Graham, and Stevenson (1982) is that anxious and fearful behavior in 3-year-olds is likely to persist over several years, and that it should certainly be the subject of further study. The results reported here suggest that temperamental differences between children assessed before the sibling's birth are systematically associated with the increase and persistence of these problems, and this second theme of the significance of temperamental differences in relation to the behavior of both child and parent recurs again and again. *Consistency* of differences among families is a third theme, apparent in the observations of interaction at each point in the study. And these consistent differences highlight the transiency of the changes in some aspects of the children's behavior at the time of the sibling's birth — the increase in demanding and fussing, and in naughtiness and sleep problems. It is helpful for parents to know how short-lived such problems are, and this encouragement is surely needed, since a fourth theme which must be emphasized is the *stress* that confronts many parents (many mothers in particular) over the year following the sibling's birth. It is all too clear that many mothers desperately need support and help, and opportunities to escape their domestic circumstances, and that such help and escape are available to very few.

eleven

Implications for Parents, Implications for Psychologists

Any analysis of the early months or years of children's lives must end with a query about the long-term significance of the patterns that it has traced. Our study ended with the babies just beginning to use language, showing themselves as powerful personalities, and taking an increasingly dominant part in family life; for the firstborn children, major changes in their lives were immediately ahead, with the beginning of school. How would these developments in the siblings' lives affect their relationship with each other? Would the marked differences in the quality of their relationship apparent during the first year persist over the next few years? We are fortunate that a colleague, Robin Stillwell-Barnes, carrying out a study of friendship and family relationships, was interested in talking to our children when they reached 6 years of age, and that the families generously agreed to participate in one further set of interviews. We are indebted to Stillwell-Barnes for giving us permission to describe briefly some of her findings. At the time of this writing, only 19 of the 40 children have reached 6 years of age, so the long-term patterns we are going to summarize must be viewed as preliminary. Although we must regard these early results with caution, it is important to give their broad outlines here. There is such striking continuity with the results from our own study that the findings on the first year of the sibling relationship are significantly reinforced.

Three Years Later

How were the 6-year-olds getting on with their younger siblings, now aged between 42 and 60 months? What kinds of activities did they enjoy together, and how did their mothers view the relationship? The first point to be stressed once again is that there were wide individual differences in the quality of the relationship between the siblings, whether the assessment was made by the mothers or reconstructed from the 6-year-olds' own comments.

Some of the children emphasized the pleasures of playing with the sibling—formal games, wildly active games, or fantasy games. Sometimes the fantasy games reached great elaboration; the enjoyment was clearly shared by both children, and understood to be shared. Here are two examples of replies to the interviewer's question "What do you really enjoy doing with your sister/brother?"

> JANE AND ROBERT P: Playing flying objects—play like we have this toy telephone. I have to be on the phone and when there's a call I tell him if it's important and if somebody wants to talk to him, and I have to think about letters doing them—I'm the secretary and he's the FO boss, boss of FO. We pretend we saw the great big spider that fits through the telephone and it came in a flying saucer, and we ring [call up] all the police and all the people who have supplies to kill him, and we tell them not to kill it 'cause it's good army man. Action Man and Cindy—he's got two Action Man and one Army Man with three suits; I have two dolls. My Cindy's the oldest and the other girl was born by another mother, but that mother died and her father is the army, one of the army men you see, and when we have camp she cooks—once she made a special omelet with baked beans inside it. Explorers—we get . . . dig and try to find things. I was digging once and found a dog tooth. He likes and I like, we both like the same.

JUDY AND CAROLE B: We play operationing. It's a game what we play with our doll we've got; it really has a bad leg, it flops down — we get things and we pretend we're operating [on] it — I like and so does she.

Several of the children (11 of the 19), however, stressed their dislike of the sibling's aggression and commented on the frequency of fights:

SANDRA AND MARIE M: I don't like her; she's horrible, she is, 'cause uhm hits, disgusting; she shouts at me, hits me, kicks me, hits me. [Does she do it much?] She doesn't do anything else.

DUNCAN AND ROBBIE K: I just don't like him, I don't know why. He fights me and I don't like it.

LAURA AND CALLUM W (pointing at bite she received from her younger brother): He does that a lot, quite a lot pinching me, he does that all over my face. I pull most of the scabs off.

The children were often quite explicit about what they themselves did that gave the sibling pleasure or pain.

DIANNE AND MARION H:
O: What do you do that really pleases your sister?
C: Tickling her — when I make up funny words or songs, like "Greedy monkeys eat greedy no greedy . . . monkeys . . . "Oh, I CAN'T remember — or "Dirty donkeys dance with dirty dogs," I think. It makes her giggle and I like her giggling, it keeps her quiet for a few minutes. When I'm doing something silly with her like carrying her like a baby if I can, but I always put her back down on a chair or settee [sofa], but she always giggles.

Sally and Trevor C:
C: I go and get his teddy for him 'cause he doesn't like upstairs on his own. Once he lost his sweets [candy] and I gave him one of mine, and when he found his he gave me one to pay me back.
O: Does it happen much?
C: A lot.

Three replies to the question "What do you do that really annoys your brother?":

Duncan and Robin K: When I fight him and he gets told off. I fight him and he fights me and he gets me down. He's a better fighter than me—he gets told off—I'm the one that *should* get told off, but I'm not.

Russell and Trish S: Tease her—get something and hang it from the ceiling and she tells Mum. [Does it happen much?] Yeah, she gets cross a lot.

Sandra and Marcie H: Hit her, hit her, kick her, tell her to shut up, pinch her. [Does it happen much?] A little.

The individual differences from family to family were evident, too, in the mothers' descriptions of the children. Some of the mothers described a relationship full of harmony and love, while others reported frequent aggression and fighting. "It's not very good really—at the moment its very *bad* . . . Last week I was pulling my hair out!!" And just as at the earlier visits, many mothers stressed the *ambivalence* of the relationship. "It comes down to love and hate, doesn't it? Some days they play so well, then other days . . . fighting about nothing at all, they make it into such a big thing."

The second point to be emphasized is that the *differences* between siblings pairs in these qualities showed strong continuity with our earlier findings. Stillwell-Barnes asked the mothers about specific aspects of the relationship — for instance, the first child's response to sharing his things with the sibling, and his response when the younger child hurt himself or was in real distress. From the child's own comments about the sibling when he was interviewed, she derived a ratio score of positive to negative comments. A rating of the sibling relationship was also derived from the mother's description of the children. The differences between the sibling pairs on each of these scores were clearly related to the differences we had found three years earlier, at the 14-month visits. Children who had shown very frequent friendly behavior to their siblings during the 14-month observations, and a high proportion of friendly rather than hostile behavior, were most likely to share willingly and happily at 6 years ($rs = 0.48$, $p < 0.05$.) Children who at 6 years responded with concern when their younger sibling was hurt had, during the observations three years earlier, made more friendly social approaches ($rs = 0.52$, $p < 0.05$), and fewer hostile approaches, to their siblings than children who did not show concern ($rs = 0.46$, $p < 0.05$). And the children who at 6 years made the largest proportion of positive comments about their sibling had been observed to make the highest proportion of friendly approaches to their sibling three years before ($rs = 0.49$, $p < 0.05$). The mothers' ratings of the sibling relationship also showed positive correlations with the observed friendly behavior of the child to the sibling at the 14-month visits ($rs = 0.40$, $p < 0.10$).

It was striking that continuity was also evident between the immediate reaction of the firstborn to the new baby sibling and his behavior at the age of 6 years. Children who had shown marked friendly interest and concern for the new baby in the first three weeks after the birth were significantly more likely to respond with concern at the 6-year visits if the younger was hurt or distressed ($rs = 0.42$, $p < 0.05$). This consistency from the earlier to the later measures was evident too when the sibling relationship in same-sex and different-sex pairs was compared. At the 6-year interview firstborn children in same-sex pairs made relatively more friendly comments about their sibling than the firstborn in different-sex pairs (a difference significant at the 5-percent level). As in the earlier study, differences in the quality of the sibling relationship were not linked to the age gap between the siblings.

What is so striking about these consistencies in the differences between sibling pairs is not simply that they span a three- to four-year interval, but that this interval involves major developmental changes in both children. The *content* of the interaction between a 6-year-old and his 4-year-old sibling, playing elaborate rule-governed and formal games such as snakes and ladders, or disputing the responsibility for "disturbance of the peace," was so totally different from the games and fights of the 2- or 3-year-old with his baby sibling. Yet the affective quality remained, for our small sample, remarkably consistent.

Developmental Issues

In following our 40 children over a period of great change in their lives, we have touched on many issues of importance for psychologists and for parents. Some of these are questions to which we can begin to suggest answers, some are questions that remain difficult to resolve. Which issues are of particular significance, theoretically and practically?

Emotional Experience and Developmental Change

Our observations of the children throughout the study have serious implications for an understanding of the relation between social and emotional experience and developmental change. They document not only the emotional impact on the first child of the arrival of the baby, and the change in patterns of family interaction that follow it, but also the emotional quality of the sibling relationship—a relationship in which pleasure, affection, hostility, aggression, jealousy, rivalry, and frustration are freely and frequently expressed. They document the salience for each child of the interaction between parent and sibling; the sensitivity with which the child assesses and reacts to the interaction of the others in his family, and the frequency and the intensity of interaction between the siblings themselves—imitation, play, combat, aid, frustration, attention, and amusement. What happens between the siblings and between the mother and the other child really *matters* to the firstborn. It is not a situation of emotional neutrality, but a situation in which the child is emotionally ready to attend to, to respond to, and, we would argue, to learn about the other persons in his world. Although we were recording the routine events of family life, to the first children these were events of major affective significance. Compare the point succinctly made by Chekhov in a letter to a friend justifying his presentation of "ordinary life" events on the stage: "People eat their dinner, just eat their dinner, and all the time their happiness is being established or their lives are being broken up" (Hingley 1966, p. 233).

At issue are two questions: First, is it possible or likely that the emotional upheaval for the elder child contributes in an important way to the developmental advances that follow the birth of the sibling? Second, what part does social interaction, more broadly considered, play in changing the first child's conception of himself and of other people during the infancy of the sibling?

On the first question, it is remarkable how often in the discussion of the relationship between affect and cognition affect is treated merely as the outward expression of a cognitive change. Despite the frequent acknowledgment that affect and cognition are inseparably linked (Freud 1938; Piaget and Inhelder 1969), developmental changes in social behavior have in fact been discussed by psychologists primarily in terms of the cognitive changes presumed to underlie them. These changes in social behavior are seen as essentially the *consequences* of cognitive change. Thus changes in an infant's behavior toward his mother over the first year are discussed in terms of the child's changing powers of memory and recall. Much less attention is paid — at least by developmental psychologists — to the possibility that affective experience may shape behavior.

Yet there is a powerful case to be made for the importance of affective experience in developmental change. In the process of differentiation of self and other, for instance, as Izard has cogently argued, the emotions of shyness and anger may well play a crucial part.

The heightened consciousness of self that occurs in shame has motivational value for developing self-identity and self-esteem. Eventually, shame anticipation motivates the development of skills and competences that increase self-worth and decrease the likelihood of experiencing shame . . . Between 4 and 6 months, the infant is capable of experiencing and expressing anger and the anger experience motivates efforts to deal with frustrating restraints and barriers. Thus anger increases the infant's opportunities to sense self-as-causal-agent and hence to experience self as separate, distinct, and capable. (1977, pp. 398–399)

It is plausible that the emotional experiences that the child undergoes after the sibling is born do contribute, in the ways Izard suggests, to a heightened awareness of the distinction between self and other and to the developmental changes that the mothers described to us.

Social Interaction and Developmental Change

The second question concerned the relation between social interaction and developmental change. Here, we should like to suggest first, the social situation we were studying is a context in which the child is particularly likely to *show* that he knows about people, and second, it is a context in which he is particularly likely to *learn* about people.

The observations of the siblings, and the comments of the firstborn to us and to their mothers, have demonstrated a wider knowledge of and interest in other people than previous studies have attributed to children of this age. The discrepancy between the capabilities that the child demonstrates in his relationships at home and those attributable to him in more "public" situations suggests that if we study children only in these public domains we may greatly underestimate their competence. The evidence from the child's conversations with the mother shows how the child's competence is realized within a supporting relationship. And the relationship with the sibling has a special significance here. The very aspects of the sibling relationship that make it so difficult to characterize in simple dimensions demonstrate the wide range of capabilities that even 2-year-olds possess. They can and do act as comforters and teachers, as devious and manipulative bullies, or as sensitive companions who can enter the play world of the other.

Concerning the role of social interaction in the child's developing powers of understanding, we obviously cannot prove that the child is learning in the particular situations we have studied, since we have not experimentally manipulated the situation and have no precise systematic indexes of "understanding." All we wish to do is to emphasize the importance of the observed interactions as *potential* learning situations, and draw attention to some parallels between those interactions and the experiments on cognitive change carried out by Doise and Mugny (1981) and their colleagues in Geneva.

There are in fact very few clear demonstrations of where or when children do learn anything of real significance to them. There are also very few studies that take real account of the role of social interaction or emotional experience in development, despite current interest in Vygotsky's (1977) proposal that social interaction plays a crucial role in developmental change. The studies by Doise and his coworkers provide a dramatic exception, an exception that is particularly important for our study, since their experiments suggest that social interaction can be crucially important in cognitive advance. The Genevan studies demonstrate that children can make dramatic advances in their ability to solve Piagetian problems when they face these tasks *with another child*, even if that child is less advanced intellectually. In interpreting their findings they draw on Vygotsky's proposals, arguing that the social interaction involved in their experiments in some way presents the child with a "cognitive conflict" between his own understanding of the problem and that of the other child. They suggest that it is the recognition and the resolution of this conflict that leads to greater understanding of the cognitive problem. Although our own study focused on children in a very different setting, and was concerned with quite different aspects of behavior, there are important ways in which the studies complement each other.

The Genevan studies show that the interaction between two human understandings, neither of which is of adult power, does in fact facilitate rapid cognitive advance in the face of determinate intellectual problems. This result has been largely interpreted by the Genevans in terms of a cognitive psychology that makes no clear reference to motivation. Its significance within such an essentially "unmotivated" cognitive psychology applies directly to our own context of sibling interaction. But this context, in its turn, through the emphasis on affective considerations that it highlights so dramatically, may well cast doubt on an interpretation of the Genevan results exclusively in terms of a cognitive psychology without reference to motivation. Our observations of the siblings show not only that the opportunities for cognitive advance are available, but that the degree of motivation for cognitive advance is of a very distinctive and intense kind. They show how important and how *interesting* the behavior of the other child is to each of the siblings. This intense interest in the other child may well be significant in explaining the particular salience of the situation used in the Genevan studies, and the dramatic nature of the cognitive changes documented. Margaret Donaldson and her colleagues have emphasized that the success with which a child tackles a cognitive task depends on the social relevance of the task for the child, and their Edinburgh experiments clearly demonstrate the force of this argument (Donaldson 1978).

Our findings show further that rapid developmental changes can and do take place in a real-life situation, very unlike the laboratory setting of the Genevan experiments. No doubts can be expressed about the "ecological validity" of the homes in which our children took their "great leap forward."

Doise and his colleagues propose that it is when a child is just on the *edge* of a developmental advance — at the "point of elaboration of a notion" — that social interaction can be most important in leading to developmental change. Now our children of 2 and 3 years old were at a stage of *beginning* to understand the dimensions and categorizations of self and other, the social rules and the norms of their world. When the sibling was born there was, as we have seen, a sharp increase in the discussion of self and other; the presence of the sibling meant too that the children were constantly monitoring the interaction between other people who mattered to them. It is at least possible that since our first children were at this particular stage, the changes in the child's "egocentric" world did indeed contribute directly to developmental changes in the children's behavior. At present this hypothesis can be only speculative, but the issue is important enough to merit further, more precise study.

Implications for Research

In many ways our study must be regarded as a pilot study. It has suggested many causal relationships that it cannot substantiate and raised many questions that it cannot address in depth. It remains a small study of a particular sample, and even its most robust findings require replication on a different sample. In what particular directions does it imply that further research would be most profitable?

One direction that we have already discussed in general terms is the theoretically and practically very complex issue of the relation between affective and cognitive development. A second direction, more manageable and of great practical importance, concerns individual differences in the vulnerability of children, and their response to environmental change. What implications do our findings on the reaction of the children to the birth of the sibling have for children's responses to other changes in their lives? Are the differences in temperament that we found to be significant also important in predicting the response of children to other potentially stressful events? If our results do have some generality, then they clearly may have clinical importance.

Another issue raised by the study, which certainly needs further investigation, concerns the pattern of connections between the way the mothers talk to their firstborn, and the later behavior of the siblings toward each other. Mothers who discussed the motives, intentions, and feelings of the baby were much more likely to use justification in control situations, to enter the child's world of pretend, and to use language for complex intellectual purposes. We have emphasized that we should not look for simple links between any one aspect of the mothers' speech and later differences in the children. But it is certainly important to examine further these differences in conversational style and their implications for the children's development. It would be particularly worthwhile to investigate, for instance, how much these differences affect the development of children's communication skills and role-taking skills. Light (1978) concluded from his study that the development of these aspects of "social sensitivity" was linked to differences in the symmetry of the relationship between mother and child, and it would be valuable to discover whether the differences in conversational style that we have described in this book are similar to, or parallel, the differences between mothers that Light derived from his interviews.

Yet another issue raised by the study is the development of the child's understanding and categorization of *self*. The comments made by our children, often only 2 years of age, provide intriguing suggestions but not hard evidence. Yet the implications are of central importance for our views on how children see themselves and other people, and the richness of the data certainly suggests that this is a viable subject for research even with such young children.

Our study has also highlighted a number of more circumscribed problems that would surely be important and practical to investigate. One is the issue of quarreling and hostility between siblings, and the role of the parents in minimizing or escalating the conflict. Our results show some intriguing differences between families with boys and families with girls. Mothers of boys were more consistent in their response to the children's negative behavior, and there were differences in the patterns of correlations over time which, if replicated in other studies, are certainly significant. We do not suggest that from our findings on this small sample, which are simply patterns of correlations, one can draw causal inferences about the link between the mothers' response to quarrels and increased aggression between siblings (or vice versa). Still, the results show that this is an issue that matters a good deal to parents and that needs careful research.

Implications for Research Strategies

Perhaps the most important methodological lesson from this study is that it is both crucially important and practically possible to study young children, with their families, in situations of real emotional significance to them. There are several other points, too, that deserve comment.

One is the extent of agreement we found between our direct observations of the children and the descriptions of them given by their mothers in the interviews. There was good accord on temperament ratings, on the first child's behavior toward the sibling in the first three weeks, on both siblings' behavior at 8 and 14 months, and on the description of anxious or unhappy behavior at 14 months. We should not generalize from this agreement in too cavalier a fashion: we certainly cannot assume that the same agreement would have been found if we had been working with questions about the mothers' own behavior, with a different kind of sample, or with interviews conducted in a clinical setting.

A second point is the importance of studying more than just a single dyad within the family—a point highlighted by the findings reported in Chapter 9, which show the complex interconnections between the different relations of mother and siblings.

A third issue concerns the methods of recording and the levels of description during the observations. It became evident during the study that it was extremely important to try to describe different aspects of family interaction at varying levels of detail. The links between the mother-child conversations in the first three weeks after the sibling birth, and the (often nonverbal) behavior of the siblings over the following year, illustrate this point. And neither a description of the children's behavior in global terms of jealousy or affection, nor a description in terms of discrete behavioral acts, could have begun to capture the complexity of the behavior of the siblings toward each other. One lesson we learned too late is that it would have been both useful and practicable to record more details of the affective quality of the sibling interaction on a systematic basis.

Implications for Parents

Books of advice for parents often lay a heavy responsibility on the parents for the jealousy and disturbance in their children: "Nothing can change the fact that a new baby is a threat to a child's security. However, whether his character will be enhanced or warped by the stress or strain of the crisis depends on our wisdom and skill" (Ginott 1969, p. 148). Close (1980) maintains that jealousy is *not* inevitable, but that it comes through the indirect suggestion of others in the family. And the Calladines (1979, p. 28) comment: "When the baby is mobile this is when sibling quarrels usually get under way

. . . how the parent handles all this determines whether or not this becomes a repetitive rivalrous situation." This is a view held by many of those with responsibility for helping families in difficulties (for instance, Einstein and Moss 1967).

To what extent did our findings support this view? There was indeed an association between the quality of the relationship between the parents and their firstborn and the quality of the relationship that developed between the siblings. But is it fair to suggest that parents are primarily responsible for the extent of jealousy and disturbance in the firstborn? Surely not. First, hostility and aggression and disturbed behavior shown by the firstborn children was clearly related to other factors as well as to the relationship with the parents. The sex constellation of the sibling pair and the temperament of the first child were both of major importance; it would be quite unjustified, indeed invidious, to suggest that the expression of jealousy and disturbance depended predominantly on the parents. The temperamental differences we found to be so important are not features of the child's behavior that parents could easily control or change. Any advice to a parent should take very serious account of the particular temperament of the child in question. Indeed, any broad generalization about the consequences of particular patterns of child rearing cannot take sufficient account of these individual differences, as any parent with more than one child well knows.

Secondly, it was in the families where the mother had a particularly close, sensitive, and harmonious relationship with her daughter that the sibling relationship was particularly difficult. It is not at all obvious that the mother should be blamed in this case—blamed for *what* precisely? Surely not for the sensitivity of her relationship with her daughter?

There are some practical lessons for parents from our findings on the reactions of the firstborn to the arrival of the new baby. For instance, it is important to try to minimize the changes in the child's life, and to try to avoid dropping too drastically the level of play and attention the first child has been receiving. For expectant mothers it is important to enlist as much help as possible for the early weeks: it is likely to be a difficult time for both mother and firstborn, and husband, grandparents, and friends should be aware that their support will be very much needed. Many mothers find it helpful to know that the increased naughtiness and demanding behavior are so common, and related in part to the child's temperament, and it is of course encouraging for them to know that these difficulties, the breakdown in toilet training, and the increase in sleeping problems are likely to improve substantially over the first months. It is also valuable to know that a child who becomes very demanding and difficult is not especially likely to get on badly with his brother or sister in later years.

We have learned, furthermore, that the moments in the early weeks when the mother is caring for the new baby are the times when confrontation is particularly likely between mother and firstborn. Mothers should certainly be prepared — ready with distractions for the first child *before* the trouble begins. Spock's view that feeding and bathing are times of particular trouble is supported by the findings of the study; however his view that breast-feeding is particularly traumatic for the first child appears from our evidence to be a trifle romantic. Mothers need not feel that by choosing to breast-feed they are increasing the distress and strain for their first child.

On the issue of whether parents should talk to their first child about the baby, the advice books disagree. While some recommend that the parents keep references to the baby to a minimum, the Calladines (1979, p. 28) specifically recommend: "Talk with your children about each other's needs, if the sibling is a baby, talk with the older one about what babies are like".

Our results certainly support this line of advice. In families where the mothers discussed caring for the baby as a matter of joint responsibility and talked about the baby as a person from the early days, the siblings were particularly friendly over the next year. Most encouraging of all, our findings show that in families where the first child was interested and affectionate toward the baby, the relationship continued to be rewarding, loving, and supportive for both children—not just for the first year, but over the next three years.

And of course the warmth of a close relationship between siblings is a source of strength and love far beyond the early years of childhood. We have been looking in this book at the very beginnings of a relationship that we know—from the writing of poets and novelists rather than from psychologists—can be of immeasurable importance throughout life. What George Eliot, or Tolstoy, or the dying Keats whose sister "walks about my imagination like a ghost" (Keats 1980) show us, with a power no developmental psychologist is ever likely to approach, is the depth and significance of that early relationship. The intensity of the joys and sorrows of the world of brother and sister are perhaps more poignantly captured in *The Mill on the Floss* than in any other work. In recognition of this, and in acknowledgment of all that our own or any comparable study must fail to reveal, we close with George Eliot's Maggie, in misery after having persuaded her brother to chop off her hair:

She sat as helpless and despairing among her black locks as Ajax among the slaughtered sheep. Very trivial, perhaps, this anguish seems to weather-worn mortals who have to think of Christmas bills, dead loves and broken friendships, but it was not less bitter to Maggie—perhaps it was even more bitter—than what we are fond of calling antithetically the real troubles of mature life . . . Every one of such keen moments has left its trace and lives in us still, but such traces have blent themselves irrevocably with the firmer texture of our youth and manhood; and so it comes that we can look on at the troubles of our children with a smiling disbelief in the reality of their pain . . . Surely, if we could recall that early bitterness, and the dim guesses, the strangely perspectiveless conception of life that gave the bitterness its intensity, we should not pooh-pooh the griefs of our children.   (Eliot 1979, p. 122)

Appendixes
References
Index

Appendix A contains the majority of the statistical tables that support the text of Chapters 3 to 10, and the tables are keyed to those chapters. Table A4.10, for instance, is the tenth appendix table for Chapter 4. Unless otherwise stated, N=40. The abbreviations M, F, C, and B (used throughout the tables) stand for Mother, Father, Child (firstborn), and Baby. Significance levels reported are for two-tailed tests:

$$
\begin{array}{rcl}
* & = & p < 0.05 \\
** & = & p < 0.01 \\
*** & = & p < 0.001 \\
\text{n.s.} & = & \text{not significant}
\end{array}
$$

Appendixes B and C discuss the methodology used in the studies and give some statistical notes.

Appendix A

Tables

Table A3.1 Numbers of firstborn children showing behavior changes from pregnancy visit to first-month visit: mothers' reports.

C's behavior	No increase	Slight increase	Moderate increase	Marked increase
Tearful	16	11	10	3
Clinging	17	12	9	2
Withdrawn	29	9	2	–
Demanding	3	13	22	2
Negative to M	9	8	22	1
Regressive	12	15	13	–
Problems related to –				
Sleeping	29	7	3	1
Feeding	37	3	–	–
Toilet training	14	4	5	3

Table A3.2 Numbers of children showing interest in the new baby: mothers' reports.

C's behavior	Absent/ rare	Some	Frequent	Constant
Verbal references and comments	8	20	12	–
Concern when B cries	16	14	9	1
Attempts to help care for B	2	16	21	1
Entertaining of B	18	11	11	–
Affectionate physical interest	10	21	8	1

Table A3.3   Numbers of children showing irritating, hostile, or imitative behavior toward the new baby: mothers' reports.

C's behavior	Never/rarely	Occasionally	Frequently
Irritates B	19	13	8
Is hostile to B	31	6	3
Imitates B	10	15	15

Table A3.4   Association between mother's state and difficulties during first months after birth: interview measures.

Association of M's feeling very tired and/or very tired and depressed with –	Chi-square	df	p level
Less than 6 hours' sleep	6.64	1	0.01
Night interrupted by B's waking frequently	8.42	1	0.01
Some/frequent difficulties with B	2.79	1	0.01
Increases in tearfulness of C	3.21	1	0.06

Table A3.5   Changes in observation measures from pregnancy to first month after birth.

Observation measures (median no. of 10-sec units/1000)	Pregnancy observation	First-month observation	p level (Wilcoxon test)
M helps	9.5	5.5	0.01
M shows	16.0	9.5	0.01
M suggests (highlights)	11.0	8.0	0.05
M prohibits	15.0	21.0	0.01
Mutual look (negative)	10.0	16.0	0.01
Confrontations (M and C)	19.0	34.0	0.04

Table A3.6 Changes in interaction bout measures from pregnancy to first-month observations.

Bout measures		Pregnancy observations	First-month observations	*p* level (Wilcoxon test)
Number of M-initiated bouts of play per 100 10-sec units		11.40	6.40	0.01
Ratio:	$\dfrac{\text{C-initiated bouts of play}}{\text{M-initiated + C-initiated bouts of play}}$	0.48	0.59	0.05
Ratio:	$\dfrac{\text{C-initiated bouts of joint attention}}{\text{M-initiated + C-initiated bouts of joint attention}}$	0.57	0.64	0.10

Table A3.7 Changes in verbal interaction from pregnancy to first-month observations.

Verbal interaction	Pregnancy	First month	*p* level (Wilcoxon test)
Number of control episodes per 100 minutes M present (median)	8.0	10.0	0.04
Number of verbal interactions per 100 minutes M present initiated by −			
Negative comment by M	7.5	12.5	0.02
Unsolicited positive comment by M	10.3	8.0	0.10
New suggestion for C's activity by M	11.3	8.3	0.02
Verbal game or fantasy suggested by M	1.6	0.6	0.03
Comment by C	17.0	37.0	0.01
Percentage of total verbal interactions initiated by M's positive comment	35.1	30.1	0.05

Table A3.8   Spearman rank correlations between measures from pregnancy observations.

	Joint play	Joint attention	M and C close	M shows	M suggests (highlights)	M prohibits	M starts interaction with prohibition
Joint attention	0.23						
M and C close	0.43**	0.62**					
M shows	0.49**	0.26	0.54**				
M suggests (highlights)	0.64**	0.42**	0.43**	0.57**			
M prohibits	−0.32*	0.23	−0.10	−0.38*	−0.30		
M starts interaction with prohibition	−0.56**	−0.41**	−0.35*	−0.36*	−0.53**	0.72**	
Confrontation	−0.31*	0.21	−0.08	−0.39*	−0.32*	0.92**	0.65**
C verbally demands play	0.52**	0.46**	0.56**	−0.21	0.46**	−0.01	−0.26
C initiates play	0.69**	−0.11	0.23	0.33*	0.53**	−0.41*	−0.42**
C wanders	−0.43**	−0.32*	−0.34*	−0.45**	−0.47**	0.32*	0.47**
C sits	−0.26	−0.07	−0.34*	−0.55**	−0.31*	0.32*	0.27
C fusses	−0.28	−0.24	−0.01	−0.15	−0.15	0.30	0.05
C verbally demands object	−0.21	0.25	0.21	0.09	−0.04	−0.15	0.18
C looks at M without M look at C	−0.32*	0.17	0.04	−0.41*	−0.26	0.44*	0.15
M affectionate tactile contact	0.00	0.12	0.02	0.03	0.14	0.24	−0.17
C affectionate tactile contact	0.12	−0.16	−0.13	0.08	0.03	0.05	0.20
M holds C	0.18	0.26	0.24	0.00	0.01	0.12	−0.22

Table A3.8   (*continued*)

Confrontation	C verbally demands play	C initiates play	C wanders	C sits	C fusses	C verbally demands object	C looks at M without M look at C	M affectionate tactile contact	C affectionate tactile contact
−0.00									
−0.30	0.45**								
0.33*	0.39*	−0.55**							
0.39**	−0.18	−0.36*	0.55**						
0.31*	−0.04	−0.20	0.24	0.01					
0.19	0.26	0.50	0.07	0.04	0.33*				
0.51**	0.00	−0.34*	0.49**	0.61**	0.31*	0.41*			
0.28	0.02	−0.05	0.10	0.01	0.17	0.13	0.00		
0.01	0.09	0.36*	−0.10	0.02	−0.20	0.09	−0.22	0.31*	
0.20	0.01	0.04	0.04	0.06	0.23	−0.05	−0.02	0.35*	0.19

Table A3.9   Spearman rank correlations between measures from first-month observations.

	Joint play	Joint attention	M and C close	M shows	M suggests (highlights)	M prohibits	M starts interaction with prohibition
Joint attention	0.27						
M and C close	0.43**	0.50**					
M shows	0.27	0.17	0.19				
M suggests (highlights)	0.48**	0.60**	0.38**	0.47**			
M prohibits	-0.41*	0.10	-0.20	-0.24	-0.11		
M starts interaction with prohibition	-0.46**	-0.41**	-0.35*	0.13	-0.38*	0.58**	
Confrontation	-0.36*	-0.03	-0.26	-0.21	-0.11	0.88**	0.69**
C verbally demands play	0.61**	0.14	0.52**	0.43**	0.48**	-0.18	-0.26
C initiates play	0.70**	0.00	0.28	0.21	0.37*	-0.31*	-0.27
C wanders	0.07	0.12	-0.09	0.24	0.06	0.06	0.07
C sits	-0.24	-0.33*	-0.20	-0.15	-0.30	0.12	0.27
C fusses	0.31*	-0.05	0.19	-0.02	0.09	0.10	-0.05
C verbally demands object	-0.12	0.01	0.02	-0.15	-0.02	0.58**	0.36*
C looks at M without M look at C	-0.14	0.09	-0.20	-0.14	-0.19	0.12	0.15
M affectionate tactile contact	-0.16	0.16	0.26	0.12	0.00	-0.02	-0.17
C affectionate tactile contact	0.07	0.05	0.04	-0.02	-0.06	0.06	0.20
M holds C	0.18	0.38*	0.20	-0.06	0.14	0.08	-0.22

Table A3.9   (continued)

Confrontation	C verbally demands play	C initiates play	C wanders	C sits	C fusses	C verbally demands object	C looks at M without M look at C	M affectionate tactile contact	C affectionate tactile contact
−0.12									
−0.23	0.43*								
0.01	−0.36*	−0.07							
0.15	0.53**	−0.20	0.08						
0.25	0.28	0.09	0.06	0.02					
0.52**	0.15	−0.17	0.13	0.07	0.29				
0.00	−0.34*	−0.15	0.17	0.27	0.21	0.02			
−0.11	−0.04	0.00	0.12	0.12	0.00	0.03	0.13		
0.04	−0.22	−0.18	0.06	0.13	0.09	0.13	0.42**	0.53**	
0.02	−0.25	0.16	0.17	0 23	0.08	−0.10	0.06	0.46**	0.11

Table A3.10   Spearman rank correlations (rs) on measures from pregnancy and first-month observations.

Measure	rs
Joint attention	0.75***
Joint play	0.38*
M suggests (highlights)	0.61***
M shows	0.60***
M prohibits	0.59***
C fusses	0.19
C wanders	0.07
C verbally demands object	0.14
C sits without playing	0.28

Table A3.11   Comparison of interactions of mother and firstborn at times when the mother was involved with the new baby and when she was not involved during first-month observations, and during pregnancy observations.

Observation measures (median/1000 10-sec units)	First-month observations			Pregnancy observations[a]
	M not feeding or caring for B	M feeding B[a]	M holding or caring for B[a]	
Joint attention	113	266***	225***	174*
Joint play	42	31	43	54*
M shows	9	15	9	17**
Mutual look (positive)	61	142**	125**	77
M suggests (highlights)	8	17*	18*	13
Confrontation	25	63**	81***	38
M prohibits	16	25*	34**	13
Mutual look (negative)	8	23*	25**	11

a. Wilcoxon matched-pairs signed-ranks test: comparison with measure when M not feeding or caring for B.

Table A3.12 Incidents of deliberate naughtiness: comparison of different contexts using Wilcoxon test.

	Pregnancy	First month	
Mean number of incidents per 1000 10-sec units in context	4.8	12.8*	
		M not feeding/ caring for B	M feeding B
		4.4	13.7*

Table A3.13 Observed behavior of firstborn after birth of sibling: relation to description in first-month interview.

First-month interview	Observation measures (median per 1000 10-sec units)	N₁ (increase absent or occasional)	N₂ (increase frequent or constant)	p level (Mann-Whitney U test)
Increase in tearfulness $N_1 = 27, N_2 = 13$	Change in C's fussing (pregnancy to 1st month)	-10	20	0.004
Increase in clinging $N_1 = 29, N_2 = 11$	Time held by M (1st month)	10	50	0.04
Increase in demanding $N_1 = 16, N_2 = 23$	C's verbal demands (1st month)	20	30	0.10
Increase in negative behavior to M $N_1 = 16, N_2 = 23$	Change in confrontation (pregnancy to 1st month)	-10	20	0.01
	Change in proportion of control episodes in conversation	10	28	0.03
	Increase in % interactions initiated by M prohibiting	-20	60	0.06

Table A3.14   Observed behavior after birth of sibling: relation to interaction with father before sibling birth.

Observation measures (median per 1000 10-sec units)	Pregnancy interview			Chi-square (4 *df*)	*p* level
	Little time with F (N = 4)	Little time but positive interaction (N = 17)	Little/moderate time but intense interaction (N = 16)		
Joint attention	160	160	260	8.2	0.10
M prohibits	25	10	11	12.5	0.01
Confrontation	30	35	20	7.8	0.10

Table A3.15   Wilcoxon test comparing interaction when mother was feeding the baby and when she was not feeding or caring for baby: breast-feeding and bottle-feeding groups.

Observation measures (median per 1000 10-sec units)	Breast-feeding group		Bottle-feeding group	
	M not feeding/caring for B	M feeding B	M not feeding/caring for B	M feeding B
Confrontation	17	13	25	63**
Incidents of deliberate naughtiness	2.5	4.4	7.4	34*
Joint play	8	13*	2	2

Table A3.16   Comparison of breast-feeding and bottle-feeding groups when mother was feeding the baby.

Observation measures (mean per 1000 10-sec units)	Breast-feeding group	Bottle-feeding group	*p* level (Mann-Whitney U test)
Joint play	13	2	0.05
Confrontation	13	63	0.05
Incidents of deliberate naughtiness	4.4	34	0.05

Table A3.17 Observed behavior after birth of sibling: comparison of home and hospital delivery.

Observation measures (median per 1000 10-sec units)	Home delivery	Hospital delivery	*p* level (Mann-Whitney U test)
Pregnancy:			
Joint play	47	14	0.02
M holds C	50	14	0.01
First month:			
Joint play	24	9	0.02
M holds C	24	9	0.05

Table A4.1 Associations between references to baby's wants and mother's references to joint responsibility for the baby.

	Chi-square	*df*	*p* level
Joint responsibility:			
M talks about B's wants	6.1	1	0.01
C talks about B's wants	11.8	1	0.001
M talks about B's wants:			
C talks about B's wants	9.9	1	0.01

Table A4.2 Association between mother's references to joint responsibility and first child's positive reaction to the baby.

	Mother		*p* level (Mann-Whitney U test)
	No reference to joint responsibility	Reference to joint responsibility	
C's positive reaction	3	5	0.05

Table A4.3   Association between language measures, and references to joint responsibility for baby and to baby's wants (N=20).[a]

Language measure (median number of conversational turns/time M present)	Comments on joint responsibility		Comments on B's needs	
	Yes	No	Yes	No
Complex cognitive use of language	12	4***	13	7*
Explores motives of others	11	4**	11	6*
Pretends	5	4**	5	4*
Justification for control (control with justification/total control)	0.39	0.20**	0.35	0.27

a. Mann-Whitney U test.

Table A4.4   Spearman rank correlations between features of maternal and child language (N = 20).

Mother	Mother			Child		
	Pretends	Explores motives	Justification in control	Complex cognitive use of language	Pretends	Explores motives
Complex cognitive use of language	0.55*	0.75*	0.43	0.69*	0.50*	0.44*
Pretends		0.51*	0.57*	0.60*	0.91*	0.43
Explores motives of others			0.41	0.51*	0.26	0.62*
Justification in control				0.30	0.51*	0.37
C's complex cognitive use of language					0.54*	0.43*
C pretends						0.19

Table A5.1   Relationship between observation and interview data.

Observational variables	Interview variables			Chi-square	p level
	Frequency of fights				
	Infrequent	Sometimes	Daily		
Percentage of C's social approaches that were friendly	82.8	56.0	45.5	6.67	0.04
Frequency of C's friendly social approaches	416	191	170	8.40	0.02
Negative touching (hit, etc.)	0.5	60.0	41.5	6.15	0.05
	Games				
	Most days	Less often			
Percentage of C's social approaches that were friendly	60.5	41.5		4.74	0.03
Frequency of C's friendly social approaches	237	177		3.01	0.08
Games	42.5	21.0		5.43	0.02
C imitates B	34.5	1.5		4.83	0.03
	C tries to comfort B				
	Not seen	Occasional	Frequent		
Percentage of C's social approaches that were friendly	45.0	53.0	70.0	8.12	0.02
Frequency of C's friendly social approaches	126	232	304	6.30	0.04
Joint physical play	1.40	43.0	29.0	5.58	0.06
	B goes to C for comfort				
	Not seen	Occasional			
Percentage of C's social approaches that were friendly	46.5	71.5		9.01	0.003
Frequency of C's friendly social approaches	170	319		8.15	0.004
C imitates B	16.5	53.0		5.90	0.02
	C imitates B				
	None or some	Frequent			
C imitates B	16	51		6.01	0.02

Table A5.2   Attempts to comfort and help baby during first month: numbers of children in three frequency categories (mothers' reports).

Behavior	Rarely	Occasionally	Frequently
C comforts B	14	13	8
C helps B	8	19	12

Table A5.3   Mothers' reports on baby's reactions when parent plays with or cuddles first child (numbers of children).

Parental behavior	B ignores	B joins in (friendly)	B attempts to push away C
M cuddles C	8	12	16
F cuddles C	5	13	14

Table A5.4   Wilcoxon test comparing social approaches of child and baby as percentages and as frequencies (median per 1000 10-sec units).

	Child	Baby	*p* level
Percentage (median) of social approaches that were friendly	55	70	0.001
Frequency of friendly social approaches	20.7	17.7	n.s.
Frequency of hostile social approaches	15.3	10.4	0.001
	Friendly	Hostile	
Frequency of friendly and hostile social approaches by C	20.7	15.3	n.s.
Frequency of friendly and hostile social approaches by B	17.7	10.4	0.001

Table A5.5 Spearman rank correlations between percentage of "mismatch" interactions and types of sibling interactions (expressed as percentage of interactions) and social approaches.

Mismatch interaction	Percentage of interactions						Percentage of social approaches friendly	
	Game	Joint physical play	C helps/ care- takes	C gives B object	Mutually friendly	Mutually hostile	C's	B's
C friendly, B hostile	0.05	−0.25	0.11	0.19	0.00	−0.10	0.36*	−0.09
C hostile, B friendly	−0.36*	−0.18	−0.49*	−0.50**	−0.68***	0.22	−0.78***	−0.18

Table A5.6 Spearman rank correlations between "types" of interaction between siblings.

Interaction	Games	Joint physical play	C gives B object	C helps B	C imitates B	B imitates C
Joint physical play	0.28					
C gives B object	0.29	0.14				
C helps B	0.40*	0.28	0.48**			
C imitates B	0.46**	−0.30	0.33*	0.59***		
B imitates C	0.42*	−0.20	0.35*	0.33*	0.53***	
C prohibits B	−0.18	−0.08	0.10	0.04	0.18	−0.07
C negatively touches B	−0.23	−0.07	−0.58***	−0.30	−0.31*	−0.38*

Table A7.1   Association between use of diminutives, questions, and playful repetitions in child's speech to the sibling, and observed friendly social approaches.[a]

	Diminutives		Questions		Playful repetitions	
	Present	Absent	Present	Absent	Present	Absent
Frequency of C's friendly social approaches to B (median per 1000 10-sec units)	24.1	17.8*	26.6	17.0*	29.8	17.0*

a. Mann-Whitney U test.

Table A7.2   Imitative behavior of siblings at 14 months: same-sex and different-sex pairs.

	Same-sex pairs (N = 18)	Different-sex pairs (N = 22)	p level (Mann-Whitney U test)
C imitates B (median per 1000 10-sec units sibs together)	46	12	<0.01
B imitates C	51	26	<0.10

Table A8.1   Tantrums and worries before the sibling birth, and percentage of sibling interactions at 14-month observations that were mutually friendly.

Tantrums (pregnancy interview)		
None/brief/2 per week (N = 28)	Long/2 per day (N = 11)	p level U test)
25	57	0.05
Worrying (pregnancy interview)		
Never (N = 23)	Sometimes/often (N = 16)	
37	24	0.05

Table A8.2 Spearman rank correlations between first child's interest in new baby and friendly social approaches 14 months later.

Frequency of friendly social approaches	rs	p level
Child	0.33	0.05
Baby	0.39	0.05

Table A8.3 Percentage of mutually friendly and mutually hostile sibling interactions at 14 months: comparison of families where first child showed signs of increased withdrawal at sibling birth with families where first child did not increase in withdrawal.

Sibling interactions	Increase in withdrawal at birth	No increase in withdrawal at birth	p level (Mann-Whitney U test)
Mutually friendly	25	41	0.05
Mutually hostile	30	18	0.01

Table A8.4 Mother's state during first month after birth of sibling, and behavior of first child to sibling at 14-month observation.

Siblings at 14 months	Feels fine/ tired but coping	Very tired and/or depressed	p level (Mann-Whitney U test)
C's frequency of friendly social approaches	13	24	0.05
C gives B object	41	75	0.01
C hits or pushes B	61	19	0.01
Joint physical play	0	32	0.05

Table A8.5 Friendly social approaches by firstborn boy and by sibling at 14 months: comparison of same-sex and different-sex siblings.

Percentage of friendly social approaches of —	Same-sex siblings (N = 10)	Different-sex siblings (N = 11)
Firstborn boy	74	41
Baby	77	63

Table A8.6 Frequency of socially directed behavior by siblings at 8 and 14 months: comparison of same-sex and different-sex siblings.[a]

Socially directed behavior (median per 1000 10-sec units)	Total sample (N = 40)		Same sex (N = 18)		Different sex (N = 22)	
	8 mo	14 mo	8 mo	14 mo	8 mo	14 mo
C:						
Friendly	19	21	23	31*	20	18
Hostile	9	15 *	11	14	7	17*
B:						
Friendly	15	20	18	31*	16	18
Hostile	2	10*	4	9 *	4	10*
Time interacting (% of time siblings together)	12	16	12	21	12	12

a. Mann-Whitney U test comparing 14-month scores in same-sex and different-sex pairs; Wilcoxon T test comparing 8-month and 14-month scores.

Table A9.1 Responses of firstborn children (percentages) to mother-baby interactions at 14 months.

M-B interaction bouts	Median	Range
C protests	23	3–59
C watches	14	0–37
C joins (friendly)	13	0–49
C hostile to B	4	0–24
C ignores	52	22–93

Table A9.2   Percentage of playful and nonplayful mother-baby interactions at 14 months that evoke friendly participation or protest by first child.

| Reaction of C | M-B interaction | | p level (Wilcoxon T test) |
	Playful	Nonplayful	
Joins (friendly)	25	7	0.001
Protests	24	21	n.s.

Table A9.3   Percentage of mother-baby interactions at 14 months that evoke protest or hostility to baby or are ignored: association with first child's reaction to birth of sibling.

Reaction of C	Increase in demands	No increase in demands	p level (Mann-Whitney U test)
Protests	29	16	0.02
Ignores	52	72	0.05
	Imitation of B	No imitation of B	
Is hostile to B	3	9	0.05

Table A9.4   Percentage of mother-baby interactions at 14 months that evoke protest or are ignored by first child: association with temperamental differences.

| Reaction of C | Temperamental trait | | p level (Mann-Whitney U test) |
	Unmalleable and intense (extreme)	Rest of sample	
Protests	32	18	0.05
Ignores	51	64	0.05

Table A9.5 Spearman rank correlations between measures of mother-firstborn interaction at first-month observation and behavior of firstborn toward younger sibling at 14-month observation.

First-month observation: M-C inter-action	C's behavior to B at 14 months					
	Girls (N = 19)		Boys (N = 21)		Total sample (N = 40)	
	Friendly (proportion)	Hostile (frequency)	Friendly (proportion)	Hostile (frequency)	Friendly (proportion)	Hostile (frequency)
Joint play	−0.63**	0.54*	0.03	0.31	−0.18	0.47*
Joint attention	−0.45*	0.32	0.06	−0.13	−0.35*	0.11
Verbal in-teraction initiated by M's prohibition	0.46*	−0.46*	0.00	0.22	0.23	−0.26
Prohibiting incidents	0.38	−0.46*	0.08	−0.08	0.04	0.31

Table A9.6 Spearman rank correlations between measures of mother-firstborn interaction at first-month observation and behavior of second child toward first at 14-month observation.

First-month observation: M-C interaction	B's behavior to C		
	C: girls (N = 19)	C: boys (N = 21)	Total sample (N = 40)
	Friendly (proportion)	Friendly (proportion)	Friendly (proportion)
Joint play	−0.56*	0.06	0.003
Joint attention	−0.08	0.17	−0.18
Verbal inter-action initi-ated by M's prohibition	0.26	0.08	−0.07
Prohibiting incidents	0.31	−0.13	−0.09

Table A9.7 First child's friendly social approaches to sibling at 14 months: association with affection for father before sibling birth.

Friendly approaches (median frequency per 1000 10-sec units)	Affection for F (pregnancy interview)		
	Little or moderate (N = 20)	Marked (N = 16)	*p* level (Mann-Whitney U test)
First child	31	18	0.01
Second child	30	15	0.01
Mutually friendly interactions (percent)	57	22	0.01

Table A9.8 First child's social approaches to sibling at 14 months: association with spanking before sibling birth.

C's approaches (median per 1000 10-sec units)	Frequency of spanking by M (pregnancy interview)		
	Never or once per week	Twice each week	*p* level (Mann-Whitney U test)
Friendly	18	24	0.05
Hostile	22	14	0.05
Mutually friendly interactions (percent)	21	51	0.05

Table A9.9 Kendall's tau partial correlations between measures of mother-firstborn girl interaction, mother-baby interaction, and sibling social approaches at 14 months.

x	=	M-firstborn girl joint play (first-month observations)
y	=	Firstborn girl's hostile social approach to B (14-month observations)
z	=	M-B playful interactions (14-month observations)

$\tau\, xy = -0.44^{**}$ $\tau\, xy.z = -0.34^{**}$

Table A9.10　Kendall's tau partial correlations between measures of mother-baby interaction, and firstborn child's social approaches to sibling.

x = M-B time interacting (8-month observations)
y = C's friendly social approach to B (14-month observations)
z = M-B time interacting (14-month observations)
$\tau\, xy = -0.28^*$　　$\tau\, xy.z = -0.23$

Table A9.11　Kendall's tau partial correlations between measures of mother-baby interaction and second child's social approaches to elder sibling.

x = M-B playful interactions (8-month observations)
y = B's hostile social approach to C (14-month observations)
z = M-B playful interactions (14-months observations)
$\tau\, xy = 0.45^{**}$　　$\tau\, xy.z = 0.44^{**}$

Table A9.12　Mother's reaction to different types of sibling quarrels.

Reaction of M (median % interactions)	Sibling prohibition	Sibling negative action	p level (Wilcoxon test)
Prohibits	16	44	0.01
Distracts	22	14	0.05

Table A9.13　Kendall's tau partial correlation between measures of mothers' reactions to sibling quarrels and sibling social approaches (firstborn boys).

x = M prohibits sibling prohibition (8-month observations)
y = C's hostile social approach to B (14-month observations)
z = M prohibits sibling prohibition (14-month observations)
$\tau\, xy = 0.49^{**}$　　$\tau\, xy.z = 0.38^*$

Table A9.14 Kendall's tau partial correlation between measures of mothers' reaction to sibling quarrels and sibling social approaches (firstborn girls).

x	=	C's hostile social approach to B (8-month observations)
y	=	M prohibits sibling prohibition (14-month observations)
z	=	C's hostile social approach to B (14-month observations)

$\tau\,xy = 0.42^*$ $\tau xy.z = 0.38^*$

Table A9.15 Consistency in measures of mothers' interactions with firstborn boys and girls from 3-week observations to 14-month observations.[a]

	Boys ($N = 21$) rs	Girls ($N = 19$) rs
M prohibits	0.74^{**}	0.34
Time in confrontation	0.71^{**}	0.22

a. Spearman rank correlations.

Table A10.1 Changes in children's behavior from first-month interview to 8-month interview: significance of change in probabilities.

Behavior change	Difference in probabilities (chi-square)	p level
Decrease in probability of marked misery	15.11	0.001
Decrease in probability of sleeping problems	16.22	0.001
Decrease in marked demand for attention	17.92	0.001
Increase in probability of marked affection for M	17.90	0.001
Increase in probability of marked affection for F	16.84	0.001

Table A10.2   Associations between behavior problems.

	Chi-square	*df*	*p* level
Miserable moods —			
and tantrums	8.4	2	0.02
and fears	8.8	2	0.02
Worries —			
and rituals	6.7	2	0.05

Table A10.3   Association between completion of toilet training and age.

	Chi-square	*df*	*p* level (Kruskall-Wallis)
Age of children with toilet training complete compared with age of those not yet completely trained	7.15	1	0.03

Table A10.4   Emergence, persistence, and disappearance of unhappy behavior: comparison of probabilities from pregnancy interview and 14-month interview.

Unhappy behavior	Persisting[a]	Not Persisting[b]	Chi-square	*p* level
Frequent miserable moods	0.69	0.31	9.20	0.01
Marked fears	0.70	0.30	5.80	0.02
	Persisting	Emerging[c]		
Worrying	0.66	0.40	10.16	0.01
Marked fears	0.70	0.42	9.16	0.01
Frequent miserable moods	0.69	0.48	10.50	0.01
Sleep problems	0.55	0.08	11.47	0.01

a. Probability that a child categorized as suffering from, for example, marked fears at pregnancy interview was still categorized as suffering from marked fears at 14 months.

b. Probability that a child categorized as suffering from, for example, marked fears at pregnancy interview was *not* so categorized at 14 months.

c. Probability that a child categorized as *not* suffering from, for example, marked fears at pregnancy interview was categorized as suffering from marked fears at 14 months.

Table A10.5 Increase in behavior problems and temperament: significant differences between those children scoring above the median on particular temperament traits and the rest of the sample.

Behavior problem	Temperament trait	Extreme group greater or less than rest of sample	p level (Fisher exact probability)
Increase in rituals	Negative mood + intensity	Greater	0.05
Increase in fears	Intensity	Greater	0.0001
	Intensity + unmalleability	Greater	0.04
Increase in worry	Negative mood + intensity	Greater	0.06
Increase in tantrums	Withdrawal	Less	0.08

Table A10.6 Behavior at 8-month interview and temperament: significant differences between those children scoring above the median on particular temperament traits and the rest of the sample.

Behavior	Temperament trait	Extreme group greater or less than rest of sample	p level (Fisher exact probability)
Constant use of comfort object	Intensity	Greater	0.04
Marked fears	Intensity	Greater	0.001
Frequent worry	Intensity	Greater	0.04
Marked rituals	Intensity	Greater	0.001
Frequent miserable moods	Intensity	Greater	0.04
Feeding problems	Intensity + unmalleability	Greater	0.04
Sleeping problems	Negative mood	Greater	0.01
Tantrums	Withdrawal	Less	0.001
Marked affection for M	Intensity	Greater	0.02
Marked affection for F	Intensity	Greater	0.02

Table A10.7   Association between reaction to birth of sibling and behavior problems at 8-month and 14-month interviews.

Behavior problem	Reaction to birth	Chi-square	df	p level
8-month interview:				
Sleeping problems	Marked increase in withdrawal > no increase	6.02	1	0.01
14-month interview:				
Frequent use of comfort object	Marked increase in tearfulness > no increase	4.04	1	0.04
Marked fears	Marked increase in tearfulness > no increase	5.69	1	0.02
Marked rituals	Marked increase in tearfulness > no increase	6.57	2	0.04
Frequent worry	Marked increase in withdrawal > no increase	3.77	1	0.05
	Marked increase in clinging > no increase	3.70	1	0.05
Frequent miserable moods	Marked increase in negative response to M > no increase	7.28	2	0.03
Tantrums	Marked increase in negative response to M > no increase	6.35	2	0.04

Table A10.8 Frequency of parental spanking.

Time of questioning	Mother	Father	Both equally	Neither	N
Pregnancy interview	22	0	6	2	30
8-month interview	24	0	8	2	34
14-month interview	27	2	4	3	36

Table A10.9 Association between reported changes (pregnancy and 14-month interviews) and observed behavior at 14 months.

Children reported to have increased in fears (pregnancy to 14-month interview)	Chi-square	df	p level (Kruskall-Wallis)
Increase in use of comfort object	3.90	1	<0.05
No decrease in wandering			
No decrease in sitting			

Children reported not to have increased in fears			p level (Sign test)
Decrease in use of comfort object			<0.001
Decrease in wandering			<0.01
Decrease in sitting			<0.01

Children reported not to have increased in miserable moods			
Decrease in use of comfort object			<0.05
Decrease in wandering			<0.01

Table A10.10   Spearman rank correlations between pregnancy, first-month, and 14-month observations.

| 14-month observation | Correlation with — | |
	Pregnancy observation	First-month observation
Joint attention	0.29	0.45*
Joint play	0.32*	0.41*
M shows	0.36*	0.42*
M suggests (highlights)	0.50*	0.53*
M affectionate tactile contact	0.32*	0.14
M prohibits	0.45*	0.57*
M initiates verbal interaction with prohibition	0.36*	0.37*
Confrontation	0.36*	0.43*
C looks at M without M looking at C	0.26	0.32
Mutual positive look	0.15	0.22
C wanders	0.07	0.28
C sits	0.09	0.31
C fusses	0.50*	0.00
C affectionate tactile contact	0.09	−0.17
C verbal demand (total)	0.32*	0.21
C verbal demand for play	0.37*	0.04

Table A10.11   Maternal irritability at 8 months.

Maternal irritability	Temperament trait	Chi-square	df	p level
Marked, frequent (daily or more)	Extreme on withdrawal < Rest of sample	6.31	2	0.04
	Reaction to birth			
	Increased tearfulness > no increase	8.37	2	0.02

Methodology

Population Studied

The families taking part in this study were collected with the help of family doctors and health visitors. The families were largely from the working class; the occupation of the father, classified according to the Registrar General, was IV (unskilled manual) for 7 families, III (skilled manual) for 12 families, III (clerical) for 13 families, and II (lower professional managerial) for 8 families. Thirteen of the mothers delivered their second baby at home. The sex composition of the children in the sample is shown below:

	Secondborn	
Firstborn	Girls	Boys
Girls	8	11
Boys	11	10

None of the mothers were in paid employment at the beginning of the study (when the mother was pregnant with the second child), but by the 14-month visit ten mothers were employed, or had been employed over the past year, on a part-time basis.

Observation Methods

The observations carried out in the home were unstructured. Observations of one hour's duration were made on at least two occasions at each of the four age-points of the study:

pregnancy, first month, when younger sibling was 8 months, and when younger sibling was 14 months. The observations were carried out by the authors, with only one observer present at each observation.In the pregnancy visits (made between one and three months before the expected date of delivery) for each family, the observer arranged to sample periods when the mother was busy with housework, and periods when she was more relaxed. In the majority of cases this meant that the visits were made during the morning. In the first-month visits the observation included at least one session when the mother was feeding the baby in the presence of the firstborn.

The observations were made in the form of a running record, in a lined notebook where each line represented 10 seconds. Time was marked by an electronic bleeper. Categories of child behavior, mother behavior, and interaction were precoded and are given below. The technique allowed the observer to record in narrative form details of the child's play and the objects played with, as well as further details of control incidents or behavior toward the sibling. During the observations the verbal exchange between child and family members and comments made by the child as he played ("self-talk") were recorded on a portable stereo tape recorder. Immediately after the observation the observer transcribed the tape recording.

Observational categories[1]

Mother (M) — Child (C)

Joint attention*   Both M and C attending visually to same focus (not necessarily both involved in same activity; child may be playing independently).

---

1. Categories marked with an asterisk include the responsibility for initiating and terminating the bout.

M holds C*	C held by M, sitting on her knee, leaning or resting on M.
M close to C*	M and C within 2 feet of each other.
Joint play*	Both M and C involved in same activity. Includes both cooking or cleaning together and playing more conventional games.
M caretakes	Attends to clothes, washes, puts on pot, and so on.
M helps	Assists C when in difficulty.
M shows	Highlights or demonstrates object or action to C.
M suggests: Highlights	Makes suggestion during child's ongoing activity that refers to child's activity; suggestion has *highlighting* connotation. For instance, if C is playing with Lego, M says, "That's a nice house. You could give it a window, couldn't you?"
Directs	Makes suggestion that has *directing* connotation, when child not involved in any activity. For example, if C has just been dressed and is standing without playing, M says, "Why don't you go and play with your Lego?"
Redirects	Makes suggestion to redirect C's activity (say, after prohibition or restraint, or confrontation between siblings). For instance, if C hits sibling, M says, "Stop it, that's enough. You could go and play Lego now, couldn't you?"

M's affectionate physical contact	M kisses, cuddles, caresses, or makes other affectionate gesture.
M prohibits	M verbally prohibits C from continuing present activity.
M restrains	M physically prevents C from continuing present activity, holds C back, or removes from situation.
M punishes	M spanks, sends to room, or the like; carries out threatened punishment after particular child action.
Confrontation	Time during which M and C are interacting in strong disagreement; this can include marked verbal disputes over control issues or physical confrontation.
Mutual look (positive)	C looks at M and gaze is returned.
Mutual look (negative)	C looks at M with glare or scowl; M same.
C looks at M	C looks at M without M looking at C.
C verbally demands play or attention	C requests help, attention, or play from M.
C verbally demands object	C requests object, toy, food, or drink from M.
C wanders	C moves about room or garden without clear purpose or activity, without interacting with other person.
C sits	C sits without playing, eating, drinking, or talking, or any ac-

	tivity other than sucking thumb or handling comfort object.
C fusses	C fusses or cries.
C gives	C gives, shows, or points out object to M.
C's affectionate physical contact	C kisses, cuddles, caresses, or other affectionate gesture.
C complies	C complies with mother suggestion (prohibition).
C uses comfort object	C sucks thumb, pacifier, bottle (not full), blanket, or particular transitional object.
C elicits pick up	C requests (verbal/nonverbal) to be held.

Additional Categories

People present	
M busy	M's activity (cooking, housework, and so forth) specified.
Joint physical play*	Both M and C involved in physical game, cuddling, romping, and the like.
C follows	C follows specified person.
C approaches	C moves purposefully toward specified person.
C investigates	C examines or explores (in answer to question "What is it?," "How does it work?," "What can it do?")

After C points or
   shows: M acknowledges

                              M ignores

                              M agrees or extends

After C verbally demands: M complies

                              M does not comply

After C elicits
   pickup: M holds

Sibling

The occurrence of the following categories of socially directed behavior shown by either sibling toward the other was recorded during each 10-second unit: (1) gives/shows object, (2) vocalizes (other than prohibition or protest), (3) smiles, (4) laughs, (5) touches affectionately, (6) approaches, (7) sits very close, (8) replicates (imitates) action of sibling while looking at sibling, (9) takes active part in joint physical play, (10) takes active part in games with sibling (such as peekaboo), (11) helps, (12) comforts, (13) prohibits sibling, (14) negatively touches sibling (hits, pokes, pinches), (15) fusses or protests at sibling's action, (16) removes toy or object from sibling. The observer also noted, in narrative form, further details about each interaction bout between the siblings: particular attention was paid, for instance, to recording the details of play or game sequences between the children, the particular actions imitated, and details of affective expressive behavior. After the observation the observer filled in a summary sheet where each interaction between the siblings was described in detail.

In the majority of the analyses reported in this book, two summary measures of sibling social behavior are used: (a) friendly social approaches, a category that included the occurrence of any of the behavioral items (1) to (12) listed above; and (b) hostile social approaches, a category that included any of the items (13) to (16).

These two measures were selected on the grounds that (*a*)

the summary measures were more stable from observation to observation than the individual fine-grain measures; (*b*) the summary measures represented a useful summary index of the behavior of each child toward the other: each of the individual fine-grain measures correlated significantly with the summary measure (the Spearman rank correlations for behavioral items included in the measures of friendly social approaches ranged from 0.73 to 0.48, and for those included in the measure of hostile social approaches from 0.81 to 0.39 (N = 40); (c) the summary measures enable us to express the results of the analyses more concisely. The results are reported both as frequency and as proportion measures. The frequency of the measures of friendly and hostile social approaches is reported per unit of observation time that the siblings were together.

Mother-Secondborn Interaction

Interactions between mother and secondborn child[2] were categorized as follows:

Playful interactions
Joint physical play, verbal games, play with objects, imitative sequences, conventional games such as peekaboo, joint attention to books, toys, or objects, affectionate contact between mother and baby.

Caretaking interactions
Mother dresses, feeds, helps, cleans the baby, or changes the baby's diaper.

Restraining interactions
Mother prohibits the baby, attempts to restrain or change his/her ongoing behavior, or spanks the baby.

Vocal interactions
Mother vocalizes to the baby without also playing, caretak-

---

2. For the purposes of this analysis, interactions between the mother and second child that included another individual (father, grandparent, or other) were excluded.

ing, or restraining (as defined above).

One or more of such interactions constituted an interaction bout between the mother and the secondborn child. The interaction bout was considered to have ended when one or both partners moved away, averted their gaze, or started some alternative activity not involving the other. Since we wished to examine the possible importance of both differences in the *time* mother and secondborn spent interacting, and differences in the *quality* of this mother-secondborn interaction, two measures from this record were used in the analyses reported in Chapter 9:

(1) *Time interacting*: the number of 10-second units of observation time during which mother and second child were interacting, expressed as a percentage of 10-second units that mother and second child were together with first child. (This excluded (*a*) units when one of the dyad looked at the other without the gaze being returned, (*b*) units when the mother carried the second child without vocalizing, playing, caregiving, and (*c*) units when the second child cried or fussed and the mother made no observable response.

(2) *Proportion of play*: the proportion of interactions between mother and second child that included play — that is, interaction including any of the following: repetitive verbal games, imitative sequences, conventional games such as peekaboo, joint attention to books, toys, or objects, joint physical play, or affectionate contact between mother and infant.

Categorization of Firstborn's Behavior

The first child's responses to all types of mother-baby interaction bouts were categorized as follows:

Joins, friendly: firstborn approaches or vocalizes in a positive way, gives toys, helps, affectionately contacts either the mother or the baby, or joins in an ongoing game or joint physical play between the mother and the baby.

Protests: firstborn makes verbal protests or demands for objects, help, attention, food; hits or pinches mother.

Joins, hostile to baby: firstborn hits, pinches, or screams at baby, takes away toys, prohibits or restrains baby.

Watches: first child watches but makes no attempt to approach or join in.

Ignores: first child continues his/her ongoing behavior and makes no attempt either to join in or to watch the mother-baby interaction.

Reliability

Interobserver reliability was assessed by comparing the records of the two observers made during hour-long home observations when both observers were present. Families who were not part of the main study sample were visited for these assessments. The reliability checks were carried out at three points in time corresponding to the pregnancy visits, first-month observations, and 14-month observations. That is, they were carried out before data collection began on the main study, in the early phases of data collection, and toward the end of data collection. Twenty-three hours of observations were used for these reliability checks; final checks were carried out with videotaped recordings after data collection was complete.

Table B.1, column (a), shows the interobserver agreement ratio (agreement/agreement + disagreement) for the observation measures used. The stabilities of individual differences in the measure of sibling socially directed behavior were assessed by computing the rank-order correlations between the measures from two observations made one week apart, for the full sample of 40 families. The Spearman Brown prophecy formula (Guilford 1954) was used to estimate the agreement. The interobservation correlations for the behavior measures are shown in column (b) of the table.

Table B1   Reliability of observation measures.

Observation measure	(a) Interobserver agreement (ratio)	(b) Interobservation agreement (Spearman correlation)
(1) M-C interaction (N = 28):		
Joint attention	0.71	0.85***
Joint play	0.88	0.71***
M shows	0.72	0.86***
M suggests (highlights)	1.00	0.70***
M prohibits	0.91	0.85***
Confrontation	0.91	0.84***
C fusses	0.66	0.70***
C wanders	0.96	0.70***
C sits	0.69	0.56**
C verbally demands object	0.91	0.64***
C verbally demands play	0.94	0.68***
C initiates verbal exchange	0.91	0.64***
C looks at M without return of gaze	0.84	0.58**
C uses comfort object	0.66	0.59**
M close to C	0.72	0.49**
Mutual look (positive)	0.88	0.62**
Mutual look (negative)	0.80	0.69***
Measures from conversational analysis:		
Verbal interaction measures (N = 26)		
Control episodes	0.94	0.82***
Initiation of verbal interactions		
M negative	0.88	0.73***
M total positive	0.96	0.82***
C	0.91	0.78***
M verbal game/fantasy	1.00	0.92***

Table B1 *(continued)*

M unsolicited positive comment	0.94	0.64***
M new suggestion	0.86	0.64***
(2) Sibling behavior:		
C friendly social approaches		
Frequency	0.84	0.54***
Percentage	0.84	0.64***
C hostile social approaches		
Frequency	0.93	0.46**
B friendly social approaches		
Frequency	0.74	0.56***
B hostile social approaches		
Frequency	0.89	0.35*
(3) M-B interaction:		
Time interacting	0.89	0.53***
Percentage of interaction bouts including:		
Play	0.98	0.68***
Caretaking	1.00	0.57***
Restraining	1.00	0.59***
(4) C's response to M-B interaction:		
Joins, friendly	1.00	0.51***
Protests	1.00	0.57***
Joins, hostile to B	0.80	0.41**
Watches	0.80	0.43**
Ignores	0.80	0.46**

The Assessment of Temperamental Characteristics Interview

This interview was developed by Sturge from other temperament assessments (such as that of Graham, Rutter, and George 1973) based on the study of Thomas, Chess, and Birch (1968).

The answer to each question on this interview is rated on a three-point scale, and the completed interview gives a total of

37 questions concerned with seven dimensions: intensity, negative mood, activity, malleability, approach/withdrawal, persistence, and assertiveness.

The scores on the separate questions were added to compile a score on each trait. This procedure involves two assumptions: that the answers to each question are on equal-interval scales, and that each question is equally important in contributing to the dimension. It is standard procedure to make these assumptions in most interview ratings of temperament and behavior; however, we are aware that the assumptions in this case may be unwarranted. Our reservations about using the temperament rating scales as equal-interval scales were particularly strong because of the nature of the behavioral differences with which the temperament assessment is concerned. In view of this, we decided to use the assessment simply to dichotomize the sample for each dimension into one group of children who scored toward one extreme, and one group that comprised the rest of the sample. When the distribution of scores was inspected for each trait, it was found that a high proportion of the children scored on or within a decimal point of the median. Since we were interested in the children who were relatively extreme in their ratings, we divided the sample for each trait into those children who scored on, below, or within a decimal point above the median, versus the rest. This accounts for the discrepancy in the size of the two groups compared for each trait. The extreme groups (those scoring above the median) were high activity, highly intense mood, high negative mood, highly unmalleable, extremely withdrawing, highly assertive, and highly persistent.

Assessment of Temperament by Observer and by Mother

After carrying out pregnancy observations (and before interviewing the mother on Assessment of Temperamental Characteristics of her child), we as observers were able to rate each child's behavior on several items in the temperament assessment interview: the child's style of play (questions on intensity, negative mood, activity, persistence); his response to frustration and his perserverance on difficult tasks (questions on malleability and persistence); his reactions to the mother's attempts to control or direct his behavior (questions on malleability, assertiveness, and intensity); and reaction to a strange person (questions on approach/withdrawal). The observer rated the child on the three-point scale for each question. According to the particular circumstances of the observation, the observer was able to rate the child on 15 to 18 questions from the temperament assessment. After the second pregnancy observation, the temperamental characteristics interview was carried out with the mother. A comparison was then possible between the ratings given by the observer and those given for the same questions by the mother.

The percentage agreement versus disagreement + agreement between mother and observer is shown below:

Temperamental trait	Agreement (percent)
Activity	57
Malleability	88
Assertiveness	90
Intensity	82
Mood	81
Persistence	83
Withdrawal	85

For six of the dimensions this agreement ranges between 81 and 90 percent. For the "activity" dimension, however, the agreement is very low: in 16 out of 18 disagreements between observer and mother, the mother rated the child as being more active than the observer did. For this reason the activity dimension was not included in the analyses. Since the temperament rating involved a three-point scale, disagreement could involve a difference of either one point or two points. Out of 434 individual questions compared, only three involved disagreements of two points.

While this comparison suggests that the mother's rating of the child on temperamental dimensions other than activity is not unduly biased by her particular perception of the child, it must be treated with caution, for it is based on a very small number of questions per dimension.

Correlations between Scores on Temperament Traits

The rank correlations between the scores on each dimension were examined, using Spearman rank correlations (Table B2). There were a number of positive correlations: those between intensity and assertiveness, negative mood and unmalleability, and assertiveness and unmalleability reaching a 5-percent level of significance.

It would be unjustifiable, therefore, to assume that the different dimensions, as assessed here, reflect independent facets of the child's temperament. They do provide indexes (albeit crude) of aspects of individual differences in children that the direct-observation categories do not cover.

Table B2　Spearman rank correlation between temperamental traits (average scores, $N = 40$).

Trait	Intensity	Assertiveness	Unmalleability	Mood	Persistence	Approach/withdrawal
Intensity		0.35*	−0.07	−0.04	−0.16	−0.07
Assertiveness			0.40*	0.18	−0.15	0.01
Unmalleability				0.45**	−0.02	−0.19
Mood					−0.12	0.25
Persistence						−0.02

*$p < 0.05$, ** $p < 0.02$.

Interobserver Reliability

The two observers rated the temperamental characteristics from 25 tape-recorded temperament assessment interviews.

The agreement ratios between the observers for the individual questions, expressed as the median for each temperament trait, are shown in Table B3. The interobserver agreement ratio is also shown for the dichotomized temperament variables.

Table B3 Interobserver agreement.

Temperamental traits	Interobserver agreement (individual questions)	Interobserver agreement (dichotomized variables)
Negative mood	0.85 (range 0.78–0.92)	0.88
Intensity	0.90 (range 0.81–1.0)	0.96
Assertiveness	0.92 (range 0.76–1.0)	0.64
Persistence	0.91 (range 0.67–1.0)	0.96
Withdrawal/approach	0.88 (range 0.83–0.94)	0.92
Unmalleability	0.86 (range 0.76–1.0)	0.68

Stability of Temperamental Assessment

The temperamental assessment interview was carried out with 13 children on two occasions, approximately a month apart. The agreement ratio for the dichotomized dimensions is shown below:

Temperamental traits	Stability agreement ratio
Negative mood	0.80
Intensity	0.72
Assertiveness	0.64
Persistence	0.72
Withdrawal/approach	0.91
Unmalleability	0.76

Since there were no significant associations between the dichotomized traits of persistence and assertiveness and the firstborn child's reaction to the arrival of a sibling, these analyses are not reported in Chapter 3 or later.

Coding of Complex Cognitive Use of Language

Each turn of both adult and child talk was scrutinized to see whether it used language in any of the ways listed below:

(1) Comparisons, similarities and differences.
(2) Recall of events occurring before recording session.
(3) Future plans for period after recording session.
(4) Linking at least two events in time, by the use of such words as "while," "when", "until," and "then."
(5) Describing purposes of objects.
(6) Giving reasons, explanations, purposes, or results of actions ("because," "in order to"). Excluded were explanations that were assertions, authority statements, or expressions of wishes ("because it is," "I want to," "I say so").
(7) Conditionals, concerned with hypothetical events ("if . . . then").
(8) Generalizations and definitions ("Pigs don't fly, birds do").
(9) Logical reasoning and inference ("so," "therefore").
(10) Problem solving, creative insight into situation. (C: We haven't got enough lollipop sticks to make it. M: Well, we'll break them in two then. M's turn coded 10.)

The codes were derived largely from the Tizard et al. (1981) classification of the cognitive uses of language, as discussed in Chapter 4. Repetitions of a remark were not coded; more than one code could be applied to a turn of talk if it included more than one instance of a complex use of language.

Appendix C

Statistical Notes

1. Regression analysis on the frequency of positive social behavior shown by the siblings at 14 months

Multivariate regression techniques impose a number of different constraints on the investigator. Two of these were of particular importance to us. First, regression techniques require a relatively large number of cases if several variables are to be examined simultaneously. We decided that with a sample of 37 we should not look at the effects of more than four independent variables at the same time. Secondly, the order in which the independent variables are entered into the regression analysis may influence the final result. In our study this order was systematically varied.

(1) Behavior of first child

Using as the dependent measure the frequency of positive social behavior shown by the first child to the baby at 14 months, the following variables were examined in a series of regression analyses:

(a) Mother talks about the baby as a person during the first-month observations.

(b) Same-sex versus different-sex sibling dyads.

(c) The proportion of interactions between mother and baby that included play.

(d) The positive reaction of the first child to the birth of the baby.

(e) The sex of the first child.

(f) The frequency of joint attention of mother and first child during the pregnancy observations.

(g) The first child's affection for the father.

The results showed that the first four variables made significant contributions to the variance in the measure of positive social behavior: (a) mother talks about baby as person ($F = 5.2$, $df = 1.33$, $p < 0.05$); (b) same sex/different sex ($F = 5.1$, $df = 1.32$, $p < 0.05$); (c) mother-baby play ($F = 4.4$, $df = 1.33$, $p < 0.05$); (d) positive reaction of first child to birth of baby ($F = 4.2$, $df = 1.31$, $p < 0.05$). The total amount of variance accounted for by these variables was 36 percent. There was an interaction effect between variables (a) and (b) ($F = 7.5$, $df = 1.31$, $p < 0.01$), which accounted for a further 18 percent of the variance.

The order in which these variables were entered into the equation did affect the amount of the variance accounted for. If variable (c) was entered before variable (a), it accounted for more of the variance than if it was entered *after* variable (a) and vice versa. This finding suggests that there was some overlap in the variance that each of the variables was accounting for. The order in which the same-sex variable was entered also affected the amount of the variance it accounted for, suggesting that there was overlap in the variance accounted for by the variables (b) same sex/different sex, (c) mother-baby play, and (a) mother talks about baby as person. The variable chosen as an index of the quality of the relationship between mother and first child in the pregnancy observations, variable (f), was significant at the 10-percent level. When the baby's positive social behavior to the first child was entered into a regression analysis, it accounted for 70 percent of the variance ($F = 81$, $df = 1.35$, $p < 0.001$).

(2) *Behavior of baby*

Using as a dependent measure the frequency of positive social behavior shown by the 14-month-old infant to the first child, the following variables were examined in a series of regression analyses: measures (a) to (e) as above, and a new variable (h), the positive social behavior of the first child to the baby at 14 months. The results showed that variables (a), (b), (c), and (h) made significant separate contributions to the variance in the measure of second child's positive social behavior (Table C1).

2. *Sex differences and variability*

Yarrow, Rubenstein, and Pedersen (1975) in a study of 6-month-olds found that the day-to-day stability of behavior was less for the boys than for the girls, and that the split-half reliability of the Bayley developmental scores was lower for the boys than for the girls (quoted in Kagan, Kearsley, and Zelazo 1978). There are certainly grounds for supposing that samples of children that have not been carefully screened for perinatal difficulties will include more boys than girls who have suffered some minor perinatal difficulties, and there is

Table C1   Regression analysis of frequency of baby's friendly social behavior.

Variable	df	F	p	Variance accounted for (percent)
(a) M talks about B as person	1.33	6.6	0.05	17
(b) Same sex/different sex	1.32	4.6	0.05	10
(c) Interaction between (a) and (b)	1.31	7.9	0.02	15
(d) C's friendly approaches	1.30	31.7	0.001	30

some evidence that such perinatal problems are associated both with variability in behavior from day to day and with a greater range of individual differences at any one time (Kalveboer 1975). To test this hypothesis we computed the rank-order correlations from one first-month observation to the next (a week later) separately for the boys and girls in the sample. The results show that in fact the correlations were higher for the boys (median $rs = 0.68$) than for girls (median $rs = 0.56$).

A second possibility is that the interaction between siblings at the 14-month observation was more variable for the boys and that, again, the sampling procedures were not adequate. The rank-order correlations from one 14-month visit to the next (a week later) for the proportion and the frequency measures of sibling behavior were computed separately for the boys and for the girls. To test for the possibility that there was a greater range of individual differences at one point in time, we analyzed separately for the boys and the girls the means and standard deviations for the first-month observation measures and for the 14-month sibling observation measures. There was no tendency for these measures to have larger standard deviations or means for the boys, or for there to be a lower stability of rank order from one week to the next.

References

The following articles contain more detailed analyses of our findings than appear in this book:

Dunn, J., and Kendrick, C. 1980a. The arrival of a sibling: changes in patterns of interaction between mother and first-born child. *Journal of Child Psychology and Psychiatry, 21,* 119–132.

_____ 1980b. Studying temperament and parent-child interaction: a comparison of information from direct observation and from parental interview. *Developmental Medicine and Child Neurology, 22,* 484–496.

_____ 1981a. Interaction between young siblings: associations with the interaction between mother and first born. *Developmental Psychology, 17,* 336-344.

_____ 1981b. Social behaviour of young siblings in the family context: differences between same-sex and different-sex dyads. *Child Development,* in press.

Dunn, J., Kendrick, C., and MacNamee, R. 1981. The reaction of first-born children to the birth of a sibling: mothers' reports. *Journal of Child Psychology and Psychiatry, 22,* 1–18.

Kendrick, C., and Dunn, J. 1980. Caring for a second baby: effects on the interaction between mother and first-born. *Developmental Psychology, 16,* 303–311.

Other reference works cited herein are the following:

Aarons, A. Z. 1954. Effect of the birth of a sister on a boy in his fourth year. *Archives of Pediatrics, 71,* 54–76.

Abramovitch, R., Corter, C., and Lando, B. 1979. Sibling interaction in the home. *Child Development, 50,* 997–1003.

Abramovitch, R., Corter, C., and Pepler, D. J. 1980. Observations of mixed-sex sibling dyads. *Child Development, 51,* 1268-71.

Adler, A. 1928. Characteristics of the first, second and third child. *Children, 3,* 14 (issue 5).

Ainsworth, M. D. S. 1973. The development of the infant mother attachment. In B. M. Caldwell and H. N. Ricciuti, eds., *Review of Child Development Research,* vol. 3. Chicago: University of Chicago Press.

Ainsworth, M. D. S., Blehar, M. C., Walters, E., and Wall, S. 1978. *Patterns of Attachment: A Psychological Study of the Strange Situation.* Hillsdale, N.J.: Erlbaum Associates.

Bandura, A., Ross, D., and Ross, S. A. 1963. A comparative test of the status envy, social power, and secondary reinforcement theories of identificatory learning. *Journal of Abnormal and Social Psychology, 67,* 527–534.

Barker, B., and Lewis, M. 1975. A multidimensional analysis of the effect of birth order on mother-infant interaction. Paper presented at the Eastern Psychological Association meeting, New York City.

Bates, E., Camaioni, L., and Volterra, V. 1975. The acquisition of performatives prior to speech. *Merrill Palmer Quarterly, 21,* 205–226.

Bernal, J. F., and Richards, M. P. M. 1970. The effects of bottle and breast feeding on infant development. *Journal of Psychosomatic Research, 14,* 247–252.

Black, D., and Sturge, C. 1979. The young child and his siblings. In J. G. Howells, ed, *Perspectives in Infant Psychiatry.* New York: Brunner-Mazel.

Blurton-Jones, N. 1972. Characteristics of ethological studies of human behaviour. In N. Blurton-Jones, ed., *Ethological Studies of Child Behaviour.* Cambridge: Cambridge University Press.

Borke, H. 1972. Interpersonal perception of young children: egocentrism or empathy? *Developmental Psychology, 7,* 107–109.

Bowlby, J. 1969. *Attachment and Loss,* vol. 1. London: Hogarth Press.

———— 1973. *Attachment and Loss,* vol. 2. London: Hogarth Press.

Bretherton, I., McNew, S., and Beeghly-Smith, M. 1981. Early person knowledge as expressed in gestural and verbal communication: when do infants acquire a "theory of mind"? In M. E. Lamb and L. R. Sherrod, eds., *Infant Social Cognition.* Hillsdale, N.J.: Erlbaum Associates.

Brim, O. G. 1958. Family structure and sex role learning by children.

Sociometry, 21, 1–16.

Brown, G., and Harris, T. 1978. *Social Origins of Depression.* London: Tavistock.

Brown, R. 1977. Introduction. In C. E. Snow and C. A. Ferguson, eds., *Talking to Children.* Cambridge: Cambridge University Press.

Bruner, J. S. 1975a. From communciation to language – a psychological perspective. *Cognition, 3,* 255–287.

_____ 1975b. The ontogenesis of speech acts. *Journal of Child Language, 2,* 1–19.

_____ 1977. Early social interaction and language acquisition. In H. R. Schaffer, ed., *Studies in Mother-Infant Interaction.* London: Academic Press.

Bruner, J., and Sherwood, V. 1976. Peekaboo and the learning of rule structures. In J. Bruner, A. Jolly, and K. Sylva, eds., *Play: Its Role in Development and Evolution.* Harmondsworth: Penguin.

Bühler, C. 1939. *The Child and His Family.* London: Harper.

Burlingham, D., and Freud, A. 1944. *Infants without Families.* London: Allen and Unwin.

Calladine, C., and Calladine, A. 1979. *Raising Siblings.* New York: Delacorte Press.

Chandler, M. J., and Greenspan, S. 1972. Ersatz egocentrism: a reply to H. Borke. *Developmental Psychology, 7,* 104–106.

Chodorow, N. 1978. *The Reproduction of Mothering: Psychoanalysis and the Sociology of Gender.* Berkeley: University of California Press.

Cicirelli, V. G. 1973. Effects of sibling structure and interaction on children's categorisation style. *Developmental Psychology, 9,* 132–139.

_____ 1975. Effects of mother and older sibling on the problem solving behavior of the older child. *Developmental Psychology, 11,* 749–756.

_____ 1976a. Siblings helping siblings. In V. L. Allen, ed., *Inter-age Interaction in Children.* New York: Academic Press.

_____ 1976b. Sibling structure and intellectual ability. *Developmental Psychology, 12,* 369–370.

_____ 1977. Children's school grades and sibling structure. *Psychological Reports, 41,* 1055–58.

_____ 1978. Effects of sibling presence on mother child interaction. *Developmental Psychology, 14,* 315–316.

Clarke-Stewart, K. A. 1973. Interactions between mothers and their children: characteristics and consequences. *Monographs of the Society for Research in Child Development,* no. 38, 6-7.

———— 1978. And daddy makes three: the father's impact on the mother and the young child. *Child Development, 49,* 466-478.

Close, S. 1980. *The Toddler and the New Baby.* London: Routledge and Kegan Paul.

Doise, W., and Mugny, G. 1981. *La Construction sociale de l'intelligence.* Paris: Interéditions.

Donaldson, M. 1978. *Children's Minds.* Glasgow: Fontana/Collins.

Douglas, J. W. B., Lawson, A., Cooper, J. E., and Cooper, E. 1968. Family interaction and the activities of young children: method of assessment. *Journal of Child Psychology and Psychiatry, 9,* 157-171.

Dunn, J. 1979. Individual differences in temperament. In M. Rutter, ed., *The Scientific Foundations of Developmental Psychiatry.* London: Heinemann Medical Books.

Einstein, G., and Moss, M. S. 1967. Some thoughts on sibling relationships. *Social Case Work, 48,* 549-555.

Eliot, G. 1979. *The Mill on the Floss.* Harmondsworth: Penguin Books.

Feschbach, N. D. 1976. Empathy in children: a special ingredient of social development. Paper presented at the Western Psychological Association meetings, Los Angeles.

Flavell, J. 1968. *The Development of Role-taking and Communication Skills in Children.* New York: Wiley.

Freud, A. 1965. *Normality and Pathology in Childhood.* New York: International Universities Press.

Freud, S. 1916. *Introductory Lectures on Psychoanalysis.* Standard edition, vols. 15-16. London: Hogarth Press.

———— 1938. *An Outline of Psychoanalysis.* London: Hogarth Press.

———— 1958. *Interpretation of Dreams.* Standard edition, vol. 4. London: Hogarth Press.

Garvey, C. 1977. *Play.* Cambridge, Mass.: Harvard University Press.

George, C., and Main, M. 1979. Social interactions of young abused children: approach, avoidance and aggression. *Child Development, 50,* 306-318.

Ginott, H. G. 1969. *Between Parent and Child.* New York: Avon Books.

Gore, F. L., and Keating, D. P. 1979. Empathic role-taking precursors. *Developmental Psychology, 15,* 594–600.

Graham, P., Rutter, M., and George, S. 1973. Temperamental characteristics as predictors of behavioral disorders in children. *American Journal of Orthopsychiatry, 43,* 328–339.

Greenwood, K., and Dunn, J. 1982. The development of communication: infants with their siblings, mothers and fathers. In preparation.

Harris, I. D. 1964. *The Promised Seed: A Comparative Study of Eminent First and Later Sons.* Glencoe, Ill.: Free Press.

Heinicke, C. M., and Westheimer, I. J. 1966. *Brief Separations.* New York: International Universities Press.

Henchie, V. 1963. Children's reactions to the birth of a new baby. Master's thesis, Institute of Education, University of London.

Hilton, I. 1967. Differences in the behavior of mothers toward first and later born children. *Journal of Personality and Social Psychology, 7,* 282–290.

Hinde, R. A. 1974. *Biological Bases of Human Social Behavior.* New York: McGraw-Hill.

——— 1979. *Towards Understanding Relationships.* London: Academic Press.

Hingley, R. 1966. *Chekhov. A Biographical and Critical Study.* London: Unwin.

Hoffman, M. L. 1975. Developmental synthesis of affect and cognition and its implications for altruistic motivation. *Developmental Psychology, 11,* 607–622.

——— 1981. Development of prosocial motivation: empathy and guilt. In N. Eisenberg-Berg, ed., *Development of Prosocial Behavior.* New York: Academic Press.

Homan, W. E. 1970. *Child Sense: A Guide for Parents.* London: Thomas Nelson.

Hood, L., and Bloom, L. 1979. What, when and how about why: a longitudinal study of early expressions of causality. *Monographs of the Society for Research in Child Development,* vol. 44, no. 6.

Hughes, M., Carmichael, H., Pinkerton, G., and Tizard, B. 1979. Recording children's conversations at home and at nursery school: a technique and some methodological considerations. *Journal of Child Psychology and Psychiatry, 20,* 225–233.

Izard, C. E. 1977. On the ontogenesis of emotions and emotion-cognition relationships in infancy. In M. Lewis and L. A.

Rosenblum, eds., *The Development of Affect.* New York: Plenum Press.

Jacobs, B. S., and Moss, H. A. 1976. Birth order and sex of sibling as determinants of mother-infant interaction. *Child Development, 47,* 315–322.

Jones, H. E. 1931. Order of birth in relation to the development of the child. In C. Murchison, ed., *Handbook of Child Psychology.* Worcester, Mass.: Clark University Press.

Jones, O. H. M. 1977. Mother-child communication with prelinguistic Down's syndrome and normal infants. In H. R. Schaffer, ed., *Studies in Mother-Infant Interaction.* (Proceedings of the Loch Lomond Symposium.) New York: Academic Press.

Kagan, J. 1971. *Change and Continuity in Infancy.* New York: Wiley.

Kagan, J., Kearsley, R. B., and Zelazo, P. R. 1978. *Infancy: Its Place in Human Development.* Cambridge, Mass.: Harvard University Press.

Kalveboer, A. F. 1975. *A Neurobehavioural Study in Pre-school Children.* London: Heinemann Medical Books.

Keats, J. 1980. Letter to Charles Brown, November 30, 1820. In Robert Gittings, ed., *The Letters of John Keats.* Oxford: Oxford University Press.

Keenan, E. O. 1975. Making it last; repetition in children's discourse. *Papers of the Berkeley Linguistic Society, 1.*

Koch, H. L. 1955a. The relation of certain family constellation characteristics and the attitudes of children towards adults. *Child Development, 26,* 13–40.

―――― 1955b. Some personality correlates of sex, sibling position and sex of siblings among 5 and 6 year old children. *Genetic Psychology Monographs, 52,* 3–50.

Kohlberg, L. 1973. Stage and sequence: the cognitive developmental approach to socialization. In D. A. Goslin, ed., *Handbook of Socialization Theory and Research.* Chicago: Rand McNally.

Lamb, M. E., ed. 1976. *The Role of the Father in Child Development.* New York: Wiley.

―――― 1978a. Interactions between 18 months olds and their pre-school-aged siblings. *Child Development, 49,* 51–59.

―――― 1978b. The development of sibling relationships in infancy: a short term longitudinal study. *Child Development, 49,* 1189–96.

Lasko, J. K. 1954. Parent behavior toward first and second children. *Genetic Psychology Monographs, 49,* 96–137.

Lawson, A., and Ingleby, J. D. 1974. Daily routines of preschool children: effects of age, birth order, sex and social class, and developmental correlates. *Psychological Medicine, 4,* 399–415.

Legg, C., Sherick, I., and Wadland, W. 1974. Reaction of pre-school children to the birth of a sibling. *Child Psychiatry and Human Development, 5,* 3–39.

Levy, D. M. 1934. Rivalry between children of the same family. *Child Study, 11,* 233–261.

_____ 1937. Studies in sibling rivalry. *American Orthopsychiatry, Research Monograph,* no. 2.

Lewis, M., and Brooks-Gunn, J. 1979. *Social Cognition and the Acquisition of Self.* New York: Plenum Press.

Lichtenberger, W. 1965. *Mitmenschliches Verhatten eines Zwillingspaares in seinem ersten Lebensjahren.* Munich: Ernst Reinhardt.

Light, P. 1979. *The Development of Social Sensitivity.* Cambridge: Cambridge University Press.

MacFarland, M. B. 1937. Relationships between young sisters as revealed in their overt responses. *Journal of Experimental Education, 6,* 173–179.

MacFarlane, J., Allen, L., and Honzik, M. 1954. *A Developmental Study of Behavior Problems of Normal Children between 21 Months and 14 Years.* Berkeley: University of California Press.

McGrew, W. C. 1972. Aspects of social development in nursery school children, with emphasis on introduction to the group. In N. Blurton-Jones, ed., *Ethological Studies of Child Behaviour.* Cambridge: Cambridge University Press.

Majoribanks, K., Walberg, H. J., and Bargen, M. 1975. Mental abilities: sibling constellations and social class correlates. *British Journal of Social and Clinical Psychology, 14,* 109–116.

Manning, M., Heron, J., and Marshall, T. 1978. Styles of hostility and social interactions at nursery, at school, and at home. An extended study of children. In L. A. Hersov and M. Berger, eds., *Aggression and Anti-social Behaviour in Childhood and Adolescence.* Oxford: Pergamon Press.

Menzel, E. W. 1974. A group of young chimpanzees. In A. Schrier and F. Stollnitz, eds., *Behavior of Non-human Primates,* vol. 5. New York: Academic Press.

Money, J., and Ehrhardt, A. A. 1972. *Man and Woman, Boy and Girl.* Baltimore: Johns Hopkins University Press.

Moore, T. 1969. Stress in normal childhood. *Human Relations, 22,* 235–250.

Moss, H. A. 1967. Sex, age, and state as determinants of mother-infant interaction. *Merrill-Palmer Quarterly, 13,* 19–36.

Newson, J. 1974. Towards a theory of infant understanding. *Bulletin of the British Psychological Society, 27,* 251–257.

———— 1978. Dialogue and development. In A. Lock, ed., *Action, Gesture and Symbol: The Emergence of Language.* London: Academic Press.

———— 1979. The growth of shared understandings between infant and caregiver. In D. Shaffer and J. Dunn, eds., *The First Year of Life.* Chichester: Wiley.

Newson, J., and Newson, E. 1968. *Four Years Old in an Urban Community.* London: Allen and Unwin.

Obendorf, C. P. 1929. Psychoanalysis of siblings. *American Journal of Psychiatry, 8,* 1007–20.

Papousek, H., and Papousek, M. 1975. Cognitive aspects of pre-verbal social interactions between human infants and adults. In *Parent-Infant Interaction,* CIBA Foundation Symposium, no. 33. Amsterdam: Elsevier.

Parke, R. D., Power, T. G., and Gottman, J. 1979. Conceptualizing and quantifying influence patterns in the family triad. In M. E. Lamb, S. J. Suomi, and G. R. Stephenson, eds., *Social Interaction Analysis.* Madison: University of Wisconsin Press.

Pawlby, S. 1977. Imitative interaction. In H. R. Schaffer, ed., *Studies in Mother-Infant Interaction.* (Proceedings of the Loch Lomond Symposium.) New York: Academic Press.

Pawlby, S. J., and Hall, F. 1980. Early interactions and later language development of children whose mothers come from disrupted families of origin. In T. Field, S. Goldberg, D. Stern, and A. Sostek, eds., *High Risk Infants and Children: Adult and Peer Interactions.* New York: Academic Press.

Petty, T. A. 1953. The tragedy of Humpty Dumpty. *Psychoanalytic Study of the Child, 8,* 404–422.

Piaget, J., and Inhelder, B. 1969. *The Psychology of the Child.* New York: Basic Books.

Podolsky, E. 1954. *The Jealous Child.* New York: Philosophical Library.

Ratner, N., and Bruner, J. 1979. Games, social exchange and the acquisition of language. *Journal of Child Language, 5,* 391–401.

Registrar General. 1973. *Great Britain Summary Tables, Census 1971 (1% Sample).* London: Her Majesty's Stationery Office.

Richman, N., Graham, P., and Stevenson, J. E. 1982. *Preschool to School: A Behavioral Study.* London: Academic Press.

Robertson, J., and Robertson, J. 1971. Young children in brief separation: a fresh look. *Psychoanalytic Study of the Child, 26,* 264–315.

Rothenburg, B. 1970. Children's social sensitivity and the relationship to interpersonal competence, intrapersonal comfort, and intellectual level. *Developmental Psychology, 2,* 335–350.

Rutter, M., Birch, H., Thomas, A., and Chess, S. 1964. Temperamental characteristics in infancy and the later development of behaviour disorders. *British Journal of Psychiatry, 110,* 651–661.

Sachs, J., and Devin, J. 1976. Young children's use of age-appropriate speech styles in social interaction and role-playing. *Journal of Child Language, 3,* 81–98.

Schaffer, H. R. 1979. Acquiring the concept of the dialogue. In M. H. Bornstein and W. Kessen, eds., *Psychological Development from Infancy: Image to Intention.* Hillsdale, N.J.: Erlbaum Associates.

Schooler, C. 1972. Birth order effects. *Psychological Bulletin, 78,* 161–175.

Sewall, M. 1930. Some causes of jealousy in young children. *Smith College Studies in Social Work, 1,* 6–22.

Shantz, C. U. 1975. The development of social cognition. In E. Mavis Hetherington, ed., *Review of Child Development Research* Chicago: University of Chicago Press.

Shatz, M., and Gelman, R. 1973. The development of communication skills: modifications in the speech of young children as a function of the listener. *Monographs of the Society for Research in Child Development, 38,* no. 5.

―――― 1977. Beyond syntax: the influence of conversational constraints on speech modifications. In C. E. Snow and C. A. Ferguson, eds., *Talking to Children.* Cambridge: Cambridge University Press.

Shotter, J., and Newson, J. 1981. An ecological approach to cognitive development: implicate orders, joint action and intentionality.

In G. Butterworth and P. Light, eds., *The Individual and the Social in Cognitive Development*. Hassocks, Sussex: Harvester Press.

Smalley, R. 1930. The influences of differences in age, sex and intelligence in determining attitudes of siblings towards each other. *Smith College Studies in Social Work, 1*, 23–40.

Snow, C. E. 1972. Mother's speech to children learning language. *Child Development, 43*, 549–555.

———— 1977. The development of conversation between mothers and babies. *Journal of Child Language, 4*, 1–22.

Snow, C. E., and Ferguson, C. A., eds. 1977. *Talking to Children*. Cambridge: Cambridge University Press.

Spock, B. 1969. *Baby and Child Care*. New York: Pocket Books.

Stendler, C. B. 1954. Possible causes of over-dependency in young children. *Child Development, 25*, 125–147.

Stern, D. 1977. *The First Relationship: Infant and Mother*. Cambridge, Mass.: Harvard University Press.

Stern, D.N., Jaffe, J., Beebe, B., and Bennett, S.L. 1975. Vocalizing in unison and in alternation: two modes of communication within the mother-infant dyad. *Annals of the New York Academy of Science, 263*, 89–100.

Stern, L. W. 1924. *Psychology of Early Childhood*. New York: Henry Holt.

Sutton-Smith, B., and Rosenberg, B. G. 1970. *The Sibling*. New York: Holt, Rinehart, and Winston.

Taylor, M. K., and Kogan, K. L. 1973. Effects of birth of a sibling on mother-child interaction. *Child Psychiatry and Human Development, 4*, 53–58.

Thomas, A., and Chess, S. 1977. *Temperament and Development*. New York: Brunner-Mazel.

———— 1980. *The Dynamics of Psychological Development*. New York: Brunner-Mazel.

Thomas, A., Chess, S., and Birch, H. 1968. *Temperament and Behavior Disorders in Children*. New York: New York University Press.

Thomas, A., Chess, S., Birch, H. G., Hertzig, M. E., and Korn, S. 1963. *Behavioral Individuality in Early Childhood*. New York: New York University Press.

Thorburn, M. 1938. *Child at Play*. London: Allen and Unwin.

Tizard, B., Hughes, M., Pinkerton, G., and Carmichael, L. 1981. Labov revisited: social class and language usage. Manuscript.

Tough, J. 1977. *The Development of Meaning.* Bristol: Allen and Unwin.

Trause, M. A., Boslett, M., Voos, D., Rudd, C., Klaus, M., and Kennell, J. 1978. A birth in the hospital: the effect on the sibling. *Birth and the Family Journal, 5,* 207–210.

Trevarthen, C. 1977. Descriptive analyses of infant communicative behaviour. In H. R. Schaffer, ed., *Studies in Mother-Infant Interaction.* London: Academic Press.

Trevarthen, C., and Hubley, P. 1978. Secondary intersubjectivity: confidence, confiding and acts of meaning in the first year. In A. Lock, ed., *Action, Gesture and Symbol: The Emergence of Language.* London: Academic Press.

Tronick, E., Als, H., Adamson, L., Wise, S., and Brazelton, T. B. 1978. The infant's response to entrapment between contradictory messages in face-to-face interaction. *Journal of the American Academy of Child Psychiatry, 17,* 1–13.

Urberg, K. A., and Docherty, E. M. 1976. Development of role-taking skills in young children. *Developmental Psychology, 12,* 198–203.

Valentine, C. W. 1946. *The Psychology of Early Childhood.* London: Methuen.

Vygotsky, L.S. 1977. *Mind and Society,* Cambridge, Mass.: Harvard University Press.

Whiting, B. B., and Edwards, C. P., eds. 1977. The effects of age, sex and modernity on the behaviour of mothers and children. Report to the Ford Foundation.

Whiting, B. B., and Whiting, J. 1975. *Children of Six Cultures: A Psychocultural Analysis.* Cambridge, Mass.: Harvard University Press.

Whiting, J. W. M. 1959. Sorcery, sin and the superego. In M. R. Jones, ed. *Nebraska Symposium on Motivation.* Lincoln: University of Nebraska Press.

_____ 1960. Resource mediation and learning by identification. In I. Iscoe and H. W. Stevenson, eds., *Personality Development in Children.* Austin: University of Texas Press.

Winnicott, D. W. 1964. *The Child, the Family and the Outside World.* London: Penguin Books.

_____ 1977. *The Piggle.* London: Hogarth Press.

Wood, D., McMahon, L., and Cranstoun, Y., 1980. *Working with Under Fives.* London: Grant McIntyre.

Wootton, A. J. 1974. Talk in the homes of young children. *Sociology*, *8*, 277–295.

Yarrow, L. J., Rubenstein, J. L., and Pedersen, F. A. 1975. *Infant and Environment: Early Cognitive and Motivational Development.* Washington, D.C.: Hemisphere Publishing Corp. (distributed by Wiley).

Yarrow, M. R., and Waxler, C. Z. 1975. The emergence and functions of prosocial behavior in young children. Paper presented at the Society for Research in Child Development meeting, Denver.

Zajonc, R. B., and Markus, G. B. 1975. Birth order and intellectual development. *Psychological Review, 82,* 74–88.

Index